American While Black

American While Black

African Americans, Immigration, and the Limits of Citizenship

NIAMBI MICHELE CARTER

OXFORD
UNIVERSITY PRESS

Oxford University Press is a department of the University of Oxford. It furthers the University's objective of excellence in research, scholarship, and education by publishing worldwide. Oxford is a registered trade mark of Oxford University Press in the UK and certain other countries.

Published in the United States of America by Oxford University Press
198 Madison Avenue, New York, NY 10016, United States of America.

CIP data is on file at the Library of Congress
ISBN 978–0–19–005354–3 (pbk.)
ISBN 978–0–19–005355–0 (hbk.)

This book is dedicated to the memory of my grandparents:

George A. and Mildred Carter and Conrey and Rutha B. Silver

Contents

Acknowledgments

THEY SAY IT takes a village to raise a child. Apparently, this is also true of books. I owe this book to the many villages I have been blessed to be a part of all these years. As a budding academic, I have been privileged to have mentors that have helped guide me along my way. Even when I was unaware, they taught me so much about who I am and the person I want to become. In high school, I had the honor to be mentored by Dr. Walter Hill, the late historian, who first made me see the value in pursuing research for "its own sake." While he introduced me to the skill of research, he was also introducing me to myself. Too often, he would tell me to dream bigger and not sell my ideas short, but he was really telling me not to sell myself short. I didn't see it then, but I do now. Thank you, Dr. Hill, for your kindness, patience, and generosity.

When I arrived on the campus of Temple University, I was overwhelmed by this place that felt so pregnant with possibility. I wanted to be lots of things when I got to Philadelphia—an anthropologist, an art historian— but it was the Department of African American Studies where I found my first intellectual home. Dr. Sonia Peterson-Lewis gave me the confidence and skill set to do, study, and be anything I wanted to be. I must also mention Drs. Abu Abarry and Nathaniel Norment, who also nurtured my growth during this time. It is rare that your mentors become your colleagues, and I am so honored to have crossed paths with you all. And I would be remiss if I did not mention the indefatigable Dr. Bettye Collier-Thomas, who taught me how to fall in love with black people across time and space through their words. What you taught me all those years ago has never been forgotten. I also have to mention Tchet Dereic Dorman, Dr. Tiffenia Archie, and Dr. David Canton for making my dreams of graduate school a reality. The Ronald McNair Program was invaluable to my choices, and I would not be here now if it were not for you. I am so thankful to Temple University for the many ways it shaped my career trajectory.

Graduate school was the place where I realized what my passion was. This, in no small part, due to the diligence of Dr. Paula D. McClain. Dr. McClain, it is because of you that this book is happening. You set me on this path, and I was unsure at first, but you are the reason I have a career. You trained me, professionalized me, and directed me when I had no idea where to go. You have been a life mentor and I am forever indebted. I am happy to say the same about the Department of Political Science at Duke University. You all gave me a strong foundation, and I thank you all for your insistence on my best. This department also gave me some of the most significant intellectual and personal relationships of my life. I am so thankful for my BLiPS crew: Victoria Defrancesco-Soto, Monique Lyle, Shayla Nunnally, and Efrén O. Pérez and Tammy Pérez. I would not have made it through graduate school, or this profession, without your help. You all have done so much to enrich my lives and you each have made me a better person because of it. I could not write this section of my life without acknowledging one of my very best friends, Dr. Jason Johnson. Though you went to that other school down the road, I am so glad we took that detour. Your friendship has been an umbrella in this rainy world. We have seen each other through a lot, and I cannot wait for a time when there is a little less happening.

In my career, I've had the pleasure of working with some amazing scholars who are even better people. The Departments of Political Science and African American Studies at Purdue University showed me what it meant to be collegial and a good departmental citizen. A young scholar could not have asked for a better set of people to be mentored by. Thank you especially, Cornelius Bynum, Rosalee Clawson, Michelle Conwell, Marlo David, Joseph Dorsey, Jennifer Freeman Marshall, Aaron Hoffman, James McCann, Venetria Patton, Keith Shimko (and Chris Olofson), Matilda Stokes, Antonio Tillis, S. Laurel Weldon, and Annette Wheeldon.

I have to thank the Mecca, Howard University, and the Department of Political Science for creating a home for me. I have never worked at a place that I have loved so much. Being surrounded by the majesty of Howard University has made me appreciate the journey so much more. Working in "truth and service" for the students of this community has been my life's great privilege; that I get to do that in the historic Department of Political Science is icing on the cake. But it has also been a distinct pleasure to work with some of the most brilliant women: Drs. Jarpa Dawuni, Keneshia Grant, and Keesha Middlemass. Lastly, to Drs. Hatem and Lashley, thank you for enduring for all of us.

Speaking of dope women, my career would not be possible if it were not for the early investment of colleagues from across campuses and disciplines. I am a fortunate woman to have so many sister-friends who care about me in such a deep and abiding way. Michelle Deveaux, I would not have written this book without you. Quite frankly, you helped me pick myself up when I didn't think it was possible, or advisable, to get up again. I whisper a small "thank you" every day to the universe for helping us find each other in that bathroom. Dr. Khalilah Brown-Dean thank you for continuing to inspire me. Dr. Lorrie Frasure-Yokley, you have made so many things in my professional life possible, and I cannot thank you enough for pulling me along even when I was unsure of the mission. Dr. Anthea Butler, you are a badass and I hope to be like you when I grow up. Dr. Natalie Masuoka, you have suffered through various stages of this project, and every time you have made it infinitely better. Dr. Jennifer Stoever-Ackerman, I feel smarter every time I talk to you, and I am so thankful we experienced Rochester together. Lastly, I have to thank my Philly family. Dr. Nina Johnson you have spoken nothing but positivity over my life, and I appreciate your giving spirit. Dr. Amada Armenta you are a truth-teller and a damn fine mixologist. Dr. Jennifer Harford-Vargas you are a ray of sunshine in the world. I have to thank my forever room-mate and vacation partner, Dr. Lee Gayle (and Obie). You guys have helped me stay moored throughout all of life's ups and downs. Thank you for allowing me into your heart and your home.

There are also many of you who I cannot thank enough for offering a kind word, your name, your intellectual energies, or just your friendship. Alvin Tillery, you have been a believer for a long time, and I thank you for your patience. Dr. Tyson King-Meadows (and Elka Stevens) I have learned about how I can grow in this profession by watching what you do, often silently, for so many of us. There are simply too many people to speak to separately, but I must acknowledge: Travis Adkins, Dawn Ambrose, Antoine Banks, Najja Baptist, Ray Block Jr., John Brehm, Nadia Brown, Nyron Crawford, Menna Demessie, Isatu Destry, Heath Fogg-Davis, Michael Fauntroy, Pearl Ford Dowe, Megan Francis, Sekou Franklin, Zinga Fraser, Andra Gillespie, Cory Gooding, Gabrielle Gray, Stacey Greene, Daniel Guillion, Alana Hackshaw, Kerry Haynie, Patrice Howard, Jarvis A. Hall, Chaunetta Jones, Julia Jordan-Zachery, Clarence Lusane, Kim Mealy, Michael Minta, Nick Nelson, D'Andra Orey, Millery Polyné, Kathy Powers, Melanye Price, Mark Sawyer, Joe Schwartz, Elsie Scott, Rick Selzer, Todd Shaw, Valeria Sinclair-Chapman, Brenda Truesdale,

Candis Watts Smith, Betsy Super, Heather Thompson, Ronald Walters, Dorian Warren, Ismail White, Janelle Wong, and Jackie Yu-Johnson. I am also thankful for the many supports I have received from the American Political Science Association and National Conference of Black Political Scientists (NCOBPS). NCOBPS family you have labored with me and I am forever grateful.

Angela Chnapko and the editorial staff of Oxford University Press, you always saw the vision of this book and ushered me to the finish line. Thank you for being such a great editor and helping me get this work to the public.

In so many ways, my life would not be possible without the love of my very large family. The Silver clan of Warrenton, NC, are unyielding in their love. There are too many of you to name, but you are all appreciated. Their support has been unwavering, especially that of my aunt and uncle, Barbara and Joe McCoy. You could not have loved me more; I appreciate the lifetime of meals, clothes, and care that you all so selflessly provide week after week. My cousins Angelia McCoy, Andrea Sorey, and Annette Lewis, I could not have asked for better companions, style-gurus, and sisters. Deena Cunningham and Bridgette Jones—thanks for always being there. My North Carolina cousins Alisha Silver, Sheron Mapp, and Jonathan Silver, you all have kept me sane and in tears (from laughing). I could not get through this life without you.

The Carter family has loved me through it all. Aunt Stephanie Davis (Uncle Charles) you were the first person I looked up to. I hope to be half the aunt you still are to me. To my other sister, Ebony Carter, you are part confidante, therapist, and co-conspirator. You've always been honest with me, and I am so lucky to call you family.

I would not have made it this far if it were not for my big sister, Dr. Portia Carter Barnes. You made me want to be the best version of myself. You are an amazing physician, teacher, principal, mom, daughter, and wife. I'm unsure how you do it all, and I am still in awe of you and all you do. To my brother-in-law, Shelby Barnes, you took me to get my first car and literally started me on this road; I thank you for how much you sacrifice to make so many things possible for all of us. Kelsey Carter, seeing you grow has been one of my joys. To my nephews Mikal, Joshua, Seth—you all have made me exceedingly proud. My niece Shelby Jaye, you are "black girl magic" personified and you are invaluable and I hope you appreciate that as you move through this world.

Last but certainly not least, I reserve my deepest appreciation for my parents Linda Silver Carter and Michael Carter. You all were the best parents I could have hoped for. You gave me the foundation to be able to do this work, and anything else I set my mind to. You are amazing co-parents and have been steadfast in your belief in me. You showed me that love is a verb, and I am grateful for all the ways you have demonstrated your care for me over the years. Thank you for the hand holding and back rubbing.

Lastly, so many past and present have prayed for me and supported me. That this book is complete is due to your efforts. Any mistakes in this book are mine alone. Thank you for loving me.

American While Black

Introduction

I CAME TO this project while a graduate student in Durham, North Carolina. At that time, the city of Durham, and the state of North Carolina, was experiencing increasing waves of immigration primarily from Mexico and other parts of South America. Much of the conversation around this "new immigration" largely focused on the dislocations between blacks and Latinos in Durham. At the time, conflict was the dominant frame used to understand the racial dynamics between these groups. This seemed wrong to me, however. I knew black people. More importantly, I listened to black people talk. My maternal family is from Warrenton, North Carolina. Warrenton is a town of less than 1,000 people that remains defined as racially black and white. Despite the demographic changes happening in that area, you must understand what happened between blacks and whites, first. My family, like so many others, is not far removed from Jim Crow and experienced the stresses and strains of old fashioned racism and the more genteel racial segregation that persists because of the racial orders of prior generations.

Being entrepreneurs has been one of the ways black people have maintained some semblance of independence from the vagaries of white supremacy. While my grandfather was a sharecropper until he was middle-aged, my uncle exhibited an independent streak and used his talent as a brick mason to work for his own firm. That firm was able to employ my other uncles, at different times, who are talented masons in their own right. As skilled craftsmen, my uncles were able to circumvent some of the workplace racism prevalent in their day. One evening as a graduate student, while visiting family, I overheard my uncle talking about a construction contract he bid on. He did not think his bid would be successful because other companies (read white) would come in cheaper because, in his words, "they hire Mexicans." This was not a jab at Mexicans, but an acknowledgment that he understood "how white people do." What "white people do" in this context is hire the cheapest labor they can find. In this case, it was newly arriving Latino immigrants. He said this with neither anger nor bitterness, but with a cold understanding of how race works. When you are black, this means that whites will opt for the cheapest labor source, not necessarily the better labor source. Far too often, "better" meant the most easily exploited. What had largely been a decision about expedience and a firm's bottom line, had morphed into a popular, racialized stereotype about Latino willingness to "work hard"; a sentiment commonly held by blacks and whites (Mindiola, Niemann, and Rodriguez 2003; National Hispanic Media Coalition 2012). Unfortunately, the flip side of this stereotype has the effect of painting black people, and even less advantaged whites, as "lazy" or unwilling to work hard by contrast. What was essentially a fiscal choice was racialized into a conversation about a group's diligence and individual drive. My uncle, a brick mason, was very aware of these realities, and this is what he was expressing in his few words. White firms used the worst caricatures of black people to justify their exploitation of immigrant laborers. This type of understanding of race and its nuances, as highlighted by the issue of immigration, is what I explore in this book.

My fundamental argument in this book is that black people respond to the "threat" of immigration by critiquing the system of white supremacy that excludes blacks through the exploitation of other groups. This means that, in the realm of labor, blacks are critiquing the practices that create imperatives for cheap labor—not the laborers. This book is not about labor relations, however. This book is about the ways in which blacks use immigration as a lens to evaluate their status as citizens. Thus, this project is essentially one of place-making. As blacks are thinking about what immigration means for the nation, they are thinking about what it means for their group. The only way this issue is given context is through their own group's racial experience, which has often found blacks struggling for belonging in the American body politic because of the white supremacy.

The goal of this book is to use immigration as a way to understand black people's opinions about race and their place in the American political landscape. It is not to say what black people ought to feel like. Rather, it is a way to understand why black people, when confronted with an issue like immigration, feel ambivalent about it. In order to understand their opinions, it is necessary to think about their relationship to white supremacy, how white supremacy structures the ways in which they receive information about immigration, and how this influences their political attitudes. Throughout this book, my primary consideration is blacks and how they understand their plight, in order to complicate the ways in which we talk about black people and their opinions. More importantly, while this work is ultimately a critique of the ways in which white supremacy structures the nature of intergroup relationships, the foil here is not white people. This is a significant intervention. Whites are not a comparison group; they are not a primary referent. In other words, white supremacy is not equal to white people. White supremacy is the system that *favors* white people and structures *all* of our life chances according to skin color, gender expression, sexuality, nationality, religion, and the like. This means all of us can participate in perpetuating the system of white supremacy regardless of whether that system benefits us individually or whether we participate in or believe in racist practice.

It would be facile to say black people would have ill-feeling toward immigrants, because that is what white people demonstrate (Banks 2016). But what my uncle said about "how white people do" demonstrated a knowledge of white supremacy at work. And that white supremacy is about reinforcing the racial hierarchy that my uncles, and so many other black people, have been resisting for centuries. By listening to black people, I came to understand that black people respond differently to the same stimulus (i.e., immigration). While this should be taken for granted, it is not (Harris-Lacewell 2004). The construction of white supremacy, and its fixation on the subordination of black people and others who cannot access whiteness, creates different constraints that structure black responses to immigration.

Consequently, whites are not only not a comparison groups to blacks in this book; they probably should not be in other spheres, either. A comparison does not make sense given the disparate experiences these groups have had in the United States. Recognizing and mining this difference is fundamental to my argument in this book. As Allport said, "the same fire that melts the butter hardens the egg" (in Hergenhahn, Cramer, and Olson 2002: 159). In this context, black people respond to the "fire" of immigration by critiquing the system that valorizes immigrants relative to their group, not the immigrants themselves. Whites, on the other hand, have often hardened their positions on immigration as the "threat" of these newcomers becomes more salient. This is not to suggest blacks are good and whites are bad. Rather, it is to understand that opinions are not homogeneous, and I contend if we want to understand black opinion then we need to theorize about black people in a way that gives priority to black experiences. We can best do this by listening to what black people have to say for themselves.

This book is dedicated to exploring the "twoness" of black public opinion on immigration. On the one hand, there is a deep commitment in black politics to the right of self-determination. The belief in individual *and* group autonomy has been part and parcel of black political struggle in the United States. The belief that group well-being is concomitant to individual well-being is long-standing and well documented in the political writings and public opinion of black people (Cohen 1999; Dawson 1994b). On the other hand, while blacks are generally not in favor of deportation as a solution to immigration, they are sensitive to the ways in which immigrants are used against them. While blacks generally do not want to see immigrants and their families harmed, they also seek to avoid the inevitable comparisons that arise from their presence. The presence of immigrants makes the anti-blackness of this nation clearer, as blacks are often lambasted for not working hard enough, not trying hard enough, or for whining about racial discrimination relative to this group of newcomers. In the American racial hierarchy, immigrants are "good" because of their values and blacks are "bad" because of their lack of values. The immigrant in this formulation becomes a straw man that leaves the foundational investment in white supremacy untouched.

My goals with this book, therefore, are to engage black people in their own words, on their own terms, to understand how their experiences influence their understanding of and encounters with immigration. The issue of immigration illuminates the ways in which black people see power circulating within and without their communities. Thus, a significant aspect of this work is to demonstrate that immigration is a "black issue." More importantly the book shows that immigration is an important issue about which black people have lots of opinions, and that can help us understand black politics more generally. Moreover, the political science literature largely frames black opinion on immigration as a matter of interminority coalition or competition; I seek to enhance and broaden that conversation.

In order to do this, I argue, it is imperative that one understand white supremacy and the ways in which it structures the relationships between minority communities. In particular, when I look at black public opinion about immigration, it is not simply a matter of the usual tropes of immigrants "taking jobs" or receiving unearned benefits, though those things exist; it is a matter of understanding the ways of white folks. If one is reading this book and wants to understand its main thrust it is this: white supremacy structures the political choices available to black people; consequently, in order to understand black opinion one has to understand the constraints of *and* resistance to white supremacy. If one does not understand white supremacy, one cannot hope to understand black politics. This is not to suggest blacks do not have political agency. They do. Yet as long as black people engage the American political system, the choices they can make for themselves and their communities are limited by these very same institutions.

While it should go without saying, black people are painfully aware of white supremacy and the ways it shows up in their lives. Most immediately, they often see it when immigrants are wielded as weapons against their communities. Of course, this is not because immigrants are doing this intentionally but because white supremacy gaslights black people, and others, into critiquing themselves and each other rather than focusing on its ill effects. This often looks like there is conflict between blacks and other minorities. What I aim to show is that conflict is not the only way to characterize the relationship. I aim to show that black resistance to immigration, where it may exist, is attitudinal only and is generally about blacks' sense of self-preservation. Black people see advocacy for their community as essential to their survival. Thus, while I may not individually feel threatened by immigration there may be reason to suspect more vulnerable members of my community might feel threatened. Why? Because whites may favor immigrants over black people in hiring decisions, housing, and other social interactions. This is very different from blacks simply being intolerant of immigrants.

I offer this book as a way to generate more conversation about the future of black politics and open the range of issues that are considered part of the canon of black political interests. Immigration is one of those issues, and in the succeeding chapters I demonstrate that blacks have a wide-ranging set of attitudes on immigration generally, but rarely do they support repressive immigration policies or support candidates who promote policies like building walls. This is not necessarily because blacks love immigrants, but because of their recognition that the white supremacy that would build that wall is the same white supremacy that marks black protestors as "racial identity extremists." Thus, as with all things, black opinion on immigration is complicated and does not fit neatly into a particular worldview. I characterize their opinions as "conflicted nativism," where they have very definite opinions about what makes one an American but do not subscribe to policies of immigrant exclusion. Finally, I think it is significant to look at the specific to get to the general. I focus a lot on what black people say in order to make sense of empirical data. It is necessary to utilize an indigenous understanding of black people in order to make sense of the statistical findings. By treating this issue holistically, it is my intention to give voice to the concerns that black people have about the health and well-being of their communities.

Outline of the Book

Chapter 1 gives the reader insight into the key ideas animating the text. In this chapter, I explore the ways in which black public opinion on immigrants has been misunderstood. I present a brief overview of how race informs black attitude formation, then a brief overview of black opinion on immigration. The major thrust of this chapter is to show the ways in which black experiences have informed their opinions on immigration. Using Chapter 2 as a foundation, I delineate the theoretical underpinnings of the text. Chapter 2 extends the discussion of black public opinion on immigration by focusing on the theoretical frame of conflicted nativism which animates much of the discussion in this book. Using blacks' historical relationship to immigration, I argue their unique experience as outsider-citizens makes them deeply ambivalent about immigration. This conflicted nativism is largely a response to white racism rather than hostility to immigrants. The key elements of conflicted nativism are identified and addressed throughout the remaining chapters of the book.

Using historical documents, Chapter 3 presents a historical view of black opinion regarding immigration. This chapter focuses on the nineteenth century and blacks' consideration of immigration as a viable political strategy for group betterment. The chief argument of this chapter is that immigration is very much a part of a black political agenda and early black engagements with immigration represented a resistance to black exclusion. Chapter 4 extends the discussion in Chapter 3 by detailing the ways in which collective memory informs contemporary black opinion. In this chapter, personal interviews are employed to connect history to contemporary black opinions on immigration. This chapter highlights the "everyday talk" blacks engage in regarding immigration. I find blacks use their past to understand present circumstances. In particular, this chapter demonstrates how blacks use the particularities of their experience to understand the ways in which racial hierarchy systematically hurts blacks. Immigration is a way to highlight the inequities of blacks' status. Through discourse I find blacks do not harbor major hostility toward immigrants. Rather, their discomfort is aimed at whites who seek to exploit others in an effort to harm blacks.

Chapter 5 uses survey data to test whether there is any empirical basis to the claims made in Chapters 3 and 4. Using a sample of 1,000 blacks from the Race and Nation Survey project, an original survey of 2,000 blacks and whites, I find blacks have some superficially nativist attitudes but are not willing to expend any political capital on the issue. Overall, blacks who view themselves as "typical Americans" exhibit more nativist attitudes, but being "proud Americans" dampens this nativist bent in their attitudes. Moreover, blacks feel more warmly toward all immigrant groups than they do to other whites, and view themselves as having more in common with Latinos. While blacks are willing to countenance a range of policies related to immigration, they remain unwilling to act on the issue. The findings in this chapter suggests blacks are not offended by immigrants despite their somewhat nativist beliefs. In short, immigration is not a salient issue for blacks, but white supremacy is.

In sum, this book is a beginning of a conversation rather than an ending. There is still much we do not understand about the nature of black politics. While blacks are treated as known quantities in American politics (i.e., they vote Democratic) there is still much we do not know about the range of issues on which they have opinions and what, if anything, those opinions mean for their political behavior. This book seeks to extend the conversation in black politics, racial and ethnic politics, interminority relations, and immigration by demonstrating the complicated, messy nature of public opinion. By exploring how blacks handle the issue of immigration in particular, I hope the book grounds the reader in the fact that black citizenship has been a long struggle and that the contemporary discourse on immigration opinion must take this into account if we are truly to understand what is going on.

1

Lies, Fairytales, and Fallacies

IMMIGRATION AND THE COMPLEXITY OF BLACK
PUBLIC OPINION

SINCE THE 1990S, there have been a variety of negative, and sometimes hostile, interactions between blacks and immigrants. From California to New York, the cleavages between native-born blacks and immigrants of color are apparent and deep (Kasinitz 1992; Kim 2004; Rogers 2004). For example, the Los Angeles Rebellion of 1992, which stemmed from the acquittal of police officers who brutalized Rodney King, was framed as the manifestation of black anti-Korean sentiment (Kim 1999; Min 1996; Min and Kolodny 1994). Although this conflagration came to encompass a range of the black community's frustrations, including mistreatment by Korean shop owners, it was also an expression of a long-simmering frustration with the disrespect of black people that long preceded Korean immigration into Los Angeles (Abelman and Lie 1995; Horne 1997).

In 1992, blacks in Los Angeles were awaiting many promised improvements to community parks, and recreation and health centers, which were agreed upon in the wake of the Watts Riots in 1968. Moreover, in March 1991 a black teenager, Latasha Harlins, was murdered by Korean shopkeeper Soon Ja Du, which exacerbated tensions between these communities. Mrs. Du and Ms. Harlins scuffled after Mrs. Du accused Ms. Harlins of shoplifting. As Ms. Harlins was leaving the store, Mrs. Du shot her in the back of the head and killed the teenager; as she lay dying, Latasha clutched the money she was intending to use to pay for the juice she was accused of stealing. Although the murder was caught on camera, Ms. Harlins' killer received no prison time. Despite being found guilty of manslaughter, Mrs. Du received five years of probation, community service, and a $500 fine. This case , which happened approximately two weeks after the Rodney King incident, was largely overlooked as another important precursor to the Los Angeles Rebellion or as an accelerant in black–Korean tensions in that city. Brenda Stevenson's 2015 book, *The Contested Murder of Latasha Harlins: Justice, Gender, and the Origins of the LA Riots,* offers an important corrective to this conversation. Still, this does not mean blacks were not already frustrated with the influx of Korean immigrant entrepreneurs in their neighborhoods. In the areas of beauty culture, liquor stores, and dry cleaners, Koreans had a virtual monopoly, particularly in poor communities. People believed that immigrants may have received government assistance such as business loans. This, coupled with immigrants' assumed lack of respect for the local community and unwillingness to hire local blacks all contributed to a complicated set of circumstances leading to 1992. Although it was untrue that immigrants received these rumored tax breaks, it has been shown that immigrants have been able to marshal resources that blacks cannot access to start businesses (Bogan and Darity 2008). Moreover, the belief in some kind of unearned assistance to immigrants was more powerful than the truth, and, given the black community's experience, the claim of tax breaks being given to immigrant businesses was credible.

In summer 2018, a protest of an Asian-owned nail salon in Brooklyn by its mostly black patrons repeated many of the same tropes of the Los Angeles conflict. That August, a dispute over an eyebrow waxing service gone awry at the New Red Apple Nails devolved into violence. A black woman customer, displeased with her service, refused to pay for her eyebrow wax despite the insistence of the salon staff that she pay for services rendered. What resulted was a brawl where the customer, along with relatives accompanying her, was accosted with broomsticks and other implements around the shop. A video of the clash went viral on social media and spurred a boycott of the Asian-owned business. Amid protests by some black residents and calls for supporting black-owned businesses, much of the historical nuance of this moment was lost. In 1990, also in Brooklyn's Flatbush neighborhood, there was an economic boycott of the Family Red Apple store after an altercation where Korean shop owner, Bong Ok Jang, attacked a Haitian patron, Ghiselaine Felaissant, over a financial disagreement. What resulted was a sustained effort by African American, Haitian, and other Caribbean activists calling for blacks to shop where they were respected. In this instance, blacks were portrayed as irrational and hostile, but as Kim (2000) noted, these protests were not spontaneous, short-term actions. Rather, they were part of a longer history of activism where "[B]lack collective actors are not mindlessly lashing out at the nearest target but purposefully reacting to the existing parameters of oppression" (p. 12). What is more, Korean immigrants were also active participants in the conflict "because each group's position is invariably defined in relation to those of other groups." Stated another way, black conflicts with other groups have a context, and that context usually has something to do with whites—who are often allowed to go unnoticed and unnamed.

Similarly, the murder of Jamiel Shaw II served to demonstrate a different type of danger immigration poses to black people. Mr. Shaw was an accomplished athlete whose football talent made him a prospect for a number of colleges, in his upcoming senior year in high school. On his return from a shopping trip he was confronted by Pedro Espinoza, a gang member, who shot Mr. Shaw after he did not identify a gang affiliation. Mr. Shaw was tended to by his father who was speaking with his son at the time of the shooting; Mr. Shaw's mother was in Iraq serving her second tour of duty. What made this case more sensational was the fact that Pedro Espinoza was an undocumented immigrant recently released from custody on other violent crimes. The family of Jamiel Shaw II sued the city of Los Angeles for wrongful death because its status as a sanctuary city protected Mr. Espinoza from deportation. Later, the family sought to rescind Special Order 40, an action which, if successful, would have revoked the city's status as a sanctuary for undocumented persons. Though both efforts by the Shaw family failed, they serve to interrupt the pattern that frames interracial conflict as the result of black aggressors and too often overlooks the role of globalized anti-blackness (Bashi 2004).

These examples allow us to see the longer trajectory of racial skirmishes between blacks and other racial minority groups, many of whom have a more recent immigrant experience. These groups increasingly find themselves in contact with one another and facing zero-sum competition for social, political, and economic services (Sonenshein 1993; Vaca 2004). While the racial conflict in these moments is often mutual, it is more often represented as evidence of racial animus on the part of blacks rather than part of a set of more complex racial dynamics where blacks may feel they are threatened. This book addresses these frequent misreadings of complicated situations or flat-out untruths. I do not believe these characterizations necessarily are ill-intentioned or malicious. Rather, it is much easier to blame black discontent and indignation as a source of conflagration rather than to interrogate blacks' righteous anger about racial (in)justice. And while immigration is not necessarily an injustice perpetrated against black people, it would be disingenuous to take no notice of the ways in which immigration has the potential to harm black people, not because immigrants are bad but because of how the racial order positions different groups and situates their needs and priorities relative to one another (King 2002; King and Smith 2005). In some ways, then, the racial conflicts we see are not anomalous but are quite predictable.

Nonetheless, the "controlling image" of angry, intolerant blacks is an easy trope to accept in a society where blacks have consistently remained at the margins.[1] However, this image belies the real frustrations and limited options blacks have for remedying their exclusion, despite their resistances (Kelley 2003). The stereotype of black intolerance has been sufficiently compelling that we have almost stopped asking questions about the racial circumstances that give rise to black attitudes toward immigration and assume blacks are simply unwelcoming. In so doing, we leave white supremacy and the institutionalization of racial hierarchy intact, because it is viewed as past and having little to do with present racial conditions. While the civil rights revolution saw the formal end of Jim Crow, the far more pernicious aspects of this system have been left unquestioned (Carter 2012, 2013; Honig 2001).

The coverage and critiques of police shootings over the years since the murder of Trayvon Martin provide a way for us to understand this phenomenon. From Dallas to Baltimore, police departments have been implicated in the deaths of black men and women. In most cases, the police officers are never charged with any wrongdoing. In the rare cases where charges are filed, convictions are often not forthcoming. Since 2005, only 33 police officers have been convicted of murder for on-duty fatalities, and only 93 have been arrested and charged with manslaughter or murder for on-duty shootings (Silva 2018). In either instance, police departments and the system that enabled these officers to carry weapons and murder nonthreatening people are allowed to pat themselves on the back for acting swiftly to discipline officers. Generally this means placing officers on administrative duty, as happened with Chicago police officer Jason Van Dyke, who was cleared internally of any wrongdoing in the shooting of Laquan McDonald. It would take over a year before any charges were filed on Officer Van Dyke for the murder of McDonald, and the McDonald case is extremely rare. In cases where officers are deemed unfit to continue in their present positions, they are often relocated to other departments. This happened in the case of Cleveland officer Timothy Loehman, who killed 12-year-old Tamir Rice, and Betty Shelby, the Oklahoma officer who killed an unarmed Terrence Crutcher.[2] In any case, the police department gets to look like they have addressed their failings by removing the troubled officers. These public shows of attrition/responsibility locate responsibility with individual officers—not the poor training, personality tests, stopgaps, and all too powerful police unions that allow officers who are unfit for duty to continue on the force. Nor do these examples address the record-keeping policies that allow officers with numerous use-of-force complaints to continue working in the field of law enforcement. The system as it exists does not indict the police officers who lie in order to cover-up the misdeeds of their colleagues on the force. Even in cases where police departments are made to pay settlements, sometimes in the millions of dollars, this does not acknowledge the systemic problem and need to reevaluate a policing culture that has moved from protecting citizens to enforcing the law in a way that paints citizens as the enemy. Rather, settlements effectively are payments that redress wrongs in a way that forestalls deeper conversations about police culture. Once payment is accepted, the tacit agreement is that the wrong has been redressed and no further correction is needed. All of these efforts are ways to preserve a dysfunctional policing culture that serves no one well, including the police officers—but the end goal is not justice. The end goal is to mollify the public by appearing to do something but offering little in the way of substantive change, such that policing culture can proceed unimpeded.

White supremacy operates in much the same way. While individuals are shamed for their individual, racist actions (such as recent incidents of whites calling the police on black people for innocuous behaviors), there is little discussion of the root causes of such behavior.[3] Of course, individual insensitivity is part of the issue, but why would anyone feel empowered to use the police in this way? Why would these white people feel they have a right to deny black people access to the same private and public spaces they inhabit? It is because white supremacy normalizes whiteness and its presence everywhere, making automatically suspect those who do not register as white. Therefore, while white people escape blame by placing responsibility on these individual bad actors, we have not asked the really important questions that would lay bare the foundation of white supremacy that these people rest easy upon. The fact that some white people call police with the expectation the police will respond and discipline the offending black bodies is the embodiment and exercise of white supremacy. Because in a white supremacist system every institution, including the police force, is there to service "the system of domination by which white people have historically ruled over and, in certain important ways, continue to rule over nonwhite people" (Mills 1997: 1–2). This is not to suggest power is evenly shared across all those people racially identified as white. What it does mean, however, is that whites may not see a difference between their white identities and those of the nation-state. According to Mills, racial identity is inexplicably bound up with space, which must be "normed and raced at the *macro*level (entire countries and continents), the *local* level (city neighborhoods), and ultimately even the *micro*level of the body itself," which makes those racialized as non-white a danger to whiteness and therefore in need of punishment. To the extent that individuals resist their coerced acquiescence to civil white authority, the police are used as the ultimate enforcers of the whims of white supremacy (Mills 1997: 43–44). The pernicious nature of white supremacy makes it appear that non-whites are in all ways suspect, troublesome, or dangerous when they are outside of white control.

In this way, racial barriers to black inclusion in housing, education, the public sphere, and employment, for example, have made it appear that their exclusion is simply a matter of happenstance. No person, group, or institution was ever responsible for Jim Crow because it was simply "how it was," and this all changed with a revision of the racial rules. There was no substantive ownership taken for Jim Crow, the institution that systematically bankrupted, undereducated, murdered, disenfranchised, and traumatized black lives. The mythology that Jim Crow was "the law" and that whites were captive adherents to the conventions of their time means that no one is responsible for the horrors of this period. Therefore, racism is bounded and contextualized, much the way we discuss slavery, as being "of the day"; no wrong was really committed, because none of these behaviors was against the law. Therefore, the mythology of racial integration maintains that when segregation laws are lifted and we became officially a post–Jim Crow, colorblind country, those behaviors dissipated because the law changed. The narrative trick that such rewriting does is to make racism the result of individual behaviors or temporary slippages in application of American ideals. Yet, what this deeply unsatisfying narrative never answers is, what about American society made Jim Crow possible?

The answer to that is white supremacy, which is *foundational* to American identity. Yet, by treating Jim Crow laws as ephemera of a bygone era, white Americans do not have to own their participation in, or at least tolerance of, a system that sought the acquiescence of non-white people to notions and practices that support white dominance (Mills 1997). Racial hierarchy where blacks occupy the nadir and whites the apex, and all other groups are figured against both whites and blacks, creates fertile ground for the interracial dustups we have witnessed across time and today.

Consequently, explorations of interminority relationships have omitted whites from their analysis because black/white racial divides are deemed outmoded, particularly as the nation's demographics suggest a more multiracial America. Thus, white supremacy, and the ways in which it structures interminority relations, continues to wield a lot of power (Anderson 2016; Betancur 2005; Mills 1997). As these calls to move from a biracial to triracial understanding of U.S. race relations become more persuasive, I argue it becomes more difficult to see the ways in which white supremacy conditions black attitudes with respect to immigration, such that black attitudes on immigration are not only about immigration but a referendum on blacks' progress (Bonilla-Silva 2004; Frank, Akresh, and Lu 2010; Lee and Bean 2007). To wit, I argue black attitudes on immigration are mediated by their understandings of black/white racial relations. That is, the best way to understand black attitude formation on immigration is to be attendant to the workings of whiteness.

This book focuses on the continuing significance of the black/white racial paradigm for understanding black public opinion on immigration. By doing so, this work demonstrates the historical and current importance of unresolved racial conflict with whites and how this informs black public opinion in the domain of immigration. Thus, this work extends the literature and insights on interminority relations by demonstrating *how* and *why* race matters in black public opinion on immigration. Additionally, I extend the literature on black politics by offering a theory of black public opinion toward immigration, which is not generally a salient issue or usual part of black political agendas. Although this has started to change, given the current spread of immigration to traditionally black areas and the increased visibility of black immigrants, a gap in the literature remains (Austin 2013; Ha 2010; McClain et al. 2006, 2007, 2011; McKanders 2010).

Black Engagement with Immigration

Although America is legally desegregated, it is far from an integrated body politic. Blacks feel this more acutely in times of increased immigration

(Borjas 2016; Borjas, Grogger, and Hanson 2006; Greer 2013; Hellwig 1978, 1982; McClain et al. 2006; Tillery 2011). While immigration may provide a net benefit to the nation, there are undoubtedly repercussions felt by the most vulnerable in the face of these new arrivals. Borjas (2016) argues that employer desires to exploit immigrant labor depresses wages for all low-skilled laborers, particularly black and Latino workers. These wages are likely not to rebound—not because of immigrants, but because the availability of more workers depresses wages for everyone. As Borjas states, "[I]mmigration redistributes wealth from those who compete with immigrants to those who use immigrants—from the employee to the employer," and this competition always leaves employees disadvantaged. Black workers do not need an advanced degree to understand the intricacies of labor exploitation (i.e., enslavement, sharecropping, convict leasing, and prison industries). Thus, when overlooking blacks' long-standing dialogue about immigration—dating back to pre-emancipation, nineteenth-century America—it becomes a lot easier to characterize the contemporary moment as if it is simply a response to present circumstances (Ferreira 1999; Jenkins 1999; Tillery 2011). Yet, blacks had a great deal to say about incoming Irish immigrants in the 1840s because they were concerned about the potential for their social elevation in the face of these new arrivals. Likewise, they were concerned Chinese Exclusion (1882) set a dangerous precedent in racial politics, even if it potentially meant they could gain a foothold in the economy (Junn 2006; Shankman 1978). Blacks, therefore, were not only concerned with the immigration of others but often considered emigration as a strategy for their racial inclusion in the United States.

Some blacks were so discontented with American racial progress that they considered leaving the United States altogether. While some blacks did emigrate to other countries, most others decided to migrate internally. Still, blacks included themselves among the world's sojourners. Proponents of black emigration believed a majority-black nation held the potential for social and political mobility because race, a necessary condition of American exclusion, would be lessened.[4] As Tillery (2011) notes, this was an extended, and oftentimes contentious, conversation, because blacks were wary of ceding their claims to America and the institutions they helped craft. Part of their reluctance to simply "move on" to the Liberian colony, or some other location, was the idea that people from other nations would be allowed to lay claim to American citizenship even though blacks were integral to forming this nation's identity. Thus, most blacks eschewed the possibility of more freedom abroad in favor of fighting for justice at home. Rather than abdicate their contributions to (European) immigrants and their descendants, they would fight against their ostracism.

Blacks' intellectual production on this matter has largely been left out of the historical record, and the present moment is often treated as the first time blacks have had an original thought about the issue of immigration. This could not be farther from the truth. With the exception of a few, such as A. Philip Randolph's anti-immigrant rhetoric rooted in his ideas regarding labor struggle, the larger black community has remained remarkably consistent in their feelings, opinions, and behaviors regarding immigrants of all colors (Carter and Pérez 2015; Diamond 1998; Ferreira 1999; Hellwig 1980; Scott 1999). Blacks have been, and I argue remain, highly ambivalent regarding immigrants (Greer 2013). In the main, blacks believe deeply in the right of all groups of people to self-determination; yet, they are wary that another group's self-determination will come at their expense socially, politically, or economically—and rightfully so, if one considers the upward trajectory of European immigrants arriving in the United States throughout the nineteenth and twentieth centuries. These immigrants surpassed native-born blacks on most measures of well-being (Hershberg et al. 1979; Jacobson 2001; Lott 1992; Parker 2009). Blacks have very real and confirmed fears that whites manipulate immigrants into turning away from potential alliances with blacks for greater social and political gains (Jacobson 2001; Katznelson 2006; Roediger 1999; Yancey 2003). For example, the interracial impetus of the Populist Movement was greatly undermined by the use of racially divisive political maneuvers. These maneuvers kept black and white workers from forming a sustained, organized body around a collective class identity (Roediger 1999).[5] Likewise, the importation of "coolie" labor in the South after slavery was a plan devised by white elites to undercut black demands for better labor practices and the expansion of civil rights (Loewen 1988; Quan 2007; Rhee 1994; Wong 1986). In the present, white employers often prefer hiring immigrant employees because they believe they are better workers; white employers also believe that immigrants are easier to exploit than native-born workers because they lack social networks that would enable them to obtain higher wages and more stable employment (Powers 2005; Saucedo 2006).

These examples demonstrate that blacks have a reasonable fear their race will continue to be an impediment in the labor market. Given the prevalence of the stereotype that immigrants work harder than native-born blacks, their concerns are not unfounded.[6] Employers generally consider black men to be "unstable, uncooperative, dishonest and uneducated" (Kirschenman and Neckerman 1991: 204).[7] Similar stereotypes exist for black women, who are often designated as "single mothers" by employers and are more likely to have their job performance assessed negatively (Kennelly 1999).[8] Although labor is only one area where blacks have a difficult time reconciling their national identity with their racial identity, it is far from an unusual circumstance (Dawson 2001; DuBois 2003[1903]). The centrality of race to America's national project as a chief signifier of inclusion and exclusion is well documented (Mills 1997; Nobles 2000; Omi and Winant 1994). That white males came to represent an unqualified membership in the polity and black people either unfit or provisional citizens, at best, is purposeful (Frankenburg 1997; Lipsitz 1995). From 1790 until 1952 "Congress made it a requirement that only 'white persons' could become American citizens," which left anyone not considered white, by whatever definition was in use at the time, without an official status with respect to the U.S. government (Martínez 2007: 336). As a result, whiteness became the chief qualification for membership, and this statute had the effect of deepening the connection between whiteness and Americanness, such that they became virtually synonymous. This is not a matter of hyperbole; experimental work of psychologists Devos and Banaji (2005) across multiple studies demonstrates that individuals see the prototypical American as racially white. What is more, for white respondents with strong national identities they found their racial and national identities to be linked in such a way that identifying as racially white became shorthand for being American. As a consequence of this American=white association, Devos and Banaji found that white foreigners were likely to be considered more American than Asian Americans born in the United States. Altogether, the authors' findings suggest that America is, at least psychologically, white-identified. Despite the implicit association between whiteness and Americanness, blacks were resistant to this characterization and less likely to subscribe to this notion.

From the end of enslavement throughout most of the twentieth century, the United States was relentless in its efforts to disaffirm black citizenship rights, devising all manner of legal and extralegal devices to prevent blacks from fully participating in the mainstream (i.e., white) public sphere (Brown 1994; Clarke 2008; Franklin 1957, 1972; Kendi 2016; Mabry 1938; Dawson 1994b; Key 1996[1949]; Muhammad 2010; Perman 2001; Reich

1996; Woodward 1974). Thus, to be included in the national polity, blacks have had to make repeated demands on the state, as bracketed Americans, to force the United States to move closer to its promise of equality. Yet, many of these efforts were routinely opposed by a majority of whites who came to signify resistance to a more racially just nation (Alderman 2000; Anderson 2016; Hoelscher 2003; Lichtenstein 2006; McMillen 1994; Moye 2004; Wells 2004; Woodward 1993). Although the norm of racial equality is publicly accepted, and overtly racist attitudes have receded, white public opinion remains firmly arrayed against affirmative policies to bring about racial equality in a range of domains (Banks, White, and McKenzie 2018; Clawson and Oxley 2012; Gilens 2000; Hancock 2004; Unnever and Cullen 2007).

I argue that the result of necessary and repeated protest activity on the part of blacks has not only yielded greater political inclusion for them, but has also produced a sense of racial insecurity (Weldon 2011). While it is the case that social movements can expand the representational possibilities of underrepresented groups, it is also the case that in an ideal circumstance, citizens should not have to fight with the state for rights they are due. This is not to suggest that the state should operate unchecked by its citizens. Rather, the allure of a democracy is that the regularity of elections and the like, which is supposed to keep representatives accountable to their constituents for their (in)actions, should also be expected to maintain the mechanisms of that accountability. That blacks have had to fight almost nonstop for the most basic citizenship rights, I argue, has engendered a feeling that they are not full citizens of this country. For blacks, partial civil rights enforcement has been the hallmark of their existence even in the post–Civil Rights Act era. Despite formal declarations, blacks have not enjoyed a full civil rights enforcement regime in this country. And while the Voting Rights Act (VRA) is only 50 years old, the Supreme Court saw fit to essentially gut the legislation that was and is a cornerstone of the Civil Rights Movement. The culmination of over a century of black organizing efforts, the VRA mandated federal oversight of designated jurisdictions that repeatedly violated the rights of blacks and other racial minorities by making them pre-clear any changes to the procedures and manner of elections in their jurisdictions. These "covered jurisdictions" had to be accountable for the ways in which their voting procedures might hinder the voting rights of groups that had experienced discrimination in the decades prior to the VRA. In the election of 2016, the gutting of the VRA led to a number of states enacting legislation to suppress black votes. According to the Brennan Center, in 2016, four-teen states added more voter restrictions in anticipation of the presidential election. These voter restrictions continued into 2017 and 2018 with legislatures in Arkansas, Georgia, Indiana, Montana, North Carolina, and Texas, to name a few, either strengthening voting laws on the books or enacting new voter restrictions (Brennan Center for Justice 2017). In 2018, on the cusp of a historic election in Georgia where the first black woman, Stacey Abrams, could be elected governor, her opponent Brian Kemp, Georgia's secretary of state, oversaw the purge of black voters in an attempt to win the election. What is more, Kemp refused to step down from office before the election and was caught on tape lamenting Abrams' get-out-the-vote efforts, saying, "if everybody uses and exercises their right to vote" it would be harmful to his campaign. This would not have been noteworthy if Kemp and his office had not been in control of the time and manner of elections. To date, his office has rescinded over 50,000 voter registrations, mostly by black applicants, and purged over 100,000 voters from the election rolls (Smith 2018). This type of behavior does not engender trust in American electoral institutions, and it is also totally predictable when one considers the arc of black politics in the United States. Malcolm X in his "Ballot or the Bullet" speech of 1964, on the eve of the Voting Rights and Civil Rights Act, best captured this sensibility. He said:

> Being here in America doesn't make you an American. Being born here in America doesn't make you an American. Why, if birth made you American, you wouldn't need any legislation; you wouldn't need any amendments to the Constitution; you wouldn't be faced with civil-rights filibustering in Washington, D.C., right now. They don't have to pass civil-rights legislation to make a Polack an American.

Because black rights have been severely curtailed and in some cases outright denied by agents of the state, either through direct or indirect means, blacks cannot rest easily on their citizenship to serve as a mark of difference between "us and them" (Kinder and Kam 2010). If we subscribe to the view of Malcolm X, the fact that blacks have had to be incorporated into the body politic through legislation does not seem to work very well; it is evidence they are not American, nor were they intended to be. In the area of voting, which is supposed to be a guarantee of citizenship, we see the limits of black national identity. The actions described above are not simply a matter of civil rights enforcement but part of an established pattern to deny black people their rights as American citizens.

Collective Memory and Black Attitude Formation

The collective memory and experience of black people has repeatedly demonstrated that being an American does not prevent one from being made an outsider within one's own country (Walters 2012). Although America has confirmed that it can and does yield to the demands of excluded groups, it does not acquiesce easily or completely to such demands (Weldon 2011). The political import of immigration in this century is once again forcing blacks to evaluate how race impedes their ability to fully enjoy the benefits of citizenship, conferred by birthright, as Americans.

This need to rearticulate a black political agenda in the face of immigration was clear in the late nineteenth and early twentieth centuries as European immigration reached unprecedented levels. Immigrants, mainly from Italy and Ireland, faced a number of circumstances reminiscent of that of blacks. Although these immigrants were allowed into the country because of the nebulous "free white persons" clause in U.S. immigration policy, their presence was not greeted with enthusiasm on the part of native-born whites (Guglielmo 2003; Ignatiev 1996; Knobel 1996; Warren and Twine 1997). In many respects, early Southern and Eastern European arrivals were not held in any higher esteem than their black counterparts (Gleeson 2001; Jacobson 2001; Barrett and Roediger 1999; Roucek 1969). Racial and cultural stereotypes often classed these immigrants as only one step above black people. As a result, it was thought that such immigrants would only be able to be partial citizens because they lacked the capacity for self-governance.[9] Yet, these European immigrants moved from being undesirables to whiteness[10] in fairly short order. The inclusion of European immigrants was predicated, at least in part, on their willingness to adopt racially prejudicial attitudes toward blacks (Jacobson 2001; Lott 1992; Roediger 1999).

Thus, new immigrant groups who were eager to be accepted as mainstream white Americans were granted admission based on their distancing themselves from blacks, some of whom tried to forge allegiances with their downtrodden European brethren (Ferreira 1999; Shankman 1980). In the Irish, particularly, blacks saw the potential for an alliance because of their shared histories of oppression (Black 2010). Intellectuals like

Frederick Douglass felt this cross-racial cooperation would be beneficial to both groups, because they could seek to resolve their mutual woes. Unfortunately, such hopes went unrealized as immigrants traded these connections for white acceptance. As Douglass (1892) noted, "The Irish, who, at home, readily sympathize with the oppressed everywhere, are instantly taught when they step upon our soil to hate and despise the Negro. They are taught to believe that he eats the bread that belongs to them. The cruel lie is told them, that we deprive them of labor and receive the money which would otherwise make its way into their pockets . . . He will find that in assuming our avocation, he has also assumed our degradation . . . Every hour sees us elbowed out of some employment to make room for some newly-arrived immigrant from the Emerald Isle, whose hunger and color entitle him to special favor . . . while a ceaseless enmity in the Irish is excited against us" (pp. 366–367). This wave of immigration was instructional for blacks. It demonstrated the strength of white supremacy to adapt to changing circumstances and coopt the "near white," who were previously harmed by white supremacist practice, in an effort to perpetuate white dominance at the expense of blacks (Bonilla-Silva 2004).[11] The ability to access the hegemony promised by white supremacy undermined the possibility of interracial collaboration and made it clear that whiteness would remain a more powerful motivator than justice. As such, assimilation to whiteness, as a sign of becoming American, was a hurdle blacks would never be able to clear.

That newcomers would be able to access levers of social mobility routinely denied black people was clear evidence that blacks were not believed to be real Americans; although they were born in this country, and their ancestors contributed to its development with free labor, their constitutional rights as citizens had limited practical value (Mills 1997; Smith 1997). Race made it nearly impossible for blacks to enjoy most immunities and protections granted by the Constitution because whites were routinely allowed to encroach on their civil rights and liberties. Still, blacks reasoned they should at least have a primary claim to inclusion in the body politic over European immigrants because they were natural born citizens (Rubin 1978). Yet, such claims fell on deaf ears as blacks watched themselves being pushed further outside of the public sphere in favor of European immigrants, who became assimilated into whiteness in a relatively short span (Jacobson 2001).

This post-1840 period of immigration underscored the potential for American inclusiveness as well as the depths of white supremacy and the limits it placed on its black citizenry. As Jim Crow laws stiffened nationally, U.S. borders were relaxed. Although blacks did not expect they would soon become favored citizens, the incorporation of European immigrants did suggest the kinds of benefits they could hope for when their time came. Decent neighborhoods, civil service employment, union-protected jobs, and other trappings of a middle-class existence that immigrants could access were things blacks expected to be available to them once they were politically incorporated. By all indicators of the time, such as lynching, rampant disenfranchisement, and various black codes,[12] blacks' hopes for the future seemed dim, but they believed in the promise of America (DuBois 1918, 1929; Mills 1997).

Despite some very convincing reasons why blacks should be restrictionist in their immigration preferences, they have not historically supported efforts to curb immigration to the United States (Diamond 1998). Generally speaking, immigration has not made it into blacks' top issues (Pew Research Center 2010). Prior to 1965, given the ever-present issue of racial segregation, it makes sense that immigration would not be at the fore of a black political agenda. Yet, even in the contemporary moment when blacks are asked about their top issues, the issue of immigration is generally not among them. According to a Gallup poll from July 2013, healthcare and unemployment were the main issues they felt confronted their group. Furthermore, blacks are the most dissatisfied with their treatment in American society of any minority group and still feel it is necessary to have the U.S. government enforce their civil rights. At the same time, less than ten percent of blacks polled felt immigration was an important issue. This is significant because this book is about black public opinion on immigration, but by my own admission, immigration is not a salient issue for blacks. Nevertheless, immigration gives us a way to think about how blacks use their race to form (racial) opinions about national belonging.

Because of their second-class citizenship status, national identity became subsumed by race as *the* operational identity for blacks because it was the key determinant of their social, political, and economic status (Gaines 1996; Shingles 1981). This does not mean that being black meant that one did not see themselves as American; the fact that blacks continued to engage all mechanisms at their disposal for greater social and political incorporation suggests they felt entitled to citizenship. It is also the case that their exclusion enabled African Americans to survive periods of the most severe disenfranchisement and mount effective challenges to discrimination domestically as well as internationally (Andrews 2004; Gill 2004; McAdam 1999; Nunnally 2012; Price 2009; Ransby 2003; Von Eschen 1997; Weare 1973). Because blacks had to create a counterpublic, they were able to create organizations, institutions, and industries that served and sustained their communities (Dawson 1994b). This resulted in a duality of black life as both black and American (Brown and Shaw 2002). Dubbed "two warring ideals" by DuBois, the tension did not result from identity politics, which is sometimes assailed as a kind of tribalism that makes integration impossible. Rather, the duality DuBois describes is the result of a white supremacy that defines blackness as a problem to be solved. For DuBois, and many others, the quest for black people is to have a country where it is "possible for a man [*sic*] to be both a Negro and an American, without being cursed and spit upon by his fellows, without having the doors of opportunity closed roughly in his face" (DuBois, [2003]1903: 2–3). Unfortunately, this desire to be full citizens remains elusive for many blacks, yet they persist in enforcing their rights claims by using every available means to hold America accountable (Weldon 2011).

Whose America? Whose Immigration?

My argument in this book is straightforward. I assert that blacks use the issue of immigration as a way to articulate their feelings about the failures of the nation-state to address *their* needs and incorporate them as full members of the citizenry. I theorize black opinion on immigration, therefore, is *mediated* by their sensibility about their lack of belonging in the body politic. More importantly, I posit that blacks view immigration through the lens of the black/white racial paradigm and are ambivalent with respect to immigration. I term this ambivalence *conflicted nativism*. Conflicted nativism comes from a sensibility that immigration will potentially harm black progress, but immigration should not be restricted, because white supremacy, not immigration, is what ultimately harms black social mobility. In short, what blacks seek is full inclusion in the public sphere, and immigration represents a potential barrier to that inclusion. I argue that this is different from anti-immigrant sentiment. Rather, it is a rational response to the myriad ways in which white supremacy has coopted those who are not black into the racial matrix in such a way as to keep blacks at the nadir of the racial order. Therefore, blacks are not anti-immigrant but anti–white supremacy. The problem is that there are few ways to articulate this position and express it succinctly.

Consequently, immigration serves as a vehicle for grievances against the white supremacy that orders American society. This does not mean blacks are monolithic in their feelings about immigration or immigrants; in the main, however, blacks do not organize or support anti-immigration campaigns.

The twin issues of race and nationhood remain a significant part of the conversation regarding black political incorporation and are rendered most visible in the domain of immigration. Blacks have a different perspective of America that is grounded in their peculiar history and experiences with this country and its institutions (Carter and Pérez 2015). Therefore, these simultaneous feelings of belonging as Americans and being excluded as blacks cannot be divorced from attempts to craft a vision of an inclusive American national identity for the black community vis-à-vis immigration. I contend that to approach these issues, one has to appreciate the legacy of black/white racial dynamics that shape the (racial) boundaries of this belonging (Holland 2012). Black responses to immigration stem from an interconnected yet tortured history, with race and national belonging related to their marginalization as Americans and their unreconciled feelings toward whites. For blacks, there is no "moving beyond" race, because America has yet to deal with the lived consequences of its racial order in the lives of black people (Carter and Dowe 2015; Shams 2015; King and Smith 2005).[13]

Black People, Black Identities: Theorizing a Black Body Politic

Although we have greatly enhanced the theoretical and practical understandings of black politics in the decades since the VRA (1965), the literature on black politics is just beginning to address the new racial realities blacks are living with as a result of new waves of immigration (Greer 2013; McClain et al. 2006, 2009; Rogers 2006). Because of an increase in non-European immigration beginning in the post-1965 period, blacks reside in a country increasingly dominated by non-black minorities. Furthermore, because of these new racial realities, the language of displacement has come to signify much of the conversation around blackness in recent decades.[14] Indeed, Latinos frequently have been described as America's "new" minority set to "dominate" or "displace" blacks as America's largest, most powerful minority group.[15]

Per the decennial census, blacks are no longer the most numerically dominant minority group in the United States.[16] Much of the conversation around minority politics has shifted to discussing Latino and Asian immigrants as important members of political coalitions in deciding elections.[17] Yet, the complicated political lives of blacks have come to occupy a lesser part of this conversation because blacks vote overwhelmingly as Democrats and have seemingly been "figured out" by the political establishment. In much the same way that blacks have come to be treated as ubiquitous in political discussions, the theoretical conversation has seemed to transcend them. Black/white racial dynamics that had been emblematic of the American racial struggle seem to have fallen from public discourse. Increasingly, scholars and others suggest there needs to be more of a focus on other minority communities who are neither black nor white (Bonilla-Silva 2004; Delgado 1997; Martínez 2007; Perea 1997; Wu 2003). In short, discussions of black people and black/white racial dynamics seem to be passé in popular discourse. Because blacks are seen as more commonplace and have seemingly been supplanted by other groups on the rise, their space in the racial conversation seems to have become less certain as American race relations have become more complex.

Because of the demographic changes wrought by immigration, some scholars suggest we need to refocus our understandings of race so they are less focused on the experiences of blacks (Feagin 2010; Mutua 1999). Along with this post-black racial conversation, the black/white paradigm seems to be treated as less relevant in discourses around race, a relic of a time that no longer exists and with limited applicability to this moment. How, then, do we talk about the black/white racial dyad in a changing America? To my mind, this paradigm has been unresolved and under-addressed for the sake of political expedience. As a result, the black/white paradigm has been ignored in plain sight, but black people have not given up on this paradigm for understanding their embodiment in this America. I contend the black/white dynamic remains a significant interpretative framework for understanding the contours of racial relationships in the contemporary United States. Blacks are the foil for whiteness (Bonnett 1998; Hartigan 1997; Lipsitz 1995; Wiegman 1999). They were the psychic backdrop upon which an idea of whiteness became visible. Thus, (white) America is rendered visible, in part, because of the uses and misuses of black bodies that became animating forces for a number of America's most significant inventions, such as anti-miscegenation laws, the war on drugs, and mass incarceration. All these efforts came to define the ideal citizen through the systematic dehumanization of black people, perpetuated by legal and extralegal institutions (Carter 2012, 2013; Feimster 2009; Hodes 1993; Wiegman 1995). Thus, it is an understatement to say the struggles represented by the black/white racial dynamic are an indelible part of the American fabric (Mills 1997). As Holland (2011) observes, "the way in which we understand how racism manifests itself is through a black/white example that belies very static, but necessary, repetitious reading of racist practice," such that we have not transcended the black/white paradigm but have continued to perfect it (p. 8). By extension, this book claims that black people read immigration as an addition to their struggle (with whites) for inclusion and recognition in the public sphere.

On the one hand, black people read immigration as an act of self-determination, which they appreciate. Much of the black diaspora's struggles can be characterized as a quest to be fully agentic beings and wresting control of their lives from oppressive forces (Bashi 1998, 2004; Carmichael and Hamilton 1967; Gaines 1996; Von Eschen 1997; Sawyer 2006; Tillery 2011). Domestically, blacks have fought strenuously for the right to move freely in this space both metaphorically and in actuality. Blacks fought against an America that curtailed their abilities to decide their community and individual needs. The long fight against Jim Crow was about liberating black people so they could progress economically, socially, and politically. The Montgomery Bus Boycott of 1955, for example, was about the ability to use public conveyances, literal movers of black bodies, in a way that honored their humanity (McAdam 1999). Black people wanted the freedom to not only move through their city unmolested on public transportation, but to also be fully actualized beings. Thus, the buses were symbolic of the many strictures that prevented black people from realizing their full potentiality. Self-determination has long been recognized by black people as the true marker of a liberated life and absolutely constitutive of a fully human experience. It was an experience explicitly denied most blacks until the official dismantling of Jim Crow in 1965, and one that many argue remains elusive (Coates 2015; Cole and Omari 2003; Franklin 1992; Hochschild 1996; McAdam 1999).[18]

On the other hand, blacks are also wary of what newcomers' posture will be toward their group, because immigration has often retarded their social progress. This is not because immigrants are malicious, but because they are self-interested in their own assimilation and often have achieved it at the expense of blacks. Whether these groups meant to hurt blacks is immaterial; white supremacy is immune to intention. Harming black people is a core dictate of this social institution. The end goal of white supremacy is white dominance, and that is only achieved through squelching those who reside on the boundaries of whiteness. Therefore, the only way for these groups to assimilate was to distance themselves from black people by being complicit in the oppression of black people. Thus, the rules of white supremacy have been such that to be associated with blackness has meant the social death of said group. Consequently, the extent to which a group can separate themselves from the stigma of blackness has correlated with increased social success.

By casting their lots with whites, immigrants could hope to gain some semblance of acceptance. This does not mean these groups, like Asians, necessarily thought of themselves as white. However, it does mean the newly arriving were relatively quick to discern that being viewed as closer to whites could vastly improve their social condition. As such, blacks have witnessed many groups achieve greater successes in fairly short order, while their community continues to occupy the lowest rungs of the racial hierarchy. Thus, the black community, despite its history in the United States, has never achieved the level of integration one might expect given their length of residence in this country.

Therefore, for black people, and those interested in understanding them, it is necessary to recognize that it is not simply a matter of moving beyond black and white. Black people are an essential part of the racial conversation and feel the need to assert their centrality into ongoing racial discourse so as to not be ignored, redefined, and/or swallowed by dialogues that would eschew their significance in American racial discourse. Moreover, much of the racial story for black people comes back to their contentious relationship with white people. It seems counterintuitive to write a book about immigration where whites feature so prominently, but that is because whites, as shorthand for white supremacy, are still prominent in the minds of blacks as they consider their racial condition (Feagin 2010; Hacker 2003; Massey and Denton 1993; Walters 2009). Immigration is a way blacks can articulate their ongoing distrust of whites and their political motives (Gay 2002; Nunnally 2012; Tate 2003). Therefore, the issue of immigration is not about immigrants per se. Rather, for black people it is about the maintenance of white supremacy and the ongoing neglect of black concerns.

Keeping this in mind demonstrates why immigration is such a useful lens through which to engage black public opinion on race.

Because immigration neither has been fully theorized nor has it been explored greatly in social science literature with respect to black people, it is ripe to demonstrate the conflicting feelings blacks have about themselves and their relationship to the nation. In particular, this work seeks to (re)assert the importance of the black/white racial paradigm for black public opinion formation. While scholars such as Masuoka and Junn (2013), Kim (2000), Betancur (2005), and Jennings (1994) demonstrate the importance of the black/white racial paradigm, the push to move beyond black/white understandings of race seem to dismiss the centrality of this formative relationship to how black people think about the world—even as that world is becoming more racially complex. Despite the important cues yielded by these works, few have taken up the significance of whites in the literature of interminority relations. In general, studies of interminority relations have looked at the racial demographics on the ground and observed that American cities are increasingly populated by blacks and other minorities.[19] Because of white flight, a lack of black mobility, and immigration, America's urban centers are increasingly non-white. Despite the negligible presence of white people in these spaces, the degree to which white supremacy continues to structure the relationships among minority communities cannot be underestimated.

Theories of Interminority Relations: Coalition, Competition, or Something Else?

The topic of interminority relations came to the fore as the racial demographics changed and America's urban centers were populated primarily by racial and ethnic minorities. As the diversity of America's urban centers increased in the 1970s because of immigration from Asia and Latin America, accompanied by white flight, researchers began to look at the relationships between minority groups (Bobo and Gilliam 1990; Eisenger 1973; Schuman, Steeh, Bobo, and Krysan 1997; Sigelman, Bledsoe, Welch, and Combs 1996). These demographic changes fundamentally altered the substance of urban minority life, which was increasingly characterized by frequent contact between and among people of color (Fong 1998). This ushered in a bevy of new studies that sought to examine the nature and structure of interminority relationships. These studies generally took two forms as researchers sought to locate either coalition or competition between racial/ethnic groups.

I first turn to coalition theories of interminority politics. After the achievements of the Civil Rights Movement and other similar social justice campaigns, a cadre of researchers began their work from the belief that experience with racial prejudice and discrimination would bring groups of color together. Because of familiarity with the joint practices of discrimination and exclusion, they theorized, groups of color had something in "common," which was the necessary adhesive for minority electoral coalitions (Fong 1998). Because none of the groups were numerically powerful enough to wrest power from the ruling white elite, they needed to coordinate their efforts to achieve greater political incorporation in America cities, particularly depending on the racial composition of the setting (Hero and Tolbert 1996). Thus, the common wisdom was that one's group was connected to other minorities excluded from the public sphere, and that minority groups would be compelled to work together.

In some instances authors indeed found coalitions to be the preferred electoral strategy of minority groups (Browning, Marshall, and Tabb 2002). As a result of being (numerical) minorities politically, economically, and socially, groups of color coordinated their efforts to achieve greater sociopolitical incorporation. This was especially true in local political contests. The 1973 election of Tom Bradley as mayor of Los Angeles was a great example of a successful minority coalition. Elected with the help of the Latino, Asian American, African American, as well as liberal Jewish communities, Bradley demonstrated the possibilities of interminority cooperation (Sonenshein 1993). And in cities as diverse as Denver, Philadelphia, Chicago, and San Antonio, coalitions did help minorities win mayoral elections (Muñoz and Henry 1986, 1990; Perry 2003).

Coalition studies yielded mixed results, more often than not revealing cleavages between minority groups. This presented a major challenge in the accompanying theory that often did not designate or consider the circumstances under which coalitions would cease to be desirable. One of the critiques of coalition theories highlighted the fact that coalitions were often short-lived (Kadushin et al. 2005). In the case of Los Angeles, the broad-based coalition that was assembled by Bradley, and ultimately elected him to the office of mayor, quickly dissipated in the face of a contest over a vacant council seat. The presence of this council seat upset the racial balance the Bradley coalition had worked diligently to devise (Sonenshein 1993). So while a cross-racial coalition did form, it was unable to sustain itself when scarce benefits, like a council seat, were up for grabs. Race mattered in these instances, and scholars of coalition studies did not offer a variegated account of the ways in which different minority groups experienced (white) racism and how this led to different needs and expectations of the government (Falcon 1988; Meier and Stewart 1991). Therefore, in instances where minority groups disagreed, coalition scholars usually defaulted to discussions of lack of leadership (Kaufmann 2003).

The appeal of coalitions was to come from this sense of shared minority status. A critical oversight of this theory was that it did not account for the highly contextual and uneven nature of America's racial project (Jacobson 2001; C.J. Kim 1999; Omi and Winant 1994). Racial groups were sorted differently in the racial hierarchy with respect to whites as well as one another (Bonilla-Silva 2004; C.J. Kim 1999; J.Y. Kim 1999; Saito 1998; Song 2004). Therefore, the (occasional) ruptures in minority relationships should have been anticipated, because the aims and objectives of these groups were highly dependent on the respective group's place in the American racial hierarchy. In these instances it was clear that minority group status had the potential to bring groups together as well as tear them apart (Fong 1998).

As scholars began to take seriously the proposition that coalition was as likely an outcome as competition, they began to look again at this idea of shared minority status—a cornerstone of the literature. For example, Kaufmann (2003) found "to the extent Latinos saw their social, economic and political opportunities tied to the status of minorities generally in the United States, the more likely they are to participate in minority led political coalitions" (p. 200). A sense of commonality enabled unity amid diversity in these communities and is indicative of the potential for mass-based coalitions between blacks and Latinos. Sanchez reinforced this finding, arguing that Latinos with a high degree of consciousness feel they have more in common with blacks. Although this does not necessarily mean automatic coalitions will form, it provides the raw material for these coalitions. This is particularly true for those Latinos who believe discrimination is a major problem for them. Still, there are significant subnational differences with respect to Latino feelings of commonality with blacks (Kaufmann 2003; Masuoka 2006; Sanchez and Masuoka 2010).

The fragility of political coalitions was made all the more apparent by intraminority tensions that cropped up in American cities, which led scholars to formulate alternative visions of interminority relations beyond the "coalition-first" model (Cheng and Espiritu 1989). Scholars, realizing the stress placed on urban resources as a result of economic recession, identified several reasons for interminority conflict: competition for limited resources, perceived association with the dominant group, and interminority prejudice.

Those studying interminority conflict from a resource-dependent perspective borrowed largely from the early work of Hubert Blalock (1967), who developed his conflict framework by studying the relationship between whites and blacks. According to Blalock (1967), competition arises in moments where there are multiple groups competing for restricted capital. The result of this competition is that one group's success retards the ability of the other group to access that resource.

In the realm of education Meier, McClain, Polinard, and Wrinkle (2004), in a cross-national comparison of multiracial school districts, examined the limited resources of administrators and teachers. Because these positions are in restricted supply, they are inherently competitive, and gains for one group will result in losses for the other; by default, groups are in zero-sum competition for these jobs. Furthermore, the authors found that when one group gains politically on the school board, their share of jobs in educational administration increases. Because jobs in educational administration are political, "African American school board members are positively associated with more African American administrators, and Latino board members are similarly associated with more Latino administrators" (Meier et al. 2004: 404). Additionally, the authors found evidence that board members support members of their own race/ethnicity while blocking the appointments of administrators not of their group. Still, a significant part of the competition story is the degree to which one can share in limited resources (i.e., city council seats) and the extent to which a group is a desirable coalition partner.

With respect to the former issue, in *The Presumed Alliance*, Vaca (2004) outlines the contours of Latino/black relationships in the twenty-first century where, for the first time in U.S. history, Latinos outnumber blacks as the predominant minority group. Instead of being a catalyst for greater cooperation between these groups, these new demographics have incited and heightened underlying tensions between them as they find themselves in increasing competition for finite social, economic, and political resources.

To illustrate, in his discussion of Compton, Vaca (2004) acknowledged the racial history of the city where whites exercised a great deal of power, which they used to exclude blacks from the city's governmental structure. Because of black activism, they eventually would become part of the city government in Compton. Rather than view this history as informing the politics of blacks in post–Civil Rights Act Compton, Vaca (2004) framed black conflict with Latinos as an irrational, unrelenting fear of Latino dominance. One of the main issues with this work is that Vaca took inherently zero-sum competitive situations and discussed them as if competition were a surprising outcome. In arenas like local elections, the competition that ensues is not necessarily the result of some deep rift between the groups. Although interracial animosity can be a culprit, competition is a rather "natural" outcome borne of the zero-sum situation and the limited resources at stake.

The history of exclusion that blacks fought against to gain positions in the Compton government is what informed their efforts, though problematic, to retain their share of power in the city. However, Vaca (2004) did not address this possibility; instead, he framed the issue as anti-Latino racism on the part of blacks and effectively left whites out of the analysis. By doing so, he missed the fundamental importance of whites who erected barriers to black inclusion, and how that informed black resistance. Blacks in Compton were not automatically anti-Latino as much as they were opposed to the potential of their group's regression into political impotence as Latinos increased their demands for representation.[20] This type of misreading of the racial landscape elides the ways in which racial inequality differentially sorts racial groups into social, political, and economic strata. As such, choices made by earlier generations of whites inform the ways in which blacks understand their circumstances in the present. Thus, the institutional rules that foster racial conflict in the contemporary moment have been nurtured in an environment of past and ongoing racial discrimination against blacks, where whites still occupy the top of the racial order. Thus, blacks are concerned about what this will mean for their group and their ability to maintain the political representation they fought for not long ago, but now see being eroded.

Although blacks and Latinos have combined efforts to achieve greater inclusion in a variety of contexts, fundamental differences over how this inclusion is supposed to look often have overwhelmed attempts at consensus building (de La Garza 1997). Efforts at coalition building have been further hampered by citizenship. Despite being intersecting conversations, issues of race and citizenship have complicated coalition efforts (Ancheta 1998; Kim 1999; Singh 2005). While blacks have consistently sought to fully realize their rights as American citizens, the lack of citizenship for Latinos, as well as some segments of the Asian community, has been a barrier to formal electoral activities such as voting.

Therefore, in Asian and Latino communities, naturalization, voter registration, and voting have presented substantial obstacles to inclusion in political coalitions with African Americans; without formal institutional power, these communities are viewed as unnecessary, or at least provisional (but not full) coalition partners (Pastor and Marcelli 2003).[21] In instances where Latinos may dominate numerically, these numbers have not necessarily translated into greater political representation as has been the case for African Americans (Vaca 2004).

Nevertheless, during many of the moments of interminority conflict, focus is on the race of the minorities involved in the immediate conflict (i.e., blacks and Latinos in the agricultural sector) rather than focusing on the racially discriminatory macro-organization of communities that constrains the available group interactions that could predict such negative outcomes. Whites seemingly have no influence on the relationship between racial minority group members. By framing moments of interminority conflict without reference to the legacy of white racism, we lose sight of the larger issues of systematic racial discrimination that inhibit the political, social, and economic inclusion of minority group members (Betancur 2005).

This book focuses on the continuing significance of the black/white racial paradigm for understanding black public opinion on immigration. By doing so, this work demonstrates the historical and current importance of unresolved racial conflict with whites and how this informs black public opinion in the domain of immigration. Thus, this work extends the literature and insights on interminority relations by demonstrating *how* and *why* race matters in black public opinion on immigration. Additionally, I extend the literature on black politics by offering a theory of black public opinion toward immigration, which is not an issue considered a salient or usual part of a larger black political agenda. Although this has started to change, given current demographic circumstances, there is still a gap in this literature.

Colorblindness and Its Discontents

Viewing blacks as triumphant over slavery and racial injustice on the one hand, and as insecure American citizens on the other hand, allows us to think differently about the narrative of black political incorporation versus that of immigrant groups, who are often wrongly compared to blacks. The disappearance of many formal barriers to equality has not led to a more open racial climate for blacks (Singh 2005). In fact, the continued presence of discrimination in the absence of a formal system of laws and practices á la Jim Crow has left blacks, and others, without a terminology to articulate opposition to inequality in an allegedly colorblind America (Omi and Winant 1994; Singh 2005). Colorblindness assumes that because official racism has been deemed illegal, people will no longer discriminate. Because formal Jim Crow policies, overturned by civil rights legislation, are often treated as racism's only form, many assume racism neither changes nor adapts to new circumstances. Where racism is found, it is treated as an individual action taken against another rather than a systemic problem (Bonilla-Silva 2006, 2015; Kinder and Sanders 1996; Sears 1988; Sidanius and Pratto 2001; Sniderman and Carmines 1997). As a result, the colorblind perspective does not acknowledge group-centered processes of racism and discrimination; in fact, they simply do not exist under its hegemony.

Therefore, under the prevailing ideology of colorblindness, group-based remedies are difficult to secure, and the usual way to deal with incidents of racism is to punish the offending *individual* rather than seek out root causes supporting this type of behavior. As a result, programs such as affirmative action and other forms of group-based redress are viewed skeptically at best and dangerous at worst, alternatively classified as "welfare" favoring undeserving minorities and "reverse racism" for harming deserving whites.

Under colorblindness, racism only exists in the minds of those who see themselves as victims, not as an objective fact. Consequently, what appears to be the result of race—poverty, infant mortality, and high rates of incarceration—is explained in nonracial terms by the (unwise) choices individuals make. Witnessing the rollback of hard-won gains of the Civil Rights Movement, such as the dismantling of affirmative action throughout the 1990s and the recent attacks on the VRA (1965), has done little to assuage black fears of their own exclusion. As such, nationhood and its ultimate symbol—citizenship—are cold comfort for blacks who fear downward mobility in the presence of newcomers (Collins 2001; Estes 2005; Gay 2006; Singh 2005). This is particularly true because whites are viewed as conspirators in black failures. In spheres such as employment and politics, whites strategically and maliciously used immigrants to undercut black social progress (Powers 2005; Shankman 1978).

My theory of *conflicted nativism* argues that African Americans shift their opinions on immigration through the lens of persistent, state-sanctioned discrimination, subjugation, and black/white racial conflict. Blacks claim preference in the sociopolitical environment on the basis of their American citizenship, despite their misgivings about their obviously disadvantaged status in the racial hierarchy (Blumer 1958; Bobo and Hutchings 1996). Blacks, however, see themselves as appreciably different from non-citizens or newly minted citizens because the stigma of blackness has not allowed them the social mobility that has been granted generations of immigrants (Bashi 2004; Frazier 1997; Tolnay and Beck 1992; Tolnay and Eichenlaub 2007). Examining the data concerning health, wealth, and poverty among African Americans, it is clear that the rising tide of American prosperity has not lifted their ships (Bell 1993; Carr and Kutty 2008). For example, black infant mortality rates are among the highest in the United States (MacDorman and Matthews 2011; Singh and Yu 1995). Furthermore, a majority of blacks continue to experience discrimination (Schuman et al. 1997), maintain high levels of unemployment (Farley 1987; McKinnon 2003; Williams and Jackson 2000), face overwhelming levels of incarceration and the consequences therein (Foster and Hagan 2009; Manza and Uggen 2006; Pettit and Western 2004), and make up a substantial portion of America's poor (Harrington 1997; DeNavas-Walt, Proctor, and Smith 2010).

My theory of *conflicted nativism* aids in our understanding of how—in a time of greater visibility and increasing social and political prominence—there remains a continuing sense of exclusion among blacks, especially in the face of new immigrants of color. As such, my research demonstrates that black public opinion with respect to immigration is less hostile and more uncertain than previously thought, and it very much remains shaped by concerns about the distinct racial context of the United States that has traditionally pitted whites against blacks (Telles 1999).

A central problem with coalition and competition theories of interminority relations is that they betray the complexity of black attitudes and ignore the historical realities of black experiences with immigration. Although this book does not seek to discard these theories—they have much to offer and are indeed an important part of the book's narrative—it does stage a theoretical intervention by incorporating the critical insights yielded by black politics and interminority relations to demonstrate the importance of memory and experience in black attitude formation, which are not typically applied to the issue of immigration (Harris-Lacewell 2004; Nunnally 2012; Tillery 2012; Walters 2009; Walton 1994). Nunnally (2012), for example, demonstrated that social trust, both interracially and intraracially, is learned from one's elders. This transmission of racial norms is learned, in part, through interactions with racial groups that have been stigmatized in American society. Similarly, Harris-Lacewell (2004) demonstrates the ways in which black people talk about race in their social spaces. By moving the focus from elites to average black people, Harris-Lacewell found a diverse, sophisticated expression of black ideologies. In both of these texts, it is social interactions with other black people in black communities that help black people identify racial inequality and provide the tools for negotiating the social and political world they inhabit. This book takes these critical insights and treats immigration as part of a larger black political agenda through which blacks to air their grievances with their unsatisfactory status in America's racial hierarchy.

Through this text, I address the nexus between race and American identity and offer the following research questions: How does race influence black public opinion on immigration? How, if at all, do blacks leverage their national identity in formulating these opinions? What is the best way to understand black public opinion? Can we attribute blacks' public opinion in the present to their historical experience of discrimination? How do contemporary experiences with discrimination affect their opinions on immigration? Lastly, how do blacks reconcile their racial and national identities?

I will address these issues in the following chapter, which looks at the role of national identity in black understandings of immigration. Conceptually, this chapter provides the theoretical underpinnings of the text as Chapter 2 highlights the continuing import of blacks' recent history of struggle for staking out a position on the issue of immigration. It is my argument that black attitudes are best characterized as "conflicted nativist" in their orientation. This means blacks express some nationalistic proclivities toward immigration, but are more concerned with highlighting their anxieties about the ongoing importance of anti-black discrimination as the real key to black exclusion. In this way, this book is not about any particular national or ethnic group; it *is* about using immigration as a lens to interrogate the complexity of black opinion in an issue area not commonly associated with a black political repertoire.

2

Citizens First?

AFRICAN AMERICANS AS CONFLICTED NATIVISTS

BLACKS HAVE SOUGHT to redefine the United States through their experience by asserting themselves as creators of American life and experience. They have insinuated themselves into the American story by defying systemic practices that sought to delegitimize their citizenship. Claiming national belonging that, at best, was tentative, black people gave expression to a sensibility that this county, with its mythology of openness, does not value blacks as Americans. Using immigration as a lens, blacks were able to identify the perniciousness of white supremacy that treated them as strangers in their own land. This difference of condition was nowhere more evident than in comparison to recent immigrants.

Immigration has occupied a part of black discursive space since the nineteenth century (Collins 1997; Diamond 1998; Ferreira 1999; Hellwig 1977, 1978, 1981, 1987; Malloy 1996; Rubin 1978; Scott 1999; Shankman 1978, 1980). Immigration had not been a national phenomenon until about 1990 when it moved past traditional receiving contexts, which largely included major cities of the North, West and Midwest. However, post-1990, immigration has spread to smaller cities of the rural Midwest and South. These "new immigrant gateways" represent a geographic dispersion of immigration that has not been seen before (Durand, Massey, and Charvet 2000; Suro and Singer 2001; Singer 2008). Nonetheless, blacks have been talking about immigration since the 1830s (Ferreira 1999; Shankman 1980). Writers as diverse as Frederick Douglass, W.E.B. DuBois, Booker T. Washington, A. Philip Randolph, and a vigorous black press all addressed the issue of immigration at some time or another (Ferreira 1999; Hellwig 1978, 1981; Malloy 1996; Shankman 1980). In many ways, blacks have seen their futures as Americans enmeshed with U.S. immigration policy (Diamond 1998; Ferreira 1999; Hellwig 1978; Shankman 1980). One of the major developments of the civil rights movement was the Immigration and Naturalization Act, which along with the Voting Rights Act (1965) and Civil Rights Acts (1964), formed a triumvirate of legislation that made America more open for native-born blacks and non-European immigrants. The Immigration and Naturalization Act was not a victory separate from the civil rights movement but was part and parcel of the movement for black inclusion. Therefore, when immigrants from Asia, the Caribbean, Africa, and Latin America arrived in the United States post-1965, it was a direct result of black struggle for inclusion. This was unlike immigrants of the early twentieth century who were favored by whites as saboteurs of black progress (Diamond 1998; Hellwig 1981). This was not the fault of the immigrants but the result of national policy and a labor market that preferred to hire Europeans over native-born blacks (Diamond 1998; Tolnay, Adelman, and Crowder 2002).

Despite the clear harms that early waves of European immigration brought to the black community, the accompanying xenophobia around these new arrivals often served as a barometer of the nation's stance on race issues. At times when the nation became more exclusionary with respect to immigrants, it is not coincidental that it also became more closed to black civil rights, because the racist logic that buttressed restrictionist immigration policy also supported black exclusion. This is because of a longstanding (but wrong) assumption that immigration, particularly from non-Protestant and non-European countries, meant whites were going to lose their cultural currency in the country (Avila 2004; Higham 1970; Leitner 2012).

Consequently, black outlets often critiqued the nation's immigration policies because they targeted certain groups in much that same way blacks were singled out by Jim Crow policies (Hellwig 1977, 1987; Scott 1999). For example, when the United States became more restrictionist with respect to Japanese immigrants, blacks viewed this as an attempt on the part of U.S. authorities to maintain white hegemony by alienating itself from its alleged core principles of "life, liberty, and the pursuit of happiness." For black critics of anti-Japanese policy, this was about more than Japanese people. This moment of prohibition demonstrated how quickly their group, barely Americans themselves, could be disinherited from U.S. citizenship. As members of the black press noted, "[C]arried to their logical conclusion, anti-Japanese policies would reinforce the idea of America as exclusively a white man's country" (Hellwig 1977: 96). What is more, many of these immigration policies used race-neutral language, but because nationality was linked with race, the effects were felt dispro-portionately by those considered non-white by whatever metric was being used at the time (Jacobson 2001; Ngai 2004; Tichenor 2002). Therefore, blacks had to make certain their advocacy of pro-restriction policies were not being made on the same racist grounds as the white majority (Hellwig 1977). Still, black criticism of racist immigration policy was not necessarily an endorsement of the foreign born. Some black writers were highly unfa-vorable toward Asian culture and suspicious of this "strange people" (Junn 2006; Shankman 1978). However, they did not appreciate the selective application of U.S. immigration control; if there was going to be immigra-tion restriction, it seemed to many blacks that the policy needed to apply equally to all newcomers, not only those outside of Europe. Although these black writers did not necessarily like foreigners, they abhorred the hypoc-risy of American racism more, and the white supremacy that supported these policies was viewed as the real enemy of black incorporation.[2]

This is not to suggest that black views on immigration were mon-olithic. In the main, however, because of their experience with racial discrimination by native-born whites and immigrants, black opinion on immigration vacillated between restriction and empathy (Hellwig 1978; Scott 1999). Although blacks viewed their status as native-born "Americans" gave them a primary claim to privilege over *all* immi-grant groups, they were often strongly opposed to the inherent racism of immigration regulations (Burns and Gimpel 2000; Diamond 1998; Hellwig 1977, 1982). Because blacks were not politically strong enough to pursue an immigration agenda of their own, they used the immigra-tion issue for their own ends, which meant that immigration became a way for blacks to critique their partial incorporation into the American public sphere. For instance, Booker T. Washington's infamous Atlanta Exposition Address (1895) was made at a time when immigrants made sporadic appearances in the South, but in a context where Washington realized Southern whites were looking at immigrants as instruments to undermine black progress. Washington used his speech to appeal to whites' sense of national brotherhood rather than white supremacy (Bonacich 1973; Loewen 1988; Rhee 1994). In this speech, Washington attempts to get blacks and whites to understand their mutual interests. In particular, he says to:

> "those of the white race who look to the incoming of those of foreign birth and strange tongue and habits for the prosperity of the South,

were I permitted I would repeat what I say to my own race, 'Cast down your bucket where you are.' Cast it down among the eight million of Negroes whose habits you know, whose fidelity and love you have tested in days when to have proved treacherous meant the ruin of your firesides. Cast down your bucket among these people who have, without strikes and labor wars, tilled your fields, cleared your forests, builded [sic] your railroads and cities, and brought forth treasures from the bowels of the earth, and helped make possible this magnificent representation of the South."

While making the case for black and white mutual aid, Washington is trying to highlight the efforts blacks have made on behalf of whites, from nursing their children, caring for them in sickness, and fighting in their wars, which in his estimation warrants whites' loyalty to blacks rather than foreigners. More than loyalty, however, Washington is making the case that blacks have earned their status as true members of the American citizenry and, for this reason, whites should demonstrate to blacks the same loyalty and eschew foreign labor.

For example, after Reconstruction, Chinese laborers were brought to the Mississippi Delta region in an effort to prevent black mobilization for increased political and economic rights. This project was largely a failure because Chinese persons quickly worked their way out of low-skill, low-wage employment and became entrepreneurs. Working primarily in small groceries, these Chinese businesses largely served a black clientele. Thus, they did not become the replacements for black laborers in the way white elites hoped. Although the efforts to lure immigrants to the South largely failed, as witnessed by Mississippi, it was nonetheless clear that whites did not view blacks as allies in the many ways Washington presented and would seek whatever opportunity presented to keep black people in a state of semi-servitude. This included, but was not limited to, using immigrants to stymie black mobility (Posadas 1982; Steinberg 2005).

Although there has been some writing on black public opinion with respect to immigration, there has been little theorizing on the substance of their national attachments and how this is reflected in their attitudes toward immigrants (Carter 2007; Carter and Pérez 2015; Diamond 1998; Greer 2013; Masuoka and Junn 2013; Rubin 1978; Thornton and Mizuno 1999). This text focuses on nativism, an expression of national identity characterized by a chauvinistic posture that exhibits as favoritism toward co-nationals and xenophobia toward outsiders. This has not generally been explored with respect to blacks (Carter and Pérez 2015). Because of this, we do not have a complete representation of how blacks understand themselves with respect to the nation state and how this manifests itself in their attitudes toward immigration.

Although blacks have been presumed to have negative attitudes with respect to immigrants, particularly in light of small, local skirmishes from Pennsylvania to California, it is necessary to know whether blacks see themselves as "prototypical" Americans with a culture to protect (Esses, Dovidio, Jackson, and Armstrong 2001; Vaca 2004; Waldinger 1996)[2] and to what extent this American identity operates to exclude "others."

In this country, one of the defining features of nativist rhetoric has been the idea that immigrants change the collective identity of a nation if they are allowed to enter unchecked. However, these movements have been underwritten by whites. The Know-Nothing movement was a white organization designed to protect the interests of white citizens.[1] Similarly, the Minuteman Project is largely fronted by whites who fear (Mexican) immigrants, particularly the undocumented, because they allegedly represent a threat to national security.[2] In the years since Donald Trump has taken office, this preoccupation with protecting American borders and culture has taken on a new relevance. Not only has Donald Trump proposed to send 15,000 armed American troops to the Mexican border to fend off asylum seekers, he disseminated a racist advertisement via his Twitter page that blamed Democrats for making America unsafe because they are "soft" on undocumented immigrants. The advertisement opened with the line, "Illegal immigrant, Luis Bracamontes, killed our people!" While the "our" in this advertisement is ostensibly Americans, given the white supremacist sympathies of this administration one cannot be certain. Donald Trump is not the only offender, as the dog whistle of "illegal immigrants" was weaponized throughout the 2018 midterm elections.

For example, in Kansas, where undocumented immigrants make up a relatively small portion of the population, gubernatorial nominee Chris Kobach (R) suggested creating a database to document these individuals, revoking in-state tuition for the undocumented, and punishing localities that offer sanctuary to these individuals (Valverde 2018). Although border protection is often framed as a matter of fairness and law enforcement, much of the anxiety around undocumented immigration is about race (Banks 2014; Pantoja 2006; Pérez 2016).[3] More concretely, much of the apprehension about immigration is about non-white people liter-ally changing the face of the nation—to the point that President Trump has proposed revoking birthright citizenship, a constitutional provi-sion and cornerstone of American identity, for the children of undocu-mented immigrants. Though an executive order would not trump the Constitution, Senator Lindsey Graham (R-SC) has doubled down on this proposal and vowed to introduce legislation to mirror Trump's suggested executive order (Lesniewski 2018). These attitudes at the national level, unfortunately, are not out of step with the attitudes of the broader public. Research has shown that the immigration debates are partly influenced by race. People are not as preoccupied about undocumented immigrants from Europe, for example (Brader, Valentino, and Suhay 2008; Burns and Gimpel 2000; Espenshade and Calhoun 1993). Thus, claims about the sanctity of American identity are highly racialized because the version of America that proponents of more restrictionist policies are attempting to preserve is not inclusive of people of color.

It would seem from the prevailing arguments that individuals are con-cerned with the degree to which immigrants will make this country less racially white. These anxieties will likely be heightened, as demographers have shown the inevitability of a waning white population in the United States. The U.S. Census estimates the United States will cease to be a white-majority country by 2043. The Brookings Institution notes these changes are largely the result of immigration that has occurred in the decades since 1965, higher birthrates among non-whites, and declining birthrates among whites (Frey 2011). California, New Mexico, Texas, and Hawaii are already majority-minority states. Although "Latino" is officially considered an ethnicity, it is unclear if Latinos are socially understood as socially white, though they can be on paper. What is more, whites—in general, but particularly white men—feel aggrieved in this changing ra-cial climate and see themselves as victims of racial discrimination amid calls to make the nation more reflective of these demographic changes (Berbrier 2000; Myers 2018). This particular display of "white fragility" makes it difficult for these types of changes to go unnoticed and unchal-lenged by whites (DiAngelo 2018).

All too often, the most effective opposition mounted by whites to the racial outsiders (in this case immigrants) who threaten their superordi-nate identity is to create an immigration regime to cordon off, detain, and/or neutralize those threats to American national identity (Tichenor 2002). This makes it difficult, then, to default to white attitudes and opinions, and makes it particularly difficult to understand whether, how, and to what degree blacks identify as exemplars of national identity (Harris-Lacewell 2003). Given their status as an excluded group within the American polity, I posit that blacks have adopted an ambivalent perspective on immigration. On the one hand, blacks believe in the right to self-determination and are empathetic to the plight of immigrants (Ferreira 1999; Hellwig 1978; Rubin 1978). This is not to suggest blacks do not value American identity or that they are unwilling to make strides toward shoring up that identity. A unique part of the black struggle for inclusion in this country has been the cooptation of American identity despite official efforts to divorce blackness from Americanness (Gaines 1996; Parker 2009; Tillery 2011). On the other hand, they recognize immigrants may represent a challenge to their group's social mobility because immigrants receive benefits based on their distance from blackness and/or have access to opportunities not afforded to blacks (Hellwig 1982). While I am not suggesting immigrants are colluding with whites to harm blacks, I am suggesting there is recognition among blacks that some immigrants are viewed as preferable to their group, and in cases where black versus non-black distinction has been made, it has not boded well for African Americans (Adelman and Tolnay 2003; Pager, Bonikowski, and Western 2009; Rosenfeld and Tienda 1999; Waldinger 1996). The important point here is that blacks do not view immigrants as a problem because they will corrupt American culture. Rather, blacks are concerned that immigrants will be *favored by whites* and thus retard blacks' ability to become full participants in the citizenry. It is my sense that while blacks may hold some nativist attitudes, these attitudes are devoid of a set of policy preferences and disembodied from mobilization efforts that would do harm immigrant communities. Historically, whites have attempted to use immigrants to dampen black demands for equality, particularly in the labor sector, which embittered some segments of the black population[4] (Hellwig 1978; Loewen 1971; Malloy 1996; Scott 1999).

Labor organizer A. Philip Randolph, made famous through his efforts with the Brotherhood of Sleeping Porters, expressed what can best be characterized as anti-immigrant views, particularly because the Pullman Corporation attempted to use Filipino immigrant labor in an effort to subvert black demands for better working conditions. More recent controversies in California regarding the specter of black workers being replaced by Latino labor have raised a similar concerns on the part of blacks who see their share of the labor market being eroded by the presence of this group (Briggs 2003). Consequently, blacks use their status as American citizens, however marginal, to claim greater status for themselves in the polity as a privilege of birthright.[5] As Hellwig (1981) notes, "if immigrant restriction did not lead to a substantial improvement in the daily lives of the average black citizen, it might at least, the leaders hoped, preserve their positions and those of their followers until a better life could be forged for all in a land of 100 percent Americans" (p. 123). Thus, black support for some limitations on immigration at different moments in time was generally about trying to ensure their group's future improvement—not necessarily a meanspirited attempt to hurt others.

For example, in "The Shape of Fear," W.E.B. DuBois (1926) argues that white reactions to blacks, as well as immigrants, was about their fear of losing their dominance. Therefore, organizations like the Ku Klux Klan, along with racist legislation advancing national origin quotas, are about maintaining a racial purity at all costs. However, DuBois believes anti-Catholicism, anti-Semitism, and the like can be distilled easily into hatred for black people. This is because "they [the American] people realized that no group in the United States is working harder to push themselves forward and upward than the Negroes" (DuBois 1926: 302). Thus, what gives rise to the Ku Klux Klan's brand of hatred is the "the fear that white America with its present machinery is not going to be able to keep black folk down," despite their attempts to use violence and legal devices to dissuade blacks from pursuing equality (p. 301). Consequently, instead of being praised for their accomplishments against great odds, blacks are punished and harassed. Therefore, by exercising their individual and constitutional liberties, blacks are pushed further to the margins of America.

Nativism and National Identity

In *Strangers in the Land,* John Higham (1970) offers a historical look at trends in nativist sentiment in the United States. Nativism is defined as a concern that some group originating from abroad threatens national identity. In the United States, these attitudes have often been expressed by whites who view immigrants as dangerous to core American values and principles that have traditionally been embodied as white, male, and Protestant. Immigrants aroused hostility based on their supposed "foreign connections," which marked them as unassimilable and potentially disloyal to the nation (Higham 1975: 4). In general, white Americans have viewed immigrants, including those from Southern and Eastern Europe, as racial and cultural dangers to the unity of this nation (Higham 1970; Huntington 2004; Jacobson 2001). Thus, eagerness to subdue foes of the "American" way of life has frequently resulted in campaigns and legislation to restrict the flow of new arrivals (Higham 1975; Knobel 1996; Jacobson 2001). For instance, the Chinese Exclusion Act of 1882 arose in response to fears that Chinese immigrants were a threat to American citizens' ability to find employment, particularly in the rail and mining industries. The hysteria created around the presence of Chinese immigrants constructed them as not only racially different from native-born Americans but also made them the first "illegal aliens" and thus criminalized their presence in this country (Lee 2002a). The Chinese Exclusion Act marks the first time a specific nationality was prevented from coming to the United States, essentially codifying the act of immigration and naturalization as the province "free white persons" (Lee 2002b). Moreover, Chinese exclusion ushered in a period of unprecedented surveillance and enforcement of national borders, particularly with Mexico, and criminalized Chinese persons already residing in the United States (Lee 2002a; Sheridan 2002).[6] Thus, by the time the National Origins Quota Act passed in 1924, immigration policy was devised in such a way as to actively preserve the notion of the United States as a white-identified country.[7] The resulting policy was such that most non-Europeans were prevented from entering the country, and the racial composition of the immigrant pool remained majority European (i.e., white).

Empirical research has shown that these types of attitudes are far from inevitable, because the presence of newcomers as such does not elicit uniformly negative associations. Strong national identity does not necessarily lead one to be a nativist (De Figueiredo and Elkins 2003). Nativism is generally understood as a chauvinistic belief in the superiority of one's country over others (Citrin, Haas, Muste, and Reingold 1994; Feshbach 1994; Hurwitz and Peffley 1999; Sidanius, Feshbach, Levin, and Pratto 1997). Patriotism generally connotes an affinity and attachment to official and unofficial symbols of a nation; this is generally viewed as a positive expression of nationalism (Citrin et al. 1994; Huddy and Khatib 2007; Hurwitz and Peffley 1999; Sidanius et al. 1997). While one should use care not to conflate these related concepts, what is clear is that nativism has a deep and persistent quality that expresses itself when a country experiences, or believes it is experiencing, an influx of "foreigners." Nativists view immigrants as threats to the nation's foundational identity and population and believe that a country is best when it rejects foreigners (Higham 1975; Huntington 2004; Knobel 1996). Although the language of nativists is often universalistic, in the case of the United States it is clear nativists believe the country is, by definition, racially white as the Founders intended. Thus, the ideal citizen as constitutionally and ideologically imagined is white and male; blacks were not envisioned as ideal citizens and neither were "non-white" immigrants, Native Americans, or women. Because the ideal citizen is already racialized as white, those immigrants not understood as racially "white" are always outside of this definitional citizenry. By relying on nationalist rhetoric of "fitness"[8] for citizenship and the like, nativists are able to make exclusionary claims about the criteria for domestic identity and belonging that appear race neutral (Lindsay 1998; Mills 1999). For instance, a commitment to Protestantism has often been used as a way to measure a group's suitability to the principles of Americanism (Tichenor 2002). Although Protestantism is not racialized on its face, it is clear that if this is a criterion of acceptance, some groups will not be included. For instance, as the United States began to receive immigrants from Ireland and Italy, the nativist response through the 1830s and 1840s was largely based on anti-Catholic religious discrimination. Because America was, by design, opposed to hierarchical authority, which is how the Catholic Church is organized, adherents of the religion were seen as opposed to the founding traditions of the republic (Higham 1970; Knobel 1996). Many white Americans viewed the Catholic Church as opposed to liberty because of its relation to monarchies and feudal governments (Higham 1975). The United States, being especially sensitive to such control because they had just defeated the empire of Great Britain in the Revolutionary War, created a government of diffuse authority. More importantly, however, Protestant Americans feared the authority of the papacy. They viewed Catholic immigrants as emissaries of the pope, sent to the United States to disrupt American institutions (Higham 1970). Because it was thought Catholic immigrants would only submit to the authority of the pope, they were viewed as being devoid of the capacity for self-government (Higham 1970). Because the ability to own and govern the self was viewed as essential for American citizenship, Catholic immigrants were, by definition, deemed unfit for citizenship. Although we have moved past this place, this Protestant bias lingers and is evidenced in our political choices. To date, John F. Kennedy, Jr. has been the only Catholic person elected to serve as President of the United States.[9]

It is generally agreed that nativism is not the same as patriotism (Carter and Pérez 2015; Citrin et al. 1994; Citrin, Wong, and Duff 2001; De Figueiredo and Elkins 2003; Schatz, Staub, and Lavine 1999; Sidanius et al. 1997). However, the degree to which nativism and patriotism are reciprocal is a source of debate (Citrin et al. 1994, 2001; De Figueiredo and Elkins 2003; Sidanius et al. 1997). Nativism is a negative type of nationalism, resulting in the discrimination and mistreatment of immigrant communities; however, patriotism is not generally associated with the same types of xenophobic responses. Usually patriots are more prepared to recognize immigrants or others who are willing to adopt the signs and symbols of their new homeland (De Figueiredo and Elkins 2003; Schatz et al. 1999). In most cases, patriots respond to newcomers without the racism and jingoism that has characterized nativists. Yet, there is some evidence that patriotism is related to classical racist ideas. The work of Sidanius et al. (1997) shows that for whites who identify with patriotic symbols, there is an increase in racist attitudes. Although the purpose of this work is not to adjudicate this debate, I think it is important to note, despite the fact there is general definitional agreement regarding nativism and patriotism, the relationship between these concepts has yet to be reconciled.[10]

While I ascribe to the definitional claims of the work on nativism, with few exceptions, this research has focused almost exclusively on whites; therefore, we do not know how these concepts operate for blacks who have a different experience. Most basically, because blacks are a racially excluded group, albeit highly visible, their incorporation as full members of the body politic remains less than fifty years old and far from complete. Thus, what authors have identified as the contours of nativist thought in the United States is informed by the attitudes and actions of whites (Citrin et al. 1994, 2001; Higham 1975; De Figueiredo and Elkins 2003). This bias in the literature continues despite the fact blacks also have written extensively on the topic of immigration from the nineteenth century onward. Comments on immigration appeared in opinion sections of black newspapers nationally. In particular, blacks were dismayed they were being overlooked in favor of immigrants. In response to national origins quotas of 1924, the black press argued that the law did not do enough to prevent Mexicans from coming to the United States, which meant blacks would now have to compete with them for menial jobs (Hellwig 1981). This position was self-interested on the part of blacks because they believed their economic and social prospects would be improved in the absence of competition from immigrants. As stated earlier, they were not as bothered by the restrictions on immigration as they were by the racial logic that gave rise to the creation of this type of legislation. What is more, the color of the immigrant did not matter as much to them, because they tended to fare worse whenever immigrants were present (Diamond 1998).

I argue that blacks' experience as insecure Americans produced a particular form of national identity I term *conflicted nativism*, which is animated by a different set of lived concerns than traditional nativism. Rather than being distressed that immigration will harm U.S. culture, black nativists are more concerned that immigration will be bad for black people. This is an important distinction to make, because it has often been the case that immigrants were feared simply because they were different. In this case the anxieties around immigration are not about immigrants per se, but about the ways in which immigrants are used against blacks in a white supremacist society such as the United States.

Race and Citizenship

From its inception, as evidenced by the Constitution, the United States was viewed as a white man's country. Although the Founding documents of the nation established this identity, federal entities, local law, and custom thoroughly reinforced this notion well into the twentieth century as formal citizenship was the sole province of (wealthy) white men (Brenkman 1993; Jacobson 2001; Collins 2001; Mills 1999; Smith 1988, 1993, 2001; Wiegman 1995). Even though black men obtained the franchise in 1868 via the 14th Amendment, it would be another century before the United States would make good on its promise of universal suffrage. Unlike many authors who see the founding vision of the United States as expansive and inclusive (Hartz 1991; Huntington 2004; Myrdal 1962[1942]; Schlesinger 1998), I argue, as do many others, that the exclusion of women, blacks, Native Americans, Asians, and others was not a perversion of the application of civic ideals but rather a *requirement* of Americanness (Brenkman 1993; Dawson 2001; Haney-López 1996; Collins 2001; Jacobson 2001; Mills 1999; Singh 2004; Smith 1993, 2001). The Supreme Court's decision in *Dred Scott v. Sandford* (1857) illustrates this point most cogently.[11] In the majority decision, the Court provided legal support for the belief that black people had no rights that a white man was bound to respect.[12] More importantly, Chief Justice Taney, in delivering the majority opinion, stated in unambiguous language that black people were never considered "citizens" by the Founders; therefore, Scott did not even have standing to bring his case. As the Court argued:

> The words "people of the United States" and "citizens" are synonymous terms, and mean the same thing. They both describe the political body who, according to our republican institutions, form the sovereignty, and who hold the power and conduct the Government through their representatives. They are what we familiarly call the "sovereign people," and every citizen is one of this people, and a constituent member of this sovereignty. The question before us is, whether the class of persons described in the plea in abatement compose a portion of this people, and are constituent members of this sovereignty? We think they are not, and that they are not included, and were not intended to be included, under the word "citizens" in the Constitution, and can therefore claim none of the rights and privileges which that instrument provides for and secures to citizens of the United States. On the contrary, they were at that time considered as a subordinate and inferior class of beings, who had been subjugated by the dominant race, and, whether emancipated or not, yet remained subject to their authority, and had no rights or privileges but such as those who held the power and the Government might choose to grant them.

The case signified the cleavages in the United States around the issue of slavery; however, using a strict constructionist approach, the Court was able to assert that the Founders never intended for those who were not white and male to be citizens of this country. For a majority of the Supreme Court, black rights were a moot point because if this group was not considered part of the citizenry at the time the U.S. Constitution was devised, they cannot simply be ushered into citizenship. Any claim to a universal acknowledgment of citizenship for black people was rejected by the nation's highest court as being a fundamental misreading of Founding documents. Because people of African descent were considered as articles of property as articulated in the Constitution, their status as outsiders was fixed.[13]

Moving from a colony to a republic, the newly minted United States developed its own criteria for national membership. Because the new republic abandoned the British form of hierarchical, aristocratic government, the polity essentially belonged to "the people" (Higham 1970).

Thus, "the people" were responsible for administering the public will, which required that citizens be able to conceive of and do what was in the best interest for the greatest number of the *members* of the republic. Consequently, the ideal citizen had to be self-possessed, with the ability to suppress his "passions" for the betterment of the polity. Hence, to be a "fit" citizen, they had to be recognized as part of the polity and have the ability to share a common vision for the progress of the nation (Brenkman 1993; Collins 2001).

As a settler republic, indigenous peoples were necessarily excluded because they were believed to be barbarians without the capacity for self-governance (Brenkman 1993; Jacobson 2001; Nagel 1997; Washburn 1965). This racial mythology was a significant element of the rationale for the conquest and usurpation of native lands in North America and other colonial enterprises (Rogin 1975; Washburn 1965). Moreover, enslaved Africans, free blacks, and their descendants were literally and figuratively kept from self-ownership (Jacobson 2001; Roberts 1997). As a physically and socially distinct category of beings, African-descended people could not, and would not, be incorporated into a republic of self-governing individuals. Unlike indigenous people, who were not fully evolved beings, they thought Africans did not have the intellectual capacity for self-government. Africans were thought to be inherently inferior groups, incapable of the perfection necessary for self-governance. Therefore, because of the explicit connection made between race and citizenship from the nation's beginning, later solidified by social custom and science, blacks were dispossessed of an American identity (Collins 1997; Jacobson 2001). Evidence of this thinking can be seen in the Naturalization Act of 1790, which granted a right of entry to free white persons and naturalization after two years of residence[14] (Jacobson 2001). In its brevity, this statute shows national belonging had nothing to do with defined territories or borders but everything to do with color.

The bond between race and citizenship would be heightened in the nineteenth century as the republic expanded westward, slavery was on the wane, and the flow of free "white" persons from Southern and Eastern Europe began to increase rapidly (Haney-López 1996; Jacobson 2001; King 2009; Ngai 2004). Latent anti-immigrant sentiment was reignited throughout these periods as concerns over labor competition and cultural preservation were heightened during moments of increased immigration. This nativist impulse remains part of contemporary immigration discourse and practice (Carter and Pérez 2015; Masuoka and Junn 2013;

Sanchez 1997). For example, California's Proposition 187 was an effort to bar undocumented immigrants from receiving medical care, educational, and social services. Service providers would be on the front lines of this effort because teachers, hospital employees, and the like would be empowered to question an individual's citizenship status. The impetus for the law was the belief that undocumented immigrants represented an undue burden to the social service system in California.[15] Although the law was framed as an attempt to stem economic hardship for Californians, many critics saw this as a discriminatory measure that unfairly targeted Latinos and Asians who only began coming to the United States in large numbers after 1965 (Adelman and Tolnay 2003; Lieberson 1980). This new immigration changed the way America looked. Yet, the persistence of English-only propositions, as well as moves to disallow social services for immigrants, indicate that policing the borders of American nationhood remains a powerful political preoccupation (Alvarez and Butterfield 2000; Espenshade and Calhoun 1993; Johnson, Farrell, and Guinn 1997; Pantoja 2006). What remains unclear is the degree to which blacks are moved to support or oppose any of these efforts.

The "Twoness" of Black Citizenship

DuBois' metaphor of "twoness," or double consciousness, is often evoked to describe the experience of being both black and American. Taken from his classic text *The Souls of Black Folk* (1903), DuBois describes the difficulties that come with retaining one's identity as a black person and trying to reconcile that with a national identity that conspires against black incorporation. Yet, despite the apt nature of DuBois' metaphor, there is still much to parse regarding how blacks view their American identity juxtaposed against the presence of the newly arrived. Much like their white counterparts, blacks were deeply engaged in their own immigration debates from the nineteenth century through the twentieth century (Ferreira 1999; Hellwig 1977, 1979, 1981; Diamond 1998; Shankman 1977, 1978). Blacks used immigration to define what national belonging and citizenship, as the embodiment and guarantor of national inclusion, meant for their community. Although opposed, on the one hand, to the racism of the white nativist movement, blacks were far less sanguine about what the continuing arrival of new immigrants meant for their own social progress. Thus, blacks developed a distinct immigration agenda that deployed their American identity as a primary claim to privilege but did *not* include immigrant exclusion as a primary objective. Rather, blacks were attempting to find a way to protect their community by putting forth a social and political agenda that made their communities' needs immediately clear and actionable. Blacks were not waiting to be overlooked; they were going to assert themselves into the conversation on immigration (Diamond 1998; Hellwig 1978, 1981; Tillery and Chresfield 2012).

As early as the 1840s, black writers and intellectuals such as Frederick Douglass were intensely concerned with how European immigration would affect the status of blacks (Ferreira 1999; Malloy 1996; Shankman 1980). Although Douglass and others were committed to the dissolution of slavery, Douglass was also sensitive to the plight of immigrants, especially the Irish (Ferreira 1999; Shankman 1980). While blacks were being enslaved in the United States, the despair of the Irish people left a lasting impression on him when he went to the country in 1845. After the publication of his life story Douglass became a celebrity of the abolitionist movement and this increased the likelihood that he could be captured and reenslaved.[16] Initially, he went to Britain seeking refuge because he was technically a fugitive and did not have freedom papers; like other blacks, even free blacks, Douglass undertook this journey as a stateless person. Not long after his arrival, Douglass traveled to Dublin where he spent several months and became supporter of Irish home rule and witnessed the worst of Irish oppression, particularly the ravages of the famine (Ferreira 1999). Upon his return to the United States in 1847, Douglass organized fundraising efforts to aid the cause of the Irish people in Ireland (Ferreira 1999; Shankman 1980). In the Irish peasant's struggles against England, Douglass saw parallels with the abolition movement in the United States. This sense of empathy and initial enthusiasm on the part of Douglass and the larger black community was dampened as the stream of Irish arrivals came to shun black solidarity and cast their lot with the native white majority (Ferreira 1999; Roediger 1999; Shankman 1980).

Not only were Irish immigrants pro-slavery in many instances, their willingness to adopt anti-black attitudes and commit violent acts against black "citizens" disquieted those who considered themselves friends of the Irish (Dooley 1998; Jacobson 2001; Roediger 1999; Shankman 1980).[17] Although Irish immigrants faced harsh treatments and discrimination, they were not enslaved in this country and could hope to advance to citizenship (Ferreira 1999; Shankman 1980). As Douglass (2003 [1855]) said, "The Irishman is poor, but he is not a slave. He may be in rags, but he is not a slave" (p. 422). This disparity in situation made native blacks resentful of the fairly easy path to citizenship created for European immigrants (Malloy 1996). The realization that immigrants could hope to find a better life, a basic right that eluded black people because of the intransigence of racism, caused blacks to be more vigorous in their challenges to white supremacy.

Although black "nativists" lacked the political capital to mount a formal institutional barrier to immigration, they developed a more forceful set of critiques of America's racist practice that denied them full citizenship for no other reason besides being born black (DuBois 1925). Because blacks appreciated the ways in which the fate of immigrants was predicated on a racial logic that had negative implications for their community, they increased their critiques of U.S. immigration policy. Thus, in black media outlets throughout the twentieth century, they used immigration policy as a way to frame their grievances with American racial policy. For example, blacks' critique of the Gentleman's Agreement with Japan in 1907 was based on the policy's exclusion of non-Europeans. For blacks who were entitled to the rights and privileges of full citizenship, the biggest hurdle to their incorporation was white racists who were committed to an ideology of exclusion (Dawson 2001; Malloy 1996). Yet, their contributions were denied in an effort to reinforce white supremacy and their place at the bottom of the American racial hierarchy (Hellwig 1978; Kim 2000; Malloy 1996). Blacks realized that shared nationality was an unreliable criterion for citizenship. This sense of racial insecurity became amplified in intra-communal dialogues about immigration (Hellwig 1977, 1978, 1981, 1987; Malloy 1996; Rubin 1978; Shankman 1978, 1980; Weill and Castañeda 2004; Wilhelm 1971). In spaces where blacks could speak to other blacks, they were preoccupied with their ongoing exclusion and were waging a decades-long fight for freedom. In the cases of other immigrant groups singled out for segregation vis-à-vis U.S. immigration policy, blacks were particularly empathetic with those groups' struggles. In the case of Japanese people, black newspapers offered an empathetic posture with regard to their exclusion and the racist grounds on which it was perpetrated. The *Baltimore Afro-American* (1920) noted the "exclusion of Japanese . . . was grounded in color prejudice." And while blacks were mostly self-interested, there was a measure of admiration for representatives of the "Orient" such as the Japanese. As Jun (2006) notes, this type of reification of the "Orient" by blacks is "appealing to disidentified black subjects who are attempting to imagine liberatory possibilities, identifications, and historical futures in spaces that have been defined as *not* the United States" (p. 1050). Yet, this positive sensibility toward Japanese citizens was not reflected in the same way when it came to Chinese exclusion. While some blacks were highly critical of Chinese exclusion, other blacks used the stereotype of the unassimilable Chinese to define their Americanness. This does not mean that blacks had the power to influence immigration policy or thwart moves toward anti-Chinese discrimination. It does mean, however, that blacks' opinions on immigration were complicated and context dependent. More to the point, blacks attitudes about immigration seemed to hang on what grounds the United States sought to exclude a particular group of immigrants. If immigrants were being excluded on their distance from American cultural values, black were going to demonstrate how much and how well they themselves approximated these American norms relative to the foreign born, in an effort to seek inclusion. Thus, blacks' opinions on immigration were highly focused on their own group's well-being.

Although the institution of formal enslavement was constitutionally dissolved in 1865, the continued denial of black civil rights significantly delayed black progress (Estes 2005). Everywhere the message to blacks was that they were not "real Americans." For almost a century, European immigrants were afforded full citizenship rights ahead of native-born blacks (Estes 2005; Jacobson 2001; Malloy 1996). Even after passage of the 14th Amendment, blacks were keenly aware that the Constitution meant nothing when it came to guaranteeing their incorporation in the polity (Dawson 2001). Although blacks had attained formal recognition as Americans, this status was in name only as they continued to face social, economic, and political disenfranchisement (Adelman and Tolnay 2003; Collins 1997, 2001; Conley 1999; Dawson 1994b, 2001; Estes 2005; Franklin 1992; Massey and Denton 1993; Sugrue 1996).[18]

As the United States was rapidly industrializing, World War I opened up factory positions, and immigration was slowing, new employment opportunities were being created for blacks in the North and Midwest (Adelman and Tolnay 2003; Collins 1997; Lieberson 1980; Sugrue 1996). Despite blacks migrating to these regions in the hope of obtaining better employment opportunities than in the South, they could not compete with immigrant workers (Collins 1997; Hellwig 1981; Malloy 1996; Lieberson 1980; Rubin 1978). Black and white workers had to deal with decreased bargaining powers as a result of the cheap labor immigrants provided. Unlike native whites, however, blacks had the additional burden of anti-black prejudice (Hellwig 1981).

Despite the fact many blacks were willing to accept substandard wages, white employers preferred hiring non-black workers (Adelman and Tolnay 2003; Collins 1997, 2001; Fairlie and Sundstrom 1997, 1999; Johnson 2004; Maloney 1995; Maloney and Whatley 1995). It was already diffi-cult competing with native-born whites for employment, but blacks took umbrage at having to compete with foreigners (Malloy 1996). Blacks felt entitled to available employment, as well as other benefits of U.S. society, by virtue of birthright. Booker T. Washington was concerned about this very thing and supported early efforts to stem immigration from Europe. Washington believed black labor was the key to social progress, which he feared might be retarded by the presence of immigrant competitors who provided cheap labor and had white skin (Malloy 1996). Thus, he surmised that limiting immigration was the appropriate manner to en-sure the upward mobility of his community (Hellwig 1978, 1981; Malloy 1996; Rubin 1978). Washington's ideas were also echoed in the black press as opinion pieces and letters to the editor often favored limiting immigra-tion (Tillery and Chresfield 2012; Hellwig 1978, 1981; Malloy 1996; Rubin 1978). Although this sentiment received some support from various cor-ners of the black community, they were in no position to push the govern-ment to place limits on immigration.

Furthermore, blacks realized that limiting or banning immigra-tion would not remedy their core problem, which was white supremacy (Hellwig 1978, 1981; Rubin 1978). Although blacks knew limiting immi-gration would substantially lessen competition in the marketplace, they also knew the only groups that would be banned would be other persons of color (Hellwig 1978; Rubin 1978). Chinese exclusion in 1882, as well as the Immigration Act of 1924, proved that the United States was less willing to limit the migration of other whites, which was a move blacks condemned (Hellwig 1978; Rubin 1978). For example, in 1921 an anonymous opinion piece published in *The Appeal*, a black writer based in St. Paul, Minnesota, states "[t]he hordes of foreigners who are planning to come to this country, if possible, are a menace to the opportunities of the native born colored working people who should be protected by appropriate legislation" (p. 2). The author recommends unnaturalized immigrants be required to pay for an annual license to work so as not to escape taxation. He sums up his piece by saying "the colored people are all citizens and taxpayers and their interests should not be overlooked" (p. 2). What this author expresses is an abiding sense that immigrants come to this country and reap all of the benefits without any of the burdens. Because black *citizens* comply with their duties, like paying taxes, but receive little to no representation, the author asserts black interests are being violated by the U.S. government. To use the often quoted language of the American Revolution, he says that blacks are currently in a situation of "taxation without representation," a blatant violation of the country's civic ideals. Immigrants are seen by this author as both a source of economic and political competition. For him, the government's reluctance to place limits on new arrivals symbolizes the country's indifference to black progress.[19] Not only are immigrants labor market competition for blacks, they are not necessarily committed to or invested in the nation in the same way as blacks.

Still, this did not negate the fact that banning immigration was a short-sighted strategy for dealing with the systemic issue of white supremacy. The opinion of this author seems to be born of frustration with the black condition, not outright intolerance of immigrants. Undergirding immigration policies were decisions made by a government helmed by whites who lacked the political desire to assist the advancement of black people. Thus, it becomes easier to attack immigrants who are closer to blacks in terms of their social location and status rather than a government that is engaged in organized, anti-black prejudice. Still, it is clear that for many black authors, going after immigrants was a classic case of picking low hanging fruit (Diamond 1998; DuBois 1929; Hellwig 1981; Scott 1999; Shankman 1982). It was easier to be critical of immigrants and express less than flattering attitudes toward them than to mount opposition to white institutions.[20] This is not to say blacks refused to confront injustice—this would be historically inaccurate. During the Nadir, the period between 1877 and 1940, black opposition was largely local in nature and was unable to achieve the sweeping changes associated with the modern civil rights movement (Logan 1954).[21] What blacks are seeking vis-à-vis immigration policy is an acknowledgment of their institutional disadvantage. Unless structural discrimination and other routine causes of black exclusion and disenfranchisement were addressed, blacks knew they would remain outside the body politic no matter what the demographic picture of the nation. Consequently, immigrant restriction, although cathartic, was seen as a less viable solution for addressing long-term community needs (Diamond 1998; Morris 2000) because even if all future immigration was prevented, it would probably change black life chances only on the margins, where it might be easier for them to obtain certain types of employment. However, the changes blacks wanted to see could only be achieved by ending white supremacy. Therefore, putting all efforts on immigration restriction would not end the entrenched problems blacks sought to remedy.

Throughout the twentieth century, blacks were uneasy about supporting efforts to exclude other communities of color, although they were not necessarily opposed to immigration restrictions if they were to be applied to all groups equally (Hellwig 1978; Malloy 1996). Although blacks were sometimes negative in their feelings toward immigrants, they were even more wary of supporting white nativist activities. They knew that in supporting exclusionist measures aimed at other minorities, they were also supporting their own degradation. After all, these anti-immigrant groups were the same groups that supported their segregation in American society (Diamond 1998; DuBois 1925; Higham 1975). Therefore, if blacks were complicit in supporting Chinese exclusion, for example, it also meant they "[agreed] with the ideology and practices of the white supremacist who wanted to retain the black American in a position of semi-servitude in his place of birth" (Hellwig 1973). Blacks, despite holding some anti-immigrant attitudes, had a fundamentally different understanding of the meaning of immigration than their white counterparts (Morris 2000; Nteta 2013). As Hellwig notes, "the America white nativists wanted to defend or resurrect was one which excluded blacks—regardless of their values—from full citizenship," which is a clear divergence in perspective from blacks (Hellwig 1982: 95). Blacks, however nativist in their opinions, were seeking to achieve full citizenship and looked at immigration restriction as an impartial achievement of that incorporation (Hellwig 1982). Although inclusion in the body politic was not something blacks were willing to negotiate away, they were also unwilling to sell their souls to achieve this end.

What differentiated blacks who held nativist opinions from white nativists was largely how they interpreted immigration (Hellwig 1982; Scott 1999). Blacks saw immigration as an important tool for diagnosing their political condition (Hellwig 1978; Malloy 1996). Immigration policy became a metric used by blacks to forecast how open the country would be to the expansion of their civil rights (Hellwig 1978, 1981, 1987; Shankman 1978). When the United States was engaged not only with the domestic issue of immigration but also with international skirmishes, such as in the Mexican American War, World Wars I and II, Korea, Vietnam, and the like, blacks used these moments to voice their grievances with their treatment at home and push for insertion into the political system, because these events magnified American hypocrisy (Dawson 2001; Dudziak 2004; Gaines 1996; Gallicchio 2000; Hellwig 1987; Parker 2009; Plummer 1996; Von Eschen 1997). As blacks made the connections between domestic and international politics, they gained a deeper appreciation of the globalization of white supremacy and the ways in which people of color were harmed by its persistence (Tillery 2011). The United States' handling of immigration, in many ways, proved the country's reluctance to recognize blacks as full citizens. Blacks now met the criterion of self-possession, yet state and federal authorities consistently undermined their constitutionally guaranteed rights as citizens. For example, European immigrants, even those who were not yet naturalized in some cases, could vote; black (male) citizens could not hope to exercise this right despite the fact they were citizens and were granted suffrage in 1870 by the 15th Amendment (Anbinder 1995; Gaines 1996; Mayfield 1993; Sheridan 2002).[22]

Therefore, blacks remained focused largely on the core issue of white racism that was more willing to extend filial bonds to foreigners than to native-born blacks (Hellwig 1981). White racism was so powerful that nationhood meant little when applied to blacks; they were provisional Americans. Because they were black, they were not included in the larger national narrative in the way some immigrants eventually were. Blacks were castaways in their own birthplace as America increasingly identified itself as a white country (Hellwig 1978). However, no matter how racist the United States, blacks never stopped using their status as citizens to push for inclusion in the public sphere (Dawson 2001; Rustin 1971; Tate 2003). More importantly, they continued to use their status as native-born Americans to separate themselves from immigrant Americans and the newly arriving (Diamond 1998; Hellwig 1978, 1981, 1987; Malloy 1996; Rubin 1978; Scott 1999; Shankman 1978). Although it was not much, Americanness was the idiom available to register their dissatisfaction with their ongoing exclusion.

Race was what kept them beneath immigrants. Race was not a useful basis for blacks to draw distinctions between themselves and immigrants as it was for whites, and was not really employed. Race, despite birthright, stood between blacks and the realization of full citizenship. But their status as American citizens, no matter how precarious, buoyed black claims and gave them the leverage to make demands on the government and demonstrate their worthiness, however small, over immigrant groups.

Conflicted Nativism

Blacks thought very deeply and critically about immigration and its consequences for their community. However, this intragroup dialogue about immigration was not of recent vintage and was not solely about immigration. Immigration helped blacks articulate their misgivings about America and its investment in white supremacy. As such, immigration opinions in black communities vacillated between empathy for newcomers and a desire for fewer arrivals. This is what I term *conflicted nativism*. This is meant to capture blacks' simultaneous opposition to white supremacist logic that is more accepting of immigrants and their own community's compassion for the plight of immigrants.[23] Therefore, immigration becomes symbolic of a lack of black incorporation into American civic and social life because of white supremacy. Thus, this ambivalence arises from blacks' use of the issue of immigration to articulate their vision for national belonging. The subtext of black discourse on immigration has been and remains about their lack of incorporation in American society and the (as of yet) unfulfilled promise of citizenship for their community, not antipathy toward immigrants as many sources in the present suggest (McClain et al. 2006b; Mindiola, Niemann, and Rodriguez 2003; Vaca 2004).

Consequently, the issue becomes less about immigrants and immigration and more about what these issues mean for black people. Blacks, despite their maltreatment, claim some form of an American identity that they use to assert the primacy of their claims in the American hierarchy (Dawson 2001). Yet, because blacks are sensitive to the potential contradictions in holding a contrarian position toward immigration, they tend to eschew outwardly hostile positions toward immigrants (Hellwig 1978; Scott 1999). After all, how can one support the cause of social justice for their community but not for all others, particularly the racially excluded?

However, this does not mean blacks are always in favor of immigrants (Gay 2006; Malloy 1996; Weill and Castañeda 2004). What it does mean is that blacks tend to have a softer position than whites on the matter of immigration (Alvarez and Butterfield 2000; Cummings and Lambert 1997; Morris 2000; Thornton and Mizuno 1999). In addition, blacks are usually skeptical of racially motivated anti-immigrant actions and appeals (Hellwig 1978). Moreover, they remain committed to the eradication of racism rather than limiting immigration. Thus, although immigration has received much attention as of late, particularly as it pertains to black and Latino relations, racism continues to be a chief issue for blacks along with governmental intervention to lessen racism's effects (Dawson 1994a, 2001; Krysan 2000; Kuklinski, Cobb, and Gilens 1997; Steeh and Krysan 1996). Thus, I argue, immigration is an issue for blacks insofar as it amplifies black insecurities and displeasure at their treatment in the nation.[24]

Dimensions of Conflicted Nativism

Although blacks have discussed immigration throughout the nineteenth and twentieth centuries, there has been relatively scant attention paid to black national identity. I think this is primarily because of a more robust set of anti-immigrant attitudes and politics among whites. Still, it can be said that blacks have harbored nativist sentiments, albeit for different reasons. This section parses the various dimensions of conflicted nativism to have a better understanding of how it presents among blacks.

It is important to bear in mind that black nativist sentiment is not totally antithetical to traditional nativist attitudes. For example, black nativists largely agree with the idea that America is a Judeo-Christian society (Carter 2007; Carter and Pérez 2015; Hellwig 1981, 1982). Also, some blacks are comfortable with the idea that to be an American one should be able to speak English (Carter and Pérez 2015). However, in practice, language proficiency and religious adherence have not protected black people from racism; therefore, as important as these criteria may be for establishing some baseline of American identity, these issues have not been significant enough for blacks to join nativist movements (Parker 2009).

One of the hallmarks of black nativism has been an avoidance of anti-immigrant organizing. Blacks have had gripes with immigrants, primarily around employment, but they have not mobilized resistance to immigration, even though they have at times joined unions or other organizations where immigration restriction was a key component. However, there have been few to no grassroots black organizations organized whose chief purpose is to exclude foreigners from U.S. soil.[25] I think this is partly because of the regional concentration of immigration in traditional receiving contexts of the North and West. It was not until the 1990s and early 2000s that Southern cities and parts of the rural Midwest became new "immigrant gateways," making immigration a truly national phenomenon (Suro and Singer 2002). Nevertheless, despite the existence of immigrants in the major cities where blacks migrated in the first half of the twentieth century, there was no real push to organize against immigrants.

Additionally, blacks traditionally have not had enough political clout to cause the government to act either in favor of or opposition to immigration. Although blacks would come to be a significant part of the Democratic Party coalition, their electoral possibilities were extremely limited (Frymer 1999). Thus, black participation in traditional forms of political activity like voting did not hold much promise for pursuing their political interests. As marginal members of the nation, black opinions regarding immigration were rarely actualized as part of a national political agenda. Furthermore, although they viewed the issue of immigration as germane to their struggle for inclusion in the American polity, black organizations like the NAACP, UNIA, Urban League, SCLC, and the like focused more on eradicating barriers to black social progress (such as educational segregation, workplace discrimination, and police brutality) rather than banning immigration. Moreover, if we examine the issues that have traditionally comprised parts of a black political agenda, immigration has typically not been considered a pressing concern. The issues that black legislators tend to address are civil rights, affirmative action, education, unemployment, housing, and other issues they believe are more immediate concerns of their black constituents (Bratton and Haynie 1999; Gamble 2007).

More importantly, conflicted nativists tend to empathize with immigrants. Although it seems contradictory, blacks usually relate to the immigrant cause. Although many blacks came to America by force, they believe in the right to self-determination. After all, making America live up to its promise was a key mantra of the black struggle in this country. Moreover, mistreatment and lack of opportunity inspired black migrants to leave the South and go North and West for better job and living opportunities during the Exoduster and Great Migration eras (Tolnay 2001; Wilkerson 2010). In some cases, blacks left the United States to live lives of dignity they felt were unachievable given the American racial climate (Akpan 1973; Clegg 2004).[26] Thus, blacks see immigrants as similar to themselves in that they want an opportunity to achieve better lives. Yet, blacks are as reluctant to aid immigrants as they are to oppose them. From their own history, blacks have seen their community harmed by immigration. Whether being displaced economically or being denied citizenship, they have seen how immigrants have been used as tools to impede their progress. Because immigration and white racism have been so inextricably linked, blacks are unable to fully support anti-immigration efforts. Although they are wary of immigration's potential outcomes, they are far more concerned about the havoc they know white supremacy routinely visits on their lives.

Finally, it is significant to understand how much conflicted nativism is informed more by whites' racism than by immigration. As mentioned previously, blacks have been necessarily preoccupied with race and racism for most of their existence in the United States. Blacks often use the nation's immigration debates as a barometer of the nation's attitudes on race relations. While the United States claimed (white) America for (white) Americans, they frequently favored immigrants over black citizens. In the political sphere, housing, education, and employment, blacks were effectively placed below immigrants because they were black (Jacobson 2001). However, this was not a result simply of European immigration. Indeed, blacks fear their economic prospects are threatened by the presence of non-European immigrants (Gay 2006; Doherty 2006). This is not necessarily because of immigrants but because of the ways in which immigrants are preferred to blacks (Powers 2005). For blacks, immigration is, and was, an inherently racial field of play that demonstrates the potency of white skin privilege. Historically, the U.S. policy of allowing European immigrants to enter the country and subsequently naturalize, while curbing the presence of non-Europeans and oppressing native-born blacks, has demonstrated the country's deep investment in white supremacy.

As such, conflicted nativists do not accept the proposition that America is a white man's country. And in the area of American immigration policy, whiteness was clearly linked to citizenship. Thus, American citizenship was largely available to any white person regardless of national origins. Blacks, though very aware of this official position, resisted this notion. In their pleas for greater inclusion, blacks deployed a universal understanding of the language of the Founders to press their claims as Americans (Bernasconi 1991; Chambers 2013). Prior to the 15th Amendment, blacks continually used the rhetoric of the Founders to challenge the racist dimensions of U.S. citizenship. Rather than allowing whiteness to coopt the language of citizenship to narrow the notion of who constituted a citizen, blacks used it to argue for a more expansive notion of citizenship. Therefore, blacks employed an alternate reading of the American ideals of "life, liberty and the pursuit of happiness" to upset the explicit, foundational understanding of whiteness as always, automatically, representative of a citizen. The black presence challenged the notion that the United States was a white man's country. In fact, the United States would not exist had black people not supplied the labor necessary for the country to develop (Baron 1983). This line of reasoning was present during the emigration debates of the nineteenth and twentieth centuries as blacks deliberated whether they should leave the United States and return to Africa or other more hospitable nations. Although some did choose to leave, most blacks were unwilling to cede their stake in America because it was *their* country.[27] Still, by 1964 the situation for black people had not changed much, as Malcolm X astutely observed in his "Ballot or the Bullet" speech. X says, "If you and I were Americans, there'd be no problem. Those Honkies that just got off the boat, they're already Americans; Polacks are already Americans; the Italian refugees are already Americans. Everything that came out of Europe, every blue-eyed thing, is already an American. And as long as you and I have been over here, we aren't Americans yet." More importantly, X notes that blacks' consistent exclusion makes them less prone to accept the idea of America. Although this has not resulted in the majority of blacks fleeing the United States, it has ensured a certain distance from identifying with all things American. This means blacks exhibit what has been called "iconoclastic patriotism," whereby they demonstrate their devotion to the nation by challenging the nation live up to its core principles of inclusion and equality (Henderson 2010; Shaw 2004). Because their race has often assured blacks' status as second-class citizens, they have been unable to deploy their skin color as a symbol of power. Thus, conflicted nativism does not hinge on race in the same way as that of white nativists; it hinges on some sense of privilege earned by struggle against American racism. Although immigration caused whites to reassert their dominance, because of the relatively stable position of blackness at the bottom of the American racial hierarchy, being racially identified as black in the United States has little social currency. As Bashi (2004) argues, blackness and the relative contempt for people racialized as black has militated against black inclusion in Western nations that are racialized as white and ardently anti-black. As a result, race for black people has proved useless in drawing distinctions between themselves and immigrants. This is true even for those immigrants deemed non-white, but who have been able to gain some esteem because they are not black (Kim 1999).

For example, in the case of Asian Americans, Kim argues that Asians are figured between blacks and whites in the racial hierarchy but on slightly different grounds. On the one hand, Asians are considered "less than" relative to whites because they are viewed as forever foreign. This process, which Kim labels "civic ostracism," suggests Asians cannot ascend to full inclusion because they are viewed as perpetual outsiders. On the other hand, Asians are considered better than blacks through a process of relative valorization. Because Asians are viewed as having better cultural values than blacks, they are seen as being above them in the racial hierarchy. Therefore, blacks have tended to use their nativity as grounds for assigning privilege and drawing distinctions between themselves and immigrants, not race.

Likewise, black nativists do not tend to use culture as grounds for discriminating against immigrants (Shankman 1982; Tillery and Chresfield 2012). Although some blacks do say unflattering things about immigrants, they do not characterize immigrants as perpetual foreigners who threaten the American identity and way of life. Blacks do not seem to believe total assimilation on the part of immigrants is necessary. Although some non-black authors, such as Samuel Huntington, seem to lament the flagging primacy of the English language and other cultural norms as anti-assimilationist, blacks do not seem to fear those characteristics in the same way (Huntington 2004; Smith 1988). For instance, a number of blacks cleave to cultural signifiers, such as names and the like, because those cultural practices have been stripped from their community (Brown and Shaw 2002; Fryer and Levitt 2004). The same is true for those blacks who may be the children of immigrants, who regard those markers of their national legacy as important to their American identity (Greer 2013; Waters 1994). Therefore, they do not necessarily see total assimilation as necessary for one to be American. This has traditionally been a central tenet of white nativism that blacks do not subscribe to.

As a result, blacks tend not to favor immigrant restriction in the same way as white nativists. From the historical record, it seems blacks are wary of allying themselves with those it deems racist, yet they understand the practical benefits of less competition from immigrants in the labor market (Hellwig 1977, 1981). Blacks have been ideologically nativist in some ways, but not politically. They are conflicted about what immigration means for them and want to protect their community from foreign encroachment, yet they are not dedicated to the politically motivated efforts to keep immigrants out, especially immigrants of color. This means they tend not to organize or manifest these interests as part of a collective political agenda.

As previously stated, immigration restriction has consistently been omitted from a larger black political agenda and has not traditionally been cited as a major issue for black people.[28] Blacks do see immigrants as threatening to their economic interests, and for that reason, immigration is important to them. My previously stated argument indicates this stance is largely the result of racism and the ways in which whites traditionally have, and continue to, manipulate immigrants for their ends, with the seeming consent of immigrants and to the detriment of blacks (Betancur 2005). Although it is understood that immigrants do not set the "rules of the game," it appears they have not been too concerned with the outcomes of their immigration for black people. For example, McClain et al. (2006) find that Latino immigrants come to the United States with negative stereotypes about blacks and are concerned with not appearing too close to them. On the other hand, blacks feel a sense of linked fate with Latino immigrants; this makes them more positive in their assessments of this group (McClain et al. 2006; Weill and Castañeda 2004).

Discussion

The purpose of this chapter has been to provide some context to the contours of black attitudes toward immigration as it relates to their national identity. Looking at both historical and contemporary moments helps clarify the nuances of black experiences as insecure citizens and how this influences their ambivalence toward immigrants, which I term *conflicted nativism*. On the one hand, blacks empathize with immigrants and their desires for self-determination. On the other hand, they are concerned that their own attempts at social progress will be harmed by the presence of immigrants.

Moreover, this chapter provides what I have termed the *dimensions* of conflicted nativism. Black people are complicated, and in the domain of immigration they have vacillated between restriction, as in the early twentieth century, and openness in the later twentieth century. In short, conflicted nativism rests on a basic sentiment that immigrants are not what is wrong with the nation; rather, white supremacy is what truly impedes blacks' ability to move ahead. Therefore, although blacks demonstrate pride in and attachment to America, they are less settled about the appropriate role of immigrants because they cannot be sure that their own social, economic, and political progress will expand in the face of new immigrants. Again, this is not because of their fears that immigrants are bad for American culture but because whites may use immigrants in an effort to thwart black progress. This was true historically, and blacks use the collective memories of these moments to inform their present attitudes on the issue. In an era of official colorblindness, white supremacy has proven more difficult to defeat. As a constitutive American ideology, it is increasingly difficult to address a phenomenon alleged not to exist and for which there is no legal protection.

In any event, blacks hold citizenship above all else as a marker of national belonging. For many black people, being a citizen is more significant than any other factor in determining American identity (Carter 2007). I think this speaks to the myriad ways that citizenship is enmeshed with black identity and blacks' articulation of national belonging. Citizenship was denied to blacks for most of their experience in the United States; therefore, the premium placed on citizenship has made it a symbol and underwriter of national belonging. Although there are many other ways one can signify their place in American society, this chapter demonstrates the key role of citizenship in black peoples' sense of national identity because it was withheld for so long.

At the same time, blacks have tried to figure out how to leverage governmental interventions for their inclusion. Because the government's immigration policy has frequently been racist, blacks have used this to gauge whether the nation would be more open to their claims for greater civil rights. For blacks, the idea that the government should be involved in their community's improvement has been difficult to reconcile with the government's policy of disallowing non-Europeans from entering the country.

Overall, this chapter emphasizes that to understand black attitudes toward immigration, it is necessary to understand the fundamental ways in which their race has shaped how they see their place in the racial hierarchy. During periods of immigration, blacks are especially insecure because they have never been full citizens. Therefore, for blacks, immigration is never solely or even principally about whether foreigners should be allowed in the country. Rather, the issue of immigration has always been about the nature of black/white racial relations and the extent to which immigration would speed or slow black progress to full citizenship.

In the end, this chapter is not about exposing blacks as traitors to the principles of equality. Neither is this chapter about presenting blacks as holding political views that are diametrically opposed to, and therefore more just than, those of their white counterparts. Rather, this chapter aims to shed light on the complexity of black opinion on immigration through time. Immigration has long occupied a place in the black imagination, and to ignore this could lead one to draw such faulty conclusions as "blacks are always hostile to immigrants and immigration."

I offer this chapter as a foray into black national identity and its linkages to expressions of nationalism, such as nativism. How these ideas have been expressed historically by blacks regarding their own groups' circumstances is the focus of the next chapter. In particular, the following chapter demonstrates how blacks envisioned themselves as emigrants and sought to employ emigration as a tool for their own liberation. By critically examining the past, the chapter demonstrates blacks' long engagement with the issue of immigration, particularly as a tool for their group's sociopolitical advancement.

3

Emigrants, Immigrants, and Refugees

EMIGRATION AS A STRATEGY FOR BLACK LIBERATION (1815–1862)

THE PREVIOUS CHAPTER outlines how American attachment has been expressed by blacks in attempts to assert their citizenship. In particular, Chapter 2 demonstrates black ambivalence on immigration, which is the result of the capriciousness of white racism. This chapter offers a different lens with which to understand African American engagements with emigration. In particular, it looks at African American attempts to use emigration as a tool for liberation and how they cast themselves as emigrants in the nineteenth century, in an effort to understand blacks' long history of engagement with the issue and its emancipatory possibility. It is worth spending time in the past to understand the present, because one cannot fully appreciate black opinion on immigration if one does not understand how African Americans, disinherited from American citizenship until 1868, utilized their liminal status to push for greater inclusion through emigration. While it seems counterintuitive that contemplations of exiting the United States would bring greater African American equality, attempts to leave America produced a vigorous intra-racial dialogue about the meanings of freedom, American identity, and citizenship for black people.

To this end, this chapter revisits the (African) colonization movement beginning in the early nineteenth century and effectively ending in 1862 with Abraham Lincoln's failed attempt to persuade free blacks to leave the United States. This historical moment's significance is often read as either a black nationalist fantasy of independence or a white supremacist project to rid the nation of free blacks. Both of these are useful, albeit limited, lenses for thinking through what repatriation meant for blacks, whites, and the nation. Going "back to Africa," and the conversations generated around repatriation in the black public sphere were paramount in how blacks defined themselves in the nineteenth century and for the future. In particular, the emigration debates gave blacks a vocabulary for highlighting the unique nature of their position as a stateless people; essentially unmoored through the process of enslavement and civil rights denial, blacks came to see themselves, in some respects, as a people with no nation. This statelessness created more than a sense of despair. Statelessness gave blacks a lexis that allowed them to register their in-between status. More importantly, as a people with no nation in a literal and figurative sense, the emigration debates gave blacks a freedom to think through the possibilities of a robust, dynamic independence. By working through these important challenges of the nineteenth century, this chapter shows that blacks have thought and continue to think deeply about emigration, not only as a political issue but one that captures the very essence of what it means for a group to have agency. Individual agency matters, because that is at the heart of who can be a citizen. In the United States, where citizenship is not defined by culture but an allegiance to certain ideals like life, liberty, and pursuit of happiness, being a sovereign person means that one is "fit" for citizenship. In this way, the purest expression of being an American is being able/free to find a place in the world, literally, and contribute to its advancement. This freedom was denied to all blacks who, during the period under study, had no status as Americans, even if free. Thus, both repatriation and colonization were immigration schemes whose sole aim was to get black people freer.

Blacks who were not wedded to the United States were seeking this ability to define themselves. They conceived novel ways of creating identity and crafting citizenship that were not defined by the machinations of whites. Rather, they defined themselves alternatively as emigrants, immigrants, and refugees, ideas that were not only more agentic but filled with prospect. How did blacks in this period come to define and redefine American identity in the face of more draconian racial policies? I contend the issue of colonization, which uses immigration as a tool for black liberation, frames blacks as central to the issue of immigration and immigration's attendant questions. More importantly, this moment not only creates blacks as emigrants and makes it possible for them to remake themselves in a non-slavery context, it gives them a space to critique the exclusivity of American citizenship and hypocrisy around freedom and democracy. Therefore, as noncitizen residents of America, blacks craft a narrative of self-remaking that predates the so-called immigrant narrative.

By repositioning African American immigration, which includes colonization, as an attempt at self-determination, I hope to destabilize notions that immigration is of little consequence to African Americans. In fact, immigration has long been a liberatory strategy discursively deployed by black people through time to demonstrate their displeasure with the direction of the United States. Whether we are exploring maroonage in Georgia, Lousiana, and South Carolina; discussing the Black Star Line envisioned by Marcus Garvey; or #blaxit, where African Americans considered moving to Africa after the election of Donald Trump, all of these movements and moments have a rich tradition in black American life and discourse. Therefore, I use this chapter to show how descendants of enslaved Africans are *central* to the immigration narrative, and, ultimately, to redefining American citizenship. Foregrounding this history moves blacks from the margin to the center of contemporary discussions regarding immigration because they were among the many people defined as not belonging to America, yet who forced America to concede to their inclusion through their commitment to remaining on this land. Nevertheless, colonization and emigration were necessary in the black public sphere because people were looking for whatever means they had available to become free. For some, this was to relocate to the shores of Africa or other hospitable climes.

Although Africa occupied much of the conversational real estate, what I demonstrate is how blacks used immigration, writ large, as an attempt to find a place where they could exercise the full measure of their humanity. Thus, as early as the nineteenth century, immigration was a way for blacks to claim and disrupt their own statelessness and what it meant to be excluded from the civic, social, and economic possibilities of American citizenship. By bringing this history into the conversation, I highlight that black public opinion about immigration is far less about who is allowed into the country and far more about the ways in which the antagonisms of white supremacy become reified and do real harm to black communities. Understood in this way, it becomes easier to see that blacks are not, in general, resistant to immigration. Instead, they are attempting to resist the grudging and conditional nature of their inclusion. Therefore, this chapter does not adjudicate whether blacks should have gone "back to

Africa" or remained in America. White supremacy renders the dichotomy moot given the ways in which anti-blackness has been exported across the world (Bashi 2004). Instead, this chapter focuses on what I feel are the real lessons of the emigration debates of this period, which is that immigration was viewed as a remedy to black statelessness. By entertaining immigration as a viable strategy for their freedom, blacks were attempting to obtain greater inclusion in America where possible.

The discussion begins with looking at how free and enslaved blacks were separated from American citizenship, and how this necessitated black movement in an effort to find some manner of freedom. Next, it analyzes how black freedom is viewed as incompatible with American identity, and how colonization becomes the method for addressing this "problem" under the auspices of black and white institutions. Taken together, the purpose of this chapter is to recast immigration as a proxy for a whole host of issues surrounding black citizenship in this earlier, seminal period, to understand the evolving nature of black attitudes on immigration. What I find is that most black conversations on immigration are about their community, not some fierce nativism that defends the nation from incursions by interlopers.

Becoming Emigrants

For most of their existence in the United States, black people were noncitizens. Regardless of status, whether free or enslaved, blacks were not deemed members of the American body politic. In fact, they were not inaugurated as full citizens until 1965. Their noncitizen status was cemented in the *Dred Scott v. Sandford* (1857) Supreme Court decision, which stated all people of African descent—whether free or enslaved— could not become citizens. Chief Justice Taney, delivering the majority opinion, stated "they are not included, and were not intended to be included, under the word "citizens" in the Constitution, and can therefore claim none of the rights and privileges which that instrument provides for and secures to the citizens of the United States. On the contrary, they were at that time [the Founding] considered as a subordinate and inferior class of beings who had been subjugated by the dominant race, and, whether emancipated or not, yet remained subject to the authority, and had no rights or privileges but such as those who held the power and the Government might choose to grant them." More importantly, the language of "alien" in this decision is used to describe blacks, as Taney uses care to preserve the right of the federal government *alone* to allow natural-ization and confer citizenship to said aliens. In observing the primacy of the federal government, Taney said the state "cannot introduce any person or description of persons who were not intended to be embraced in this new political family which the Constitution brought into existence, but were intended to be excluded from it" in the minds of the Founders.

However, this sensibility did not begin with Chief Justice Taney and the Supreme Court. Prior to *Dred Scott*, blacks were already having to relocate to have some measure of agency. Because of the limited sphere in which they were allowed to operate as free citizens, many blacks were forced to become emigrants. Most definitely, their moves often were guided by the desire to achieve better opportunities—but they were also driven by a real fear that their freedom would not last long if they were to remain too close to their former owners (Trotti 1996). This forced mobility challenges the notion of "choice," which is often central to emigration, but blacks knew freedom often required some movement (Berlin 1975, 2000). This usu-ally meant moving to "free states," larger cities, or going abroad.[1] This "choice," whether to stay in the United States or go, is where the colo-nization movement, considered as early as 1804, becomes significant. Although the term *colonization* was employed at the time, it is an inaccu-rate representation of this project. This project was a repatriation plan, not colonization as properly understood. Black people were not empowered to take land and extract wealth for the betterment of blacks living in the United States, which is what colonization implies.[2]

Quite simply, early colonization efforts were attempts by free blacks to move themselves out of the United States and into a space, preferably with blacks at the helm, to be truly independent. Efforts at these types of settlements were made as early as 1804, with a small number of blacks moving to Haiti after the Haitian Revolution (1791–1804). However, the most well-known attempts were made by Paul Cuffee in 1815, as he and other free blacks made one of the earliest recorded attempts to resettle in Africa. Although the maiden trip proved disastrous, it provided an op-tion and opportunity to those blacks willing and able to take advantage. Despite the fact they employed the term *colonization*, which was common parlance, they saw themselves as emigrants, and in some cases refugees,[3] and deployed these terms deliberately. Thus, their primary motivation for entertaining this idea was the potential creation of better lives, much in the way of other immigrant groups. If we consider this moment in light of the fact that blacks, free and enslaved alike, were a stateless people,[4] it makes clear that blacks have long been steeped in conversations around immigration.

Blacks born in the United States were without a country until the 14th Amendment was enacted in 1868, which conferred upon them some semblance of citizenship. To this point, blacks represented a "nation within a nation," to borrow from W.E.B. DuBois.[5] Consequently, I argue that movement on the part of blacks, domestic and international, represented an act of *emigration* because any place they went, whether to the northern states of this country or to the shores of Africa, was an attempt to start over and try to achieve some version of a "good life."[6] This is an important intervention because it inserts blacks into the conversation of immigration long before the later nineteenth and twentieth centuries. Because blacks are thought to be "native," they are rarely considered to be more than mere commenters on immigration. Additionally, black immigration is considered to be largely the product of the late twentieth century and has an African or Caribbean face (Greer 2013; Rogers 2006). Although this is significant, I want to revisit black Americans' intimate connections to immigration as a practice of self-remaking where limited options were available. As I highlight throughout, blacks very much saw themselves as sojourners, and this longer view helps us understand black opinion in the contemporary moment. It is necessary then to look at how blacks redefined this movement and its usage within their own communities during this period, and their eventual rejection of this plan.

These community driven efforts were, in some ways, usurped by white organizations that had the same end goal but divergent reasons for pursuing colonization. What this movement often turned into under the auspices of whites was moving free blacks to make life more convenient for whites. As such, I think it vitally important to include the voices of blacks, how they saw themselves, and how they understood American citizenship in the face of a nation unwilling to claim them.

Colonization and the "Negro Problem"

As early as 1815, Paul Cuffee[7] took at least 38 free blacks to Sierra Leone,[8] before the existence of any U.S. government entity working for the purpose of repatriating blacks to Africa. Concerns about what to do with free blacks appeared in the late eighteenth century and hastened in the wake of the so-called Prosser Rebellion of 1800. The attempted rebellion, spearheaded by Gabriel and over twenty other enslaved persons, petrified white Virginians.[9] White lives were fair game because black resistance to enslavement did not preclude violence against whites and necessitated cooperation between free and enslaved blacks. Thus, in anticipation of the next rebellion, whites not only cracked down on the already limited liberties of blacks in Richmond, but other states and localities followed suit, hoping to thwart potential revolts. Although these places had not experienced a rebellion, they were being proactive in dissuading black protest. What is more, moments like the Prosser Rebellion and the reactionary responses from whites seemed to draw them closer to the institution of enslavement. It also seemed to confirm their ideas of a black and white difference that made their living in harmony impossible.

Thomas Jefferson, for example, was a supporter of early efforts at colonization, arguing in 1811 that it was "the most desirable measure which could be adopted for gradually drawing off this part of our population" (personal correspondence to John Lynch). This was a particular concern in the South, where blacks in some jurisdictions outnumbered whites.[10] Nevertheless, blacks and whites seemed to agree that blacks would be unable to become part of the citizenry, albeit for different reasons.

Early black pro-emigration supporters were not monolithic in their reasoning. Yet, there was a common sensibility that America was too committed to its racism to let black people be free. This was expressed by Abraham Camp, a free man living in the Midwest circa 1818, who said "we love this country and its liberties, if we could share an equal right in them; but our freedom is partial, and we have no hope that it ever will be otherwise here; therefore we had rather be gone;" he goes on to say such a move would "open the door of freedom for us" (Aptheker 1973). What Mr. Camp and others felt was a profound sense of frustration with their lack of autonomy in the United States, despite constitutional musings about the protection of freedom. Although Camp expressed a love of this country, he could not see how he and other blacks would be able to make a life, because whites made it too difficult for blacks to do the most mundane tasks. This was because, as David Walker so forcefully expressed in his Appeal to the Colored Citizens of the United States (1829), whites were unwilling to treat blacks as equals. As Walker states, "Treat us like men, and there is no danger but we will all live in peace and happiness together. For we are not like you, hard hearted, unmerciful, and unforgiving." For Walker, interracial harmony was achievable if only whites ceased investment in black degradation. However, whites preferred to use colonization as a way to further their investment in racism rather than redress their own racism, making the prospect of leaving the United States more of an inevitability than a choice.

The American Colonization Society (ACS) stepped into this breach in 1816 as they saw repatriation of blacks to Africa as a way to deal with the "problem" of free blacks. The group, composed of anti-slavery Quakers and slaveholders, believed the most humane way to prevent rebellion and bring about peace between blacks and whites was to return them to their homeland. They believed if free blacks were not present, it would quell the spirit of rebellion among the enslaved and forestall collaboration between free blacks and those enslaved. Likewise, free blacks would have the opportunity to live without the color prejudice they faced in this country. It was reasoned this was the most beneficial solution for all parties involved.

Still, there were more nefarious reasons why some whites supported colonization. A belief in black criminality was as common then as it is now, and many whites felt that blacks without the benefit of masters would devolve into a permanent class of criminals (Berlin 1975; Fitzhugh 1966; Higginbotham and Jacobs 1992). Because blacks were believed to be susceptible to vice, some whites felt they would become a scourge on the nation and unable to be socialized into American culture. Therefore, sending them back to Africa was ultimately saving whites from having to deal with the inevitable fallout of black freedom. In either case, the ACS was composed of a number of whites who believed blacks' return to Africa would fix current problems and prevent future skirmishes between the groups. Undoubtedly, it was believed that by exorcising the black population, the system of enslavement by white people would be made safer.

In some ways, Walker's take on colonization was not too far afield, because whites' support of colonization seemed purely self-interested. For example, Thomas Jefferson in his *Notes on the State of Virginia* thought there was too much resentment on the part of blacks for them to coexist with whites. Jefferson's commitment to scientific racism dictated that blacks would never be able to be educated to citizenship, which made colonization a far more appealing alternative than actually treating black people like human beings. This was because Jefferson and others lacked a fundamental understanding, or at least refused to admit, that white racism was the root cause of black suffering. Blacks did not want to leave the United States, but the push was great. Of course, the sense that the ACS was uninterested in black well-being was not helped by the fact that Henry Clay[11] and John Randolph,[12] both slaveholders, were founders of the organization. Still, for all of the potential advantages offered by colonization, the removal of blacks from the United States was slow to become a main-stream political issue. Aside from resolutions passed by Virginia, Indiana, Georgia, and Tennessee legislatures barring the entry of free blacks, the national political climate did not support mass emigration, particularly among blacks as the targeted group.[13]

Although there was a real sensibility among whites that something had to be done with free blacks, there was no consensus as to what to do about them. On the one hand, the nation's founding documents enshrined principles of self-determination; on the other hand, America was invested in enslavement and black dehumanization, as the protection of slavery and the three-fifths clause attest. The ACS was framed as a partial solution to the ongoing conflict created by having free and enslaved blacks existing simultaneously. ACS efforts focused solely on free blacks, as they were defined as the problem. By attempting this strategy, the ACS tried to serve multiple masters on the pro- and anti-slavery fronts (Forbes 1990).[14] Thus, some early supporters of ACS framed the organization's colonization scheme as a type of "moral obligation" to pay penance for the sin of enslavement. Still, other whites simply viewed colonization as the best of all possible outcomes. The primary issue facing pro-colonizing white forces was how to convince free blacks, and whites skeptical about pledging the necessary resources, this was a practical and desirable solution to their mutual problems.

Given the abolitionist sentiment of the period and concerns about the feasibility of this scheme, proponents knew they needed federal support to achieve their ends. Federal government backing meant the ACS would have the tactical and financial means to do the initial surveying and eventual relocations. More importantly, federal government patronage legitimized their efforts. Federal support brought the colonization movement from the fringes of American politics and made it official policy of the U.S. government.[15] Undoubtedly, the pedigrees of the ACS's founding signatories, as well as the common interest in solving the "Negro problem," made it possible for the ACS to obtain federal funding and the other assistance it needed to make black emigration a reality.

While government support was key to the success of the movement, it meant little if they could not convince free blacks to leave the country voluntarily. Therefore, a significant portion of the ACS's time was spent figuring out how to convince blacks that leaving the United States would be advantageous. Thus, the ACS was prepared to make blacks an offer they could not refuse. "With the promise of equality, a homestead, and free passage," they reasoned blacks would be more likely to leave (Sherwood 1917). For blacks so inclined, the ACS was correct.[16] Blacks who saw Liberia as the only possibility were willing to risk the homeland they knew in an attempt to create a new vision of nationhood that was inclusive of black people. Regardless of the risks of infectious disease, an inhospitable native population, and the general unknown, those who braved the journey did so not necessarily because they had faith in the ACS, but because they were willing to bet on themselves. They gambled on their own industry to provide a measure of progress in their lifetimes in their new country. Of course, many of those who opted for relocation faced many difficulties adjusting to their new environs, but this was nothing compared to living under the yoke of white supremacy. William Burke, an emigrant from Virginia and formerly enslaved by Robert E. Lee, wrote this of his experience in Liberia:

> Persons coming to Africa should expect to go through many hardships, such as are common to the first settlement in any new country. I expected it, and was not disappointed or discouraged at anything met with; and so far from being dissatisfied with the country, I bless the Lord that ever my lot was cast in this part of the earth. The Lord has blessed me abundantly since my residence in Africa, for which I feel that I can never be sufficiently thankful.

In a similar fashion, Mrs. Rosabella Burke stated, "I love Africa and would not exchange it for America." The positivity of these letters rests, in part, on the prosperity the Burkes found in Liberia. Mrs. Burke became an entrepreneur and Mr. Burke a Presbyterian minister, and they were able to become part of the upper echelon of the Liberian emigrant community. Their enthusiasm for Liberia was informed by their ability to reach their full potential. There were not the same barriers to success and social mobility in Liberia as existed in the United States. The push of white supremacy was more powerful for emigrants than the pull of familiarity. Nevertheless, the majority of blacks chose to stay in the United States rather than emigrate. It is estimated that in the 150-year existence of the ACS, only 12,000 blacks were transported to Liberia. Therefore, those who chose to emigrate were atypical of most blacks at the time.

The internal conversation blacks were having vacillated between leaving and staying; the merits of both positions were understood by all, as blacks had to grapple with what it meant to be both free and black. Being free but black negated all claims to American citizenship, so in what ways would a free black populace define itself in relationship to the United States? These were unresolved questions, but the colonization debates helped clarify the nature of white supremacy and the ways in which blacks were harmed by America's continued devotion to its maintenance and practice.

Under the law, there was not much light between free blacks and poor whites. Consequently, the delicate balance that elite whites were able to maintain under enslavement, by selling poor whites the promise of upward mobility, ceased to operate in the same way when dealing with free black people. If blackness was as much about a status as it was about ancestry, then how were free blacks to be treated? Freedom and blackness seemed to be oxymoronic. If black people could ostensibly walk around and occupy a station identical in most dimensions to that of poor whites, then what separated black people from the family of citizenship? Because enslavement would remain in force throughout the nineteenth century, this was not a query that required an answer.[17] Still, the specter of a strata of free blacks raised anxieties because they would eventually make demands to be incorporated into the body politic. In fact, citizenship and inclusion remained a part of the black political agenda even as they contemplated colonization.

The Black Counterpublic and the American Colonization Society

In the black public sphere, the issues of colonization and enslavement were not understood as "Negro problems." Rather, the problem black people had was white supremacy, regardless of whether they decided to live in the United States or abroad. Enslavement, properly understood, was the result of a dogged adherence to a worldview that denigrated non-Europeans as less than human. In this way, the treatment of African people was not surprising given the ways in which their humanity was questioned and outright denied. Consequently, as blacks were considering the options before them in the nineteenth century—to stay or to go—they considered solutions that addressed these deeper concerns.

In January 1817, at a meeting of blacks in Philadelphia, it was determined by attendees that colonization was not a viable solution for the problems facing the black community. Not because the attendees were against Africa, but they felt that if blacks left the United States, they would concede to the false belief that America belonged to whites. Blacks had paid for permanent status in the United States with their blood. They wrote:

> Whereas our ancestors (not of choice) were the first successful cultivators of the wilds of America, we their descendants feel ourselves entitled to participate in the blessings of her luxuriant soil, which their blood and sweat manured; and that any measure or system of measures, having a tendency to banish us from her bosom, would not only be cruel, but in direct violation of those principles, which have been the boast of this republic (Aptheker 1973).[18]

In this meeting, attendees frame blacks as "true Americans" because they and their ancestors labored to make America possible. Moreover, because enslavement remained a fact of American life, these convention goers were unwilling to migrate while members of their community remained enslaved. They resolved they would never "separate ourselves voluntarily from the slave population in this country; they are our brethren by the ties of sanguinity, of suffering, and of wrong; and we feel that there is more virtue in suffering privations with them, than fancied advantages for a season" (Aptheker 1973). In this statement, free blacks were demonstrating their solidarity with less fortunate blacks who were suffering under slavery. Although free blacks had their freedom and could enjoy greater possibilities abroad, they were expressing a sense of linked fate with the enslaved. They reasoned that to exit at this point would have simply extended the life of slavery rather than providing them with greater autonomy. As such, free blacks would only have the most illusory gains while enslavement survived, and emigrating would not have made this less true. Some argued that all emigration would establish was a precedent for black removal.

Many blacks saw the ACS as simply the handmaiden of yet another racist project that sought the exclusion of black bodies from the public sphere. Even for those blacks who may have been seduced by the idea of perfect equality, they could not trust the motives of confirmed racists. Or, from a more charitable perspective, they could trust the very same people who supported the forced removal of Native Americans to *not* provide for their best interests with a plan that looked an awful like forced emigration. As participants of the Third Annual Convention of the Free People of Color resolved, "the life giving principles of the Society [ACS] were totally repugnant to the spirit of true benevolence," and the "inevitable tendency of this doctrine was to strengthen the cruel prejudice of their opponents, to still the heart of sympathy to the appeals of suffering Negroes, and retard their advancement in morals, literature and science, in short, to extinguish the last glimmer of hope and throw an impenetrable gloom over their fears and most reasonable prospects" for freedom and inclusion (Mehlinger 1916). Consequently, it was a matter of principle, not necessarily preference, that caused the majority of free blacks to turn their backs on the ACS and its goals.

This was not a decision easily made; blacks had dialogues throughout the period dedicated to debating the merits of colonization. Some of the earliest meetings of free blacks were held in Philadelphia, home of many independent black organizations like churches, newspapers, and benevolent societies. Representatives met to hear proposals for emigration to other parts of the world, mainly Canada. The impetus for these early meetings was the increasing hostility of state legislatures to free black settlers, as well as the everyday incursions against their dignity. Free blacks were not only facing restrictions on their movements in the wake of slave revolts, but throughout the 1830s and 1840s some states, like Indiana, refused to allow blacks to enter the state at all. This was shocking, because Indiana was never a slave state. Still, the black presence was defined as an incursion that needed to be beaten back. Where they were not outright banned, other states like Ohio required free blacks to register and pay a tax to reside in the state. This was intolerable, and the Ohio delegation of free blacks was the most in favor of blacks relocating to Canada to escape the confines of American race relations. For all of its anti-emigration fervor, the free blacks seemed to be supportive of black Ohioans as well as others who sought refuge elsewhere. Yet, they were opposed to emigration as a matter of national policy to address race relations.

Still, emigration was something to consider given the racial climate of the day. In September 1830, the first of several Negro conventions was convened in Philadelphia for the purpose of discussing the problems facing blacks and their possible remedies. Hosting delegates from the mid-Atlantic and greater Northeast region, a chief concern was the issue of colonization. The ACS had been founded in the previous decade, and blacks, both pro- and anti-emigration, had yet to formulate an official response to the policy on behalf of the larger community.

As reported by the *Anglo-African* "in 1829–30, the colored people of the free States were much excited on the subject of emigration: there had been an emigration to Hayti [*sic*], and also to Canada, and some had been driven to Liberia by the severe laws and brutal conduct of the fermenters of colonization in Virginia and Maryland. In some districts of these States, the disguised whites would enter the houses of the free colored men at night, and take them out and give them from 30 to 50 lashes, to get them to consent to go to Liberia" (Aptheker 1973). Given the racial environment, this meeting was handled with a great deal of urgency. Free blacks wanted some relief from the ongoing stream of abuses against them; therefore, bondsmen and emigration had to at least be considered.

At this Philadelphia convention, emigration to Canada was the primary issue. In a time where there seemed no safe place for blacks, Canada's offer of sanctuary was taken seriously. By the conclusion of the meeting, there was a great deal of support for emigration to Canada. Conventioneers stated that "every man whose sable skin divests him of his freedom, and impairs his usefulness in this country," should seek a home up North (Hazard 1830: 143). They reasoned Canada was more convenient for organizing purposes given its proximity to the United States; it was already "civilized," and Canadians were open to blacks. Although pro-Canada, the same convention goers were ardently anti-ACS. They argued that the ACS's true purpose was "white interests," which they seemed to define broadly as a commitment to anti-black prejudice. In considering Canada, blacks were not professing sympathy with the ACS mission but were thinking about their own survival. They had been cast out of several states, like Ohio, and the rest of the country was not doing much to make blacks feel like stakeholders in the nation. For those on the fence about emigration, Canada was seen as the most preferable option for a short-term move. Relocating there made it possible to observe what was happening at home and held out the hope for relocation back in the United States once the institution of enslavement was abolished. In either case, blacks on both sides of the debate felt very strongly they were doing what was in the best interests of their community.

Although some blacks did move to Canada, the spirit of support for emigration dissipated in subsequent conventions. Not only had prominent blacks like Frederick Douglass, Absalom Jones, and Richard Allen come out squarely against emigration, it was unclear what these other countries would offer blacks (Garrison 1832). Although they promised unfettered access to the bounties of Africa, blacks were unsure this would actually come to pass. Most blacks had no direct linkages to Africa beyond the psychic. Most importantly, they questioned how they would be independent if they relied on the financial resources of white patrons. For those few blacks who wanted to go, many reasoned they would do so on their own dime. They did not want a handout from whites regardless of their stated intentions. Accepting money from whites to return to Africa seemed like a bribe and implied they could be bought, which was a bit too close to replicating the conditions of slavery they were trying to escape.[19]

It is in this vein that blacks made their most consistent and persuasive anti-emigration argument: to leave the United States would be forfeiting their contributions to the development of this nation. Although remuneration would never come to them, if they simply left it would be as if they never existed in the first place. Therefore, blacks were going to be steadfast in their commitment to staying in the country and eradicating slavery, thereby denying whites this most primordial claim: that it was whites who built the country. Consequently, the colonization movement never really captured the imaginations of a majority of blacks.

Still, by engaging the issue of emigration, blacks were able to frame colonization in such a way as to bring America's failures to light while also showing their nebulous position with respect to America. Although some blacks did genuinely believe emigration to be a viable alternative to their continued oppression, these conversations drew attention to the desperate situation facing blacks because of the practice of white supremacy, which was foundational to the United States. Thus, much of the dialogue blacks had about emigration was about their being scapegoated as dangers to domestic tranquility, their statelessness, and being asked to remove themselves from the country rather than having whites reform their behaviors.

Moreover, because ACS's sole focus was *free* black emigration, the ACS did not work on securing manumissions for the enslaved or abolition of enslavement for most of their existence, which did little to evoke black faith in the organization (Burin 2005; Forbes 1990). For black opponents of emigration, to support the ACS plan was tantamount to enabling the continuation of slavery. By defining (free) blacks as the problem and removing them from the country, slavery would remain intact because there would no longer be a direct confrontation to the peculiar institution and fewer supporters to offer refuge to fleeing slaves should they escape. Those in the ACS missed this crucial distinction and would ultimately find their plan to be a failure, not because there was no sympathy for their cause but because in this instance, principle trumped self-interest.

Emigration and Elevation

Although black critiques of emigration were swift and bold, there were some who believed emigration was a viable solution. Henry Highland Garnet, Martin Delany, David Walker, William Wells Brown, and many others encouraged blacks to consider the possibilities of leaving the United States to secure their futures. In 1852, Delany published *The Condition, Elevation, Emigration and Destiny of the Colored People of the United States.* In this text, Delany argues many of the same points as his anti-emigration brethren. Namely, the ACS is a cover for racists and is not motivated by an interest in the social ascendance of blacks, but rather the base desires of slaveholders to continue their degradation of blacks. He designates "the American Colonization Society as one of the most arrant enemies of the colored man, ever seeking to discomfit him. . . . We believe it to be anti-Christian in its character, and misanthropic in its pretended sympathies" (Brotz 1991: 47). Because of their outright refusal to help blacks unless they self-deported to Africa, the ACS could not purport to care about black interests. Indeed, Delany felt the ACS, with its continued focus on black removal, was trying to extricate blacks from their birthright as the true makers of America.

Despite his misgivings about the aims of the ACS, Delany understood the situation of blacks in the United States was too precarious for free blacks to remain. This sensibility was furthered by the passage of the Fugitive Slave Act of 1850. The act, part of the Compromise of 1850 between southern slave states and northern non-slave states, allowed for the capture and extradition of escaped blacks back to their owners. Although this was framed as a simple, lawful return of property, free blacks like Delany knew this was an extremely dangerous statute, because without freedom papers, blacks had no way of proving their status as free people. Even though the line between free and slave was narrow, Delany reasoned this law made it thinner still. To his mind, the Fugitive Slave Act made free blacks vulnerable to unscrupulous slave catchers who were known to kidnap and sell blacks, irrespective of status, down river. Solomon Northup's 1853 memoir *12 Years a Slave* brought more attention to this practice, but he was far from the only free black person who met this fate. Deeper still, the North offered little to no protection for blacks because the region was not invested in the well-being of black people. Although the mythical North promised freedom, it offered little more in the way of security for the well-being of black people. Northern racism was no less vitriolic or exclusionary (Melish 1999; Tate 1998).

Therefore, Delany and other blacks set their sights on relocation for safety reasons. However, it is interesting that Delany was less sanguine about the ACS's proposed return of blacks to the colony of Liberia. Liberia was billed as a free black nation, but Delany stated frankly what all others knew—Liberia was a colony of the United States, not a free country. Although Delany wanted there to be an opportunity for the "civilization and enlightenment of Africa," he did not see this future in Liberia because "it originated in a deep laid scheme of the slaveholders of this country to *exterminate* the free colored of the American continent." Because Liberia depended on the United States for survival, Delany felt Liberia was "but a poor miserable mockery—a burlesque on a government" (Brotz 1991: 78). Because Liberia was being propped up by American slaveholding interests, he reasoned this was not a place for free black people because Liberians would be at the beck and call of American policymakers. Consequently, freedom would never be found in Liberia.

However, the world was bigger than Africa and, according to Delany, there was a place for black people. Like the citizens who attended the Philadelphia convention in 1831, Delany felt the Americas were among the most viable places to begin looking for relocation opportunities. Either south to Mexico or north to Canada, Delany argued, would be useful because they were beyond the jurisdiction of the United States and could not be pressed into slavery. Moreover, these countries were proximate enough that those escaping enslavement could seek freedom relatively close by. As he stated, "fly to the Canadas, as well the number of the twenty-five thousand already there," until a more suitable place could be found (Brotz 1991: 80). In Canada there would be a ready community, and it was easier to locate there than some place across the ocean. Further, the proximity of Canada and Mexico allowed free blacks to continue their abolition activism with greater effect. In Mexico there was a sizable population of African-descended people, and while the weather in Mexico may have been preferable to Canada, the freedom was the same and that was the object. Of course, there were more possibilities, but what Delany and others were more concerned with was that whatever the locale, there should be room for black people of all positions. Thus, it was not enough to simply leave America—the aim was to move toward opportunity for upward group development educationally, socially, economically, and politically. Wherever that place was, it had to be financed and operated by blacks for blacks. That place was *not* the United States.

Delany was not alone in his sentiments regarding black emigration. James T. Holly, a noted clergyman who eventually settled in Haiti, had long been involved in the emigration movement by the time he relocated to Haiti in 1861. Prior to his relocation, Holly spent time in Canada, and from there he took black Americans and Canadians with him to Haiti, where he became a citizen. For Holly, Haiti's distinction as the first black republic demonstrated black peoples' capacity for self-government, which had not been allowed to flourish under white rule. Haiti was the most obvious place for blacks to locate if they wanted to experience freedom and the full realization of their talents, because the Haitian people had a history of resistance, nation building, and were independent of white control.

Haiti was distinguished because the revolution was a movement of enslaved people who fought for their right to self-determination and that of other blacks. Because of Haitian efforts, blacks had a place where they could see a realized national project helmed by blacks—an opportunity unavailable on the continent of Africa because of colonization. Therefore Haiti, with a stable government, industry, and independence, presented blacks with an opportunity for self-improvement and an obligation for group advancement. As Holly states, "rather than to indolently remain here, asking for political rights," blacks should seek Haiti, which he felt "will solve all question respecting the Negro, whether they be those of slavery, prejudice or proscription" (Brotz 1991: 170). Even if blacks received rights in the United States, Holly believed these were of little value because blacks were still viewed as inferior beings by the majority of Americans. If blacks wanted to be treated as equally human, they needed to relocate to a space where that proposition was a given, not a debate. The only choice was Haiti, where blacks occupied all statuses in society, and the reign of white supremacy had been ejected.

For Delany, Crummell, Holly, and later Marcus Garvey, colonization to Africa was not just an opportunity for self-enrichment but an obligation to their "benighted brethren" who were not yet Christianized. Going back to Africa would allow blacks to fulfill their desires for office holding and social enrichment, but would also fulfill their Christian duty of spreading the gospel to nonbelievers. In this way, Africa was the fulfillment of a terrestrial and spiritual destiny. Therefore, Africa was instrumental to the material and spiritual progress of black Americans. However, for all their philosophizing about Africa, it was not as if pro-colonizing forces did not feel the pull of America. Garnet said this of his home country in 1848:

> America is my home, my country, and I have no other. I love whatever good there may be in her institutions. I hate her sins. I loathe her slavery, and I pray Heaven that ere long she may wash away her guilt in tears of repentance. I love the green-hills which my eyes first beheld in my infancy. I love every inch of soil which my feet pressed in my youth, and I mourn because the accursed shade of slavery rests upon it. I love my country's flag, and I hope that soon it will be cleansed of its stains, and be hailed by all nations as the emblem of freedom and independence (Brotz 1991: 202).

However, that day was much too far off for Garnet and others who would pursue their emigrant dreams under the auspices of the African Civilization Society (the Society). Founded in 1858, with Garnet as its first president, the Society viewed itself as significantly different from the ACS on a few different fronts. For starters, this was an organization that counted blacks among its founders. Garnet, like the other members, believed if black people were going to be in charge of their own destiny, they had to be the main drivers of the project. As Society members stated, the "ulterior objects in encouraging emigration shall be—Self-Reliance and Self-Government, on the principle of an African Nationality, the African race being the ruling element of the nation, controlling and directing their own affairs" (Brotz 1991: 194). This meant the role of whites was defined as "aiders and assistants," but this was going to be a black-led movement leading to a black-led nation. More importantly, in Article II of the constitution for the Society, the chief aim of this organization was defined as "the civilization and Christianization of Africa, and the descendants of African ancestors in any portion of the earth, wherever dispersed" (Brotz 1991: 191). This is significant because although the Society also had the goal of teaching cotton cultivation to the continent, African souls were its first priority. In fact, Crummell (1860) stated that black emigration to Africa was critical because of the lack of a Christian presence on the continent, as in the Caribbean and other parts of the African diaspora. The destruction of slavery was not mentioned until Article III of the organization's founding constitution.

The programmatic goals of the Society,[20] while parochial, patriarchal, and problematic, were an attempt to develop salvation as well as industry on the continent independent of slave labor. Most importantly, the Africa Civilization Society was not interested in the forced removal of blacks for the appeasement and comfort of whites. Garnet believed in emigration as the primary way for blacks to achieve the agency they needed and desired. Only a short time after the founding of the Society, its constitution was amended to bring more clarity to the organization's mission.

In revisiting the Society's mission, it was decided the Society would not encourage the general emigration of black people. Rather, it was committed to "aid only such persons as may be practically qualified and suited to promote the development of Christianity, morality, education, mechanical arts, agriculture, commerce, and general improvement" (Brotz 1991: 194). This was in keeping with the aims of the Society as primarily a proselytizing organization, but it was also elitist. Until this time, proponents of emigration had encouraged blacks to leave the United States with promises of the possibility for becoming better selves without the hindrance of race. Yet, by the 1861 adoption of these supplemental clauses it was clear that the notion of progress would and should be limited to the "carefully selected and well recommended," which seemed to leave out the majority of free blacks who were particularly in need of the possibilities emigration would bring. As such, emigration had been redefined and reimagined by the Society as the province of skilled blacks and not those who would be seeking literacy and other education after freedom.

Emigration and Framing Black "Americanness"

Although scholars may disagree about the level of altruism of the ACS and the Society, blacks of the time were far less measured in their critiques of these organizations, particularly the ACS. Blacks viewed the ACS as racist, complicit in the maintenance of enslavement and white supremacy. Specifically, blacks made several important claims about ACS that caused a majority of them to refuse the overtures of this group (Mehlinger 1916).

As stated previously, the chief complaint from blacks was the ACS's concern for preserving white dominance by the removal of free blacks. For many blacks, the idea that whites were genuinely concerned with their well-being was hard to accept. Not to say white allies did not exist, but the idea that southern planters would support any movement that would help them achieve independence and a better quality of life was doubtful (Burin 2005). After all, it would be foolhardy to trust the motives of those who did not believe black people were human beings and wanted to maintain their abjection at home while claiming to support their freedom abroad. In the case of the ACS, blacks felt the organization was talking out of both sides of its mouth. ACS members wanted blacks to believe its aims of relocating them were in their best interest, but they were in league with the very same people who were the cause of black suffering. Because of these connections, the ACS had little credibility with free blacks. Although some blacks did believe they would be better off should they repatriate to Africa, it escaped few of them how contradictory it was to work toward their interests with the very same people who usurped their freedom.

By avoiding the issue of enslavement, the ACS tacitly supported the foundation of white supremacy. Blacks critical of the ACS felt the organization was using emigration as a vehicle to foster white solidarity (Garrison 1832; Mehlinger 1916). By working with white racists, their sympathizers, and making the displacement of free blacks their core mission, the ACS effectively told blacks their suffering was their responsibility. If they would simply move, their lives would improve. It was not whites that needed to change; rather, it was black existence that needed to be changed. The basic message was that if not for black people, white people would behave.

This opposition to emigration by free blacks also stymied the efforts of the Society. Although the Society was a black-run organization that did not subscribe to the notion of forced removal, their steadfast commitment to leaving the United States raised the cockles of many blacks, none more prominent than Frederick Douglass. The noted abolitionist, statesman, author, and former slave was unwavering in his opposition to the proposals of the ACS and the Society. For Garnet, president of the Society, Douglass had particular venom as Garnet publicly suggested that Douglass had not been clear in his opposition to colonization and, in fact, could offer no reason to oppose the scheme. In some of his most plainspoken writing, Douglass proffers multiple reasons for his objection to the entire idea of colonization.

It is important to note that Douglass did not oppose one's individual choice to emigrate. For Douglass, it was a matter of free will. If some blacks wanted to go to Africa, he was unopposed, but he felt this expression of free will could not be framed as an imperative or obligation of all black people. He also thought the Christianization and civilization of African people was a worthy goal, and this was not a point of contention for Douglass and men like Garnet and Delany. Furthermore, Douglass chafed at the idea that "Africa, not America, is the Negro's true home"

(Brotz 1991: 264). For Douglass (1969), the belief that blacks were not "real Americans," shared by blacks and whites, was dangerous and sustained by emigration schemes because it supported the same ideas that led to black denigration and exclusion from the body politic. If it was believed that blacks in America were simply displaced Africans, then they had no claims to citizenship, rights, or respect. Despite the anti-black, pro-slavery sentiment of the time, there was reason to be optimistic the United States could change and turn away from the institution of slavery if all efforts, black and white, were directed against this institution.

Douglass felt strongly by conceding that America held no possibilities for blacks, it allowed bigotry to flourish. Rather than challenging America to live up to its promise of equality, sending blacks to Africa simply let whites off the hook and did not force them to confront black humanity. In some ways, Douglass presented emigration as a distraction from the real issue which, to his mind, was the abolition of slavery. America was not black people's problem. Instead, a commitment to an institution that depended on the dehumanization and usurpation of the agency of another was the problem.

By simply leaving enslavement untouched, emigrationists were not going to have a better chance of defeating the institution in Africa. In his skepticism, he writes there is "no reason to believe that any one man in Africa can do more for the abolition of that trade, while living in Africa, than while living in America" (Brotz 1991: 265). According to Douglass, the non-Christian slave traders of West Africa were no more willing to end their centuries-long participation in enslavement than those in the United States. He felt the emigrationists would be less successful in Africa at defeating slavery because there was already a strong abolitionist movement here, and more institutional arrangements that supported the ending of the institution. In the end, for Douglass, colonization was a fool-hardy scheme that duped black people into believing their lives would be easy anywhere else, and it capitulated too much to racism. For opponents of colonization, the scheme was a failure because it rested on the idea that blacks were not American. Blacks were American by birth, and leaving this country would not change that fact. The only thing emigration would ac-complish is letting the racists and the bigots win by allowing them to con-tinue in their belief and practice that America was a white man's country.

Nevertheless, one of the most damning charges against emigration was made by pro-colonization supporter President Abraham Lincoln. Soon to be known as the "Great Emancipator" because of his signing of the Emancipation Proclamation in September 1862, in the month before this order's passage Lincoln was still working out some way for blacks to be sent "back to Africa." In the midst of the Civil War, President Lincoln argued to a committee of free blacks, headed by Edward M. Thomas, that theirs was a mutual suffering. Blacks suffered because whites would never see them as their equals, and whites suffered because a free black presence was too much to bear. This is how Lincoln begins his conversation to a group of heretofore unconvinced blacks committed to remaining in the United States. Although Lincoln attempts to draw parallels between the white and black experiences, he is very clear in his belief and support of the notion that the United States is a white man's country. In his attempt to reason with blacks, he argues that "on this broad continent, not a single race of your race is made the equal of a single man of ours" (Fredrickson 1975: 55). In short, free blacks could not hope to attain equality with whites regardless of their status. For Lincoln, the strife of the nation was the result of slavery and the presence of black people.

Lincoln thought the problem of black resettlement was about their selfish desire to be close to whites. If free blacks simply would see that "his comfort would be advanced by it [colonization]," they would cease wanting to live in the United States. Because whites did not wish to be discomfited by the presence of blacks, Lincoln reasoned that if some number of them started to leave the country, this would encourage whites to consider ending enslavement. He says:

> But you ought to do something to help those who are not so fortunate as yourselves. There is an unwillingness on the part of our [white] people, harsh as it may be, for you free colored people to remain with us. Now, if you could give a start to white people, you would open wide a door for many to be made free. . . . If intelligent colored men, such as are before me, would move in this matter, much might be accomplished. It is exceedingly important that we have men at the beginning capable of thinking as white men, and not those who have been systematically oppressed.

Lincoln suggests that rational blacks would see that if they simply offered a good faith gesture to whites by leaving the country, then whites would be less reluctant to give up enslavement as a practice. Yet, Lincoln overlooked the economic and psychic imperatives of remaining invested in the system of enslavement. Moreover, Lincoln's claim that blacks would gain far more from leaving than they would lose if they stayed rested on the assumption that blacks could not hope for a better future as long as they remained in proximity to whites. In short, for Lincoln white supremacy was not the problem, blacks were, because they disrupted whites' ability to deny their equality.

For Lincoln, the disruptive presence blacks presented far outweighed any potential gains to be had by their continued presence in the United States. Although he hoped blacks would leave, he obviously had not taken into consideration how essential blacks were to the functioning of the United States. Not only were blacks an essential part of the labor force, they were a significant part of white identity formation. The black presence was necessary for the functioning of an effective white supremacist system. If blacks were suddenly deported to Liberia or Central America, as Lincoln proposed, how would white identity function? The visibility of blackness, as marked by physical differences, gave whiteness a raison d'etre (Mullen 1994). If blacks were suddenly gone, not only would the economic life of the nation be upset but the substance of a white identity.

To be identified as racially white carried with it a presumption of autonomy and freedom and gave all whites at least partial membership in the polity. Even though the revision of citizenship requirements would expand to include poor whites at the conclusion of slavery, white privilege was used as an inducement to forge unity among upper and lower class whites. Prior to the introduction of grandfather clauses and the like, poor white men were not guaranteed the right to vote because they were not property owners; they were seen as not being real stakeholders in the American enterprise. It was believed that a full citizen had to have material possessions to have a stake in the nation-state. It was reasoned that the propertied classes provided funds to direct local, state, and national projects, and thus had a better sense of the general will. They were the leadership class; these were the men who were the most learned and able to discern the complexities of policy, to sort out what was the greater good. This paternalism meant that those without the full possession of the self in terms of property, autonomy, and the other markers of the ideal citizen were subject to the whims of this property-owning class. Consequently, the kind of "blanket whiteness" that covers all people with white skins is a modern invention. The type of liberated whiteness we are familiar with today is the result of enslavement, immigration, and the abolition of the institution of slavery. This is not to suggest these are the only causes for the development and evolution of whiteness, as Jacobson (2001) aptly demonstrates. Nevertheless, when blacks were enslaved, lesser whites had a way to discern their place in the American racial hierarchy. They were better than the enslaved, even if they had no status to show for it (Roediger 1999). However, this sensibility of being barely better-than was threatened as slavery waned because without slavery, who were poor whites?

Therefore, to be white was already to be valued by the republic. It was unclear what freedom meant for blacks, who were certainly not citizens and were not even thought of as entirely human. Consequently, the specter of free blacks caused a real crisis for whites, because if black did not automatically equal slave, then what separated white from back? The result was a type of juridical and emotional limbo for free blacks, who were noncitizens of the nation but expected to perform the duties of citizens (i.e., paying taxes) without any of the guarantees and protections of citizens. This partially explains the disconnect between emigrants and those who remained in the United States. Although proponents and opponents of colonization could agree the living conditions of blacks in America were undesirable at best, they differed significantly as to the cause. More importantly, they disagreed about what they saw as the possibility for America to reform itself into a racially inclusive nation.

Discussion

What this chapter seeks to demonstrate is that this moment referred to as *colonization* be reconsidered as a moment of em/immigration for blacks. The opinions of black America would vacillate greatly on the question of whether they should leave or stay in the United States. Where one ended up in that conversation largely depended on whether one believed the United States was fundamentally a racist country, or if there was room for blacks to become part of the founding vision of the nation that had yet to be fulfilled. For those who believed the United States was closed to demands for black inclusion, emigration seemed like a viable alternative. However, for those who were ethically opposed to emigration, there was some acknowledgment that true freedom may prove elusive in an American context.

The language of "colonization" belies the fact that this was essentially a forced removal of blacks—not through violence but by creating an environment so hostile and inhospitable that blacks would prefer leaving the country rather than continue to stay. Although the ACS necessarily did not use violence, their flaccid response to the institution of slavery made them untrustworthy partners in the repatriation of blacks to Africa. If neither white supremacy nor enslavement were going to be challenged, blacks could not safely rely on the goodwill of whites for their safe resettlement abroad, when whites were so profoundly misguided at the outset of the process.

Consequently, although emigration represented a proactive, rational response to the dangerous conditions posed by continued residence in the United States, the ties of racial fealty proved the deciding factor. This is significant because although the majority of blacks had decided against emigration, the issue became a way for blacks to air their grievances. Acknowledging blacks both as em/immigrants and as a community with a long-standing vested interest in the question of immigration firmly places American blacks as more than observers within historical and contemporary conversations around immigration.

As such, blacks placed themselves directly in the discourse surrounding immigration. By discursively positioning themselves as immigrants within, blacks were not eschewing American identity per se. Rather, they were attempting to highlight American hypocrisy with respect to them. Thus, emancipation was only the first step in black freedom. For proponents of emigration, a full exodus of the black population from the United States was the next step toward full freedom.

As Martin R. Delany[21] states in his famous pamphlet *The Political Destiny of the Colored Race on the American Continent*, "the color of the blacks is a badge of degradation, acknowledged by statute, organic law, and the common consent of the people" (1854: 340). Thus there was no way to remove the mark of race, because this color coding was too ingrained in white American minds. Therefore, if blacks wanted to be free, Delany states that black attentions should "be turned in a direction toward those places where the black and colored man comprise, by population, and constitute by necessity of numbers the *ruling element* of the body politic," because it is only then that blacks could be recognized as equals. This would never be the case in the United States. Thus, continuing to stay in the United States, or any other majority white country, was a fool's errand because whites had sought the destruction of nonwhite people the world over.

In the early period of abolition beginning in the early nineteenth century, blacks were more than passive recipients of the organizing efforts of whites. They were active as abolitionists. Free blacks saw their fates inextricably linked to those of their enslaved brethren because of the color prejudice engendered by white supremacy; of course, asserting that freedom became especially difficult as the country increasingly stymied black efforts through legal and extralegal means. As a result, free blacks often felt as claustrophobic as those enslaved because they were threatened with (re)enslavement, and their freedom of movement became increasingly curtailed—not to mention the continual violations of their most basic human rights and their lack of inclusion in the citizenry despite their birth in this country. Consequently, many blacks saw themselves as outsiders within, and many felt they needed to leave this place to secure some type of life for themselves and their loved ones. Whether it was free blacks leaving the slave South, or the strictures of the relatively freer North, blacks saw themselves as emigrants (from the South) and immigrants (to other parts of the world).

As members of a globally oppressed group, blacks knew there were few spaces that would welcome their presence and even fewer locales that would allow them to be full participants. However, supporters of colonization were undeterred, because whether it was Haiti, Canada, or the continent of Africa, it had to be preferable to the racial limbo in which they existed. Thus, the first immigrants that blacks acknowledged and were concerned with were themselves.

This chapter pulls the lens back on the immigration debates in black America by highlighting the many internal dialogues black communities were having in this country regarding emigration. From the early nineteenth century through the beginning of the Civil War, and again in the twentieth century, black America entertained a number of possibilities including emigration that would lead to their elevation. Although emigration was not heavily supported in black communities, I do not read colonization as a failed project. Rather, I view these early emigration conversations as demonstrating blacks' ambivalence about this issue, which helps to frame the major argument of this text. That is, blacks have always viewed immigration as a major concern for their group. Although this has not necessarily come in the form of advocacy for or against a given immigration policy, what I want to show is that blacks have thought long and hard about the issue, and their sensibilities about immigration are informed by what immigration will mean for the sociopolitical advancement of their group. In this chapter in particular, what I demonstrate is that blacks see themselves as (internal) immigrants because they had to leave their homeland, generally the southern region of the country, to live relatively more freely. Moreover, this movement did not necessarily stop with moving to the mythical North, but for some included moving abroad. Although immigration in the form of repatriation to the continent of Africa was much discussed, it demonstrates the degree of conflict American-born blacks felt about their continuing presence in this country, particularly as the majority of blacks remained in bondage and the United States was thoroughly committed to the continuance of the institution. By examining the historical record, it is apparent blacks were unsettled about what to do with respect to immigration, primarily because white supremacy was not being directly confronted.

Using interview data, the next chapter highlights the "everyday talk" of blacks about immigration. In this series of interviews, it becomes clear that blacks use the past to understand their present circumstances. Through the particularities of their circumstances, I am able to show that blacks use immigration as a way to critique their systematic exclusion from the body politic. This offers a more nuanced analysis of black public opinion that is often characterized as being in opposition to immigration.

4

(Re)Remembering Race

COLLECTIVE MEMORY AND RACIAL HIERARCHY
IN THE PRESENT

IN THE PREVIOUS chapters I have outlined my core argument that black attitudes toward immigration are mediated by feelings about their own partial incorporation into American society. Insofar as blacks care about immigration, it is because it provides a vehicle to air their grievances regarding their current circumstances, which they view as being the result of past and ongoing racial discrimination. This chapter provides an analysis of discourse that demonstrates the ways in which black people dialogue about race and its connection to immigration. This chapter does not argue that the relationship between the past and present is linear; it does argue that to understand black attitudes, it is necessary to appreciate how black people relate the past to their present (Dawson 1994a; Harris-Lacewell 2004; Walters 2009). In this chapter I demonstrate how collective memory bonds the past to the present and provides the connective tissue between the realities of black people's lived experiences and their attitudes about immigration. What I am able to show is that blacks' present worldview is steeped in their collective memory of their community's struggles for racial equality (Kachun 2009; Nunnally 2012; Shackel 2003; Walters 2009). Consequently, immigration is necessarily seen through a black/white racial lens, and the immigration issue is used by blacks as an indicator of their group's progress. I demonstrate that blacks exhibit a complicated range of responses to immigration, which I characterize as ambivalent and far more uncertain than appreciated. Using the community of Durham, North Carolina, as a case study, I explore the uniqueness of this locality, especially in terms of its long fight to end school segregation, to make more general claims about the importance of the past in understanding present attitudes. I first move to a discussion of Durham and the particularities of the city and state that make it a compelling case for understanding the ways in which race informs and constrains black public opinion with respect to immigration.

Durham: Black Progress and Racial Retrenchment in North Carolina

Durham, North Carolina, was one of the success stories in black America in the late nineteenth and early twentieth centuries. The home of black entrepreneurship and middle-class progress, the many cultural and educational institutions that catered to the city's black population concealed the vast economic and racial disparities seen in many other parts of the country where blacks lived. Because blacks occupied so many places of power in the city, it masked the rather draconian racial climate of the state at large. Durham had so many blacks registered to vote by 1965 that it was not covered by the pre-clearance requirement of the Voting Rights Act[1]. Still, Durham had deep racial problems that remain to this day.

Part of the Upper South, North Carolina was viewed as relatively progressive compared to its slave-owning cousins in Virginia and South Carolina, owing to its relatively small slave markets (Johnson 1937). Nevertheless, the bugaboo of race has permeated every fiber of the state's being. The durability of black and white racial dynamics, like other southern states, remains a dominant feature of the city's and state's political landscape.[2] Despite the great waves of immigration beginning in the late nineteenth and early twentieth centuries that characterized the North, the South remained a fundamentally biracial space. North Carolina, despite its identity as a quasi-liberal state, is undoubtedly Southern and as steeped in the legacy of enslavement and Jim Crow as any other place.

Durham, one of North Carolina's oldest cities, has been influenced by that same legacy of slavery. Tobacco, for which the city was renowned, had been the source of the city's growth. Tobacco was central to the relationship between blacks and whites both during and after slavery. Well into the 1940s and beyond, the city's tobacco factories were a source of employment for most Durham residents, as well as the locus of much racial animus between blacks and whites (Greene 2005).

A considerable black middle class existed in the city for many decades, which makes Durham unique with respect to comparable places.[3] Black Durham was anchored by three very important institutions. The North Carolina Mutual and Life Insurance Company, founded in 1898, is the oldest and largest black owned and operated insurance firm in the country.[4] The Mechanics and Farmers Bank—chartered in 1907, opened in 1908, and still around today—was one of the most fiscally sound black owned and managed financial institutions to cater to an African American clientele.[5] And finally, what is now known as North Carolina Central University (NCCU) opened its doors in 1910 under the leadership of Dr. James E. Shepard with a mission to educate Negro men and women; this institution was integral to the city's sit-in movement during the 1950s and 1960s campaign for civil rights. These bodies served as important organizing institutions of the city's black community but were unable to completely shield its members from the indignities of racism.

Despite the presence of these organizations, more blacks were employed by the tobacco manufacturing industry than in black institutions (Gershenhorn 2001; Green 2005; Jones 1984). These low-paying, low-skilled jobs were a far cry from the wealth that black Durham was known for. Black Durham has always been stratified economically into the "haves" and "have-nots." Although at certain moments the class differences in this community have led to some intraracial hostility, race has been the most salient unifying force among black Durham residents.

Although poor and middle-class blacks led very different lives, the space they were allowed to inhabit as a whole was limited. Discrimination in Durham was not about class but about race. Monetary resources did not necessarily bring physical and social mobility. Despite black residents such as C.C. Spaulding[6] being viewed as gatekeepers of the black community, the financial resources wielded by Spaulding and others were unable to stem the tide of white racial prejudice in Durham. Geographically constrained by segregation, blacks were not only barred from participating in the white public sphere, they were physically removed from the presence of whites. As the map demonstrates, blacks were relegated to clearly defined communities that created and reified patterns of inequality. All areas marked with a "D" were majority black and poor, the areas were deemed "risky" by the insurance authority; consequently, the homes in these areas were undervalued and because of redlining, it was nearly impossible to obtain a mortgage. This made maintain the city's color line easier as official and unofficial authorities conspired to keep Durham's

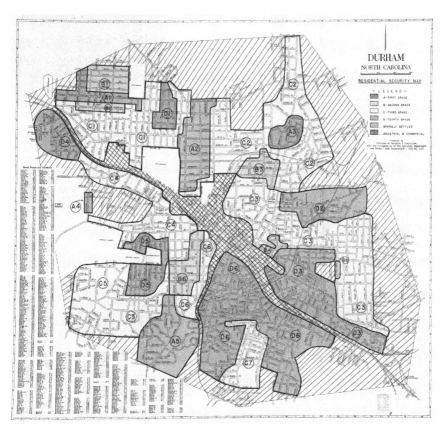

MAP 0I

communities segregated (Rothstein 2017). This segregation unwittingly provided the fodder for black collective organization. The Hayti neighborhood, located in area D6, was established in the late 1880s outside the Durham city limits, and was the hub of much of black life in the city (Litwack 2004; Rabinowitz 1976). Blacks developed a parallel business and social community in Hayti for the provision of goods and services (Anderson 1990).[7] This was not unique to Durham; black enclaves were created out of necessity to serve the economic, social, educational, and political needs of black communities, both North and South.

The literal and figurative separation of blacks and whites was also replicated in tobacco factories, where labor and workspace were segregated according to gender and color (Hunter 1997; Jones 1984). Although tobacco factories paid better than agricultural work, blacks worked the "dirty" jobs in factories and did so in separate buildings from whites; in tobacco factories, this work consisted of "sorting, cleaning and stemming" tobacco (Jones 1984: 444). It goes without saying that such racial hierarchy was reflected in differential earnings and in the unsafe working conditions blacks were subjected to. Poor ventilation, lack of safety equipment, verbal and physical abuse, and often sexual abuse for black women were standard practices in Durham's tobacco factories (Bynum 1992; Griffin and Korstad 1995; Jones 2009). These exploitative business practices overlapped with the social customs of the day that denigrated blacks.

Blacks in Durham did not experience these effects uniformly. Black women were particularly vulnerable to (sexual) abuse and low wages on the job (Greene 2005; Jones 1984). In Durham, as in other parts of the country, black women were more likely than their white counterparts to work outside the home (Greene 2005; Hunter 1997; Jones 1984; Wolcott 1997, 2001). This made them vulnerable to all manner of sexual misconduct on the part of employers. Black women fortunate enough to gain employment with one of the city's black firms were somewhat insulated from such sexual harassment (Brown and Valk 2004; Kelly 2010). Yet, for a number of black women who worked outside the home, the workplace was fraught with all types of dangers (Collins 1990; Greene 2005; Kelley 1993; Jones 2009). For those who needed the wages, albeit substandard, there was often no alternative. Unfortunately, for black women this added injury was usually without resolution because the code of (racial) justice in the South did not include any penalty for white men who transgressed the boundaries of black female sexual autonomy (Collins 1990; Edwards 2005, 1991; Greene 2005; Hodes 1997; McGuire 2010; Mitchell 1999; Roberts 1997; Wiegman 1995; West 1999).

Even though race was experienced disparately by class and gender, black Durhamites coalesced around their racial identity (Greene 2005). Racial segregation, though oppressive in most ways, enabled blacks to develop the resources necessary to resist the city's segregation (Greene 2005; Weare 1973). The entrepreneurial community played a vital yet complicated role in the city's race relations. Because black elites were able to access the city's white power structure, their role with respect to the larger black community was strained (Greene 2005). This tension was caused by the dual responsibilities and functions served by the black middle class. In addition to being arbiters on behalf of their community, black elites also served a quasi-police function with respect to the city's black populace when racial tempers flared and resulted in open defiance of white supremacist practices (Anderson 1990; Greene 2005). In these instances, black elites seemed to collude with white authorities to mollify black residents and quell conflicts. In so doing, black elites achieved greater gains for themselves owing to their ability to access their white counterparts. Unfortunately, the interests of black elites did not always result in the most equitable outcomes for the majority of blacks (Anderson 1990).

Still, the black business community was a much needed and utilized resource. Not only did they provide money for civil rights efforts, they also had access to physical space, which was necessary for organizing. Because of the nature of the industries these entrepreneurs were involved in, such as funeral homes, insurance, and beauty care, they had organizational skills, capital, and space essential for building thriving businesses and supporting burgeoning political movements on the part of blacks (Boyd 2000; Brown and Valk 2004; Gill 2004; Greene 2005; Holloway 2002; Silverman 1998; Brady, Verba, and Schlozman 1995). Moreover, by serving a racially homogeneous clientele, black businesses were able to access large swaths of the community that allowed them to facilitate social movement networks (Gill 2004; Holloway 2002; Silverman 1998). In a perverse way, the activism of the black community was greatly enabled by Jim Crow segregation. Freed from the capriciousness of white employers, black entrepreneurs were able to support a number of civil rights organizations and their political activities. The organizing activities that many of these ladies and men participated in would have guaranteed their termination and expulsion from the white employment sector. By controlling their own purse strings, black entrepreneurs did not have to fear economic retaliation by whites.[8]

The "independence" provided by segregation gave them the space to formulate a black counter-public resistant to the denial of their civil rights and liberties (Brooks 2005; Dawson 1994b; Squires 2002). From all corners, the black community began to demand everything from the provision of basic city services to better education for their children (Anderson 1990). Mirroring the larger civil rights movement, black Durham organizers concentrated much of their efforts on integrating institutions of higher education. This tactic of integrating educational institutions was chosen because *Plessy v. Ferguson* (1896) established the "separate but equal" clause, which maintained separate black institutions were permissible if they were equal to white institutions. Black institutions were rarely equal to white institutions, which was abundantly clear when looking at the state of black schools relative to their peer white schools. As a result, the constitutionality of these institutions was challenged for violating the "equality" standard, with the thought that if states were unable to meet the mandate of maintaining the same institutions for black and white students they would be forced to integrate these institutions. Thus, if integration of educational institutions could be achieved, then this would clear the way for the integration of public accommodations and other parts of segregated life. In this way, education was a small piece of a comprehensive strategy toward ending Jim Crow segregation.

Although blacks were not prohibited from applying to white colleges in the state, it was clear they would not be accepted. Furthermore, the North Carolina College for Negroes, the only historically black college in the city, did not have any graduate or professional programs.[9] Thus, it was a certainty that black students would have to relocate to obtain a graduate degree because there were no schools in the state offering professional training to black students. This reality made segregated education in North Carolina ripe for legal challenge.

Challenging Jim Crow

Durham attorneys Conrad Pearson and Cecil McCoy, with the assistance of NAACP attorney William Hastie and the support of C.C. Spaulding, sought to test admissions criteria using college student Thomas R. Hocutt as a test case (Anderson 1990; Gershenhorn 2001). Hocutt was a student at the North Carolina College for Negroes and was the only student brave enough to volunteer for the undertaking in 1933. Hocutt, accompanied by his attorneys, attempted to enroll in the University of North Carolina at Chapel Hill's (UNC) pharmacy school, where he was summarily denied admission because of his race. This denial gave the attorneys grounds to sue, because neither the university nor the state had any professional programs for blacks at this time. Soon after filing the lawsuit, the support that Pearson, McCoy, and Hocutt received from black elites evaporated amid intense pressure from their white allies (Gershenhorn 2001). Even among those whites considered racial liberals, support for equality ended at calls for integration of the public sphere (Carter 2012, 2013). Although some whites believed Hocutt should be able to pursue graduate education, they felt he should do so at a black university.

Of course, Hocutt's case presented a number of problems for blacks and whites, albeit for different reasons. C.C. Spaulding, who initially supported the Hocutt case, withdrew his public support because he did not want to upset the rather pleasant relationships he enjoyed with local whites. A racial moderate, Spaulding continued his advocacy of the case privately as he both recognized the importance of pushing a more racially inclusive agenda while maintaining friendships with whites for his commercial and community interests. James Shepard, the president of NCCN and a racial gradualist, at no point supported the NAACP and Hocutt's efforts. First and foremost, Shepard's college received funding through the state legislature. By necessity he had to adopt a far more conciliatory tone to maintain this funding, which was already lacking and subject to the whims of white state legislators. What is more, Shepard was rightfully concerned that the admission of blacks to predominantly white institutions meant less incentive for the state to put resources into black colleges for more robust degree programs (Brown 2002; Gasman 2013; Harvey, Harvey, and King 2004; Kelly 2010). For these reasons, Shepard believed the Hocutt case was not only wrongheaded but had potentially deleterious and unforeseen consequences on the long-term viability of black institutions such as the one he helmed. As such, Shepard saw the Hocutt case as an opportunity to leverage the state into granting more money to black institutions to serve the graduate and professional needs of students in the state.[10] Consequently, Shepard did not provide an official university transcript for Hocutt's application.[11] Shepard's refusal to provide Hocutt with an official transcript gave the University of North Carolina a nonracial reason to reject his application, which they did, although it was a suspect claim. Still, it is necessary to put Shepard's actions in context. The NCCN relied on the state for funding, and this was during the Great Depression, which meant the already meager funding was more threatened. By taking away Hocutt's individual opportunity, greater group gains were achieved. However, Shepard's individual beliefs and actions were not the sole reason that Hocutt's attempts to register at UNC were unsuccessful.

White moderates were also opposed to Hocutt's admission to Chapel Hill. They saw Hocutt's exclusion as necessary to preserving the sanctity of their institutions. Segregation, as a physical manifestation of white supremacy, was foundational to UNC and institutions of like mind; by rejecting Hocutt they were by extension protecting their institutions and white supremacy (Carter 2012, 2013). Then president of UNC Frank Porter Graham believed segregation was wrong, but was unwilling to lobby against the Board of Trustees and their desire to keep UNC racially white (Gershenhorn 2001). Indeed Graham, like other whites who believed in interracial cooperation, were prepared to pursue professional schools for blacks only so long as their own universities and full integration were off the table. In this sentiment, Shepard and Graham were unified. Thus, both white and black elites privately attempted to get Hocutt and the national NAACP to vacate the case.[12] In fact, UNC officials offered Hocutt guaranteed funding for his out-of-state tuition as an inducement to leave the case. It was feared that a finding in favor of Hocutt would be a slippery slope that would not only put their beloved institutions at risk, but also their children and white women (Hodes 1997; Vander Zanden 1959). This preoccupation that racial integration would lead to miscegenation was one of the more persuasive arguments for maintaining segregation. If black people, particularly black men, became the social equals of white men, then it would only be a matter of time before they desired to have the ultimate symbol of social equality with white men—white women. This "race mixing" would serve to weaken white gene pools and create social chaos for America. Of course these fears were largely unfounded, but they were powerful and had the intended consequence of cooling white sympathies toward the project of racial integration. On the other side, black elites were concerned that failure to get Hocutt to leave the lawsuit would harm their educational institutions and send the message to white elites that they did not hold sway over their communities.

When the case finally received a hearing, the state court affirmed the university's decision to refuse Hocutt's admission. Although the courts ruled UNC could not be compelled to admit black students, there was still hope among black North Carolinians that the state legislature would pass a bill to pay the tuition of black students seeking professional or graduate degrees out of state. The bill failed, and no subsequent cases challenging segregation in higher education in North Carolina were pursued. The NAACP decided Hocutt was not the type of plaintiff it needed in a state as resistant to integration as North Carolina; Hocutt was not a stellar student, and both blacks and whites agreed that another filing of the case was undesirable.[13] Although *Hocutt* may have been collateral damage on the road to racial progress, it cannot be denied that even in its failure, the *Hocutt* case was part of the lineage of other legal challenges to segregation in higher education.

Missouri ex. rel. Gaines v. Canada (1938) in Maryland is one case inspired by the legal maneuverings in *Hocutt*. The Supreme Court ruled "state universities admit blacks to graduate or professional schools unless equivalent instruction were available at black institutions" (Anderson 1990). *Missouri ex. rel. Gaines* effectively pushed the issue of integration in higher education down the road, but also opened a range of opportunities for black students. The Hocutt case also helped the North Carolina College for Negroes obtain funds to build a law school and other facilities to improve the university. In 1939, the state legislature granted a charter for the founding of a law school at North Carolina College for Negroes.[14] Rather than integrate the white institutions already in existence, the previously resistant state legislature opted to build the capacities of historically black colleges and universities (HBCUs). Furthermore, activism in Durham reached an apex.

A number of organizations and individuals began advocating for public works projects, attacked primary and secondary school segregation through the law, raised the prominence of the NAACP in the state, increased voting efforts, and aggressively lobbied city council for better representation (Anderson 1990; Elliott 1996; Payne 1989). One of the major forces for change in the city was the Durham Committee on Negro Affairs (DCNA) founded in 1935. A group of some "150 blacks representing every aspect of black life," were called together by C.C. Spaulding, who was subsequently elected as DCNA's first chairman, to form this collective action group (Anderson 1990: 373).

One of the DCNA's major undertakings was voter registration; at the close of the 1920s there were only 50 blacks registered to vote in Durham (Anderson 1990; Morris 1986; Newton 1957). By 1943, Durham County had the highest number of black registered voters in the state of North Carolina. The inroads made in voter registration proved successful as blacks were able to wield a modicum of political power in the city for the first time. Although a gradual process, blacks were eventually able to elect blacks to "positions on commissions and boards, a few public offices, a fire station manned by blacks, a few black policemen and recreational facilities," such that by 1953, Rencher N. Harris became the first black person elected to the Durham City Council (Anderson 1990: 373).[15] By 1958, Harris became the first black person on the Durham City Board of Education. This newfound political power gave black residents the resolve necessary to battle segregation in public schools and other public accommodations, which proved to be some of the most difficult and enduring fights between blacks and whites in the city.[16]

Like many of their Southern counterparts, Durham's white residents were not anxious to formulate a more open community. Not only were the public schools not ready to integrate following *Brown v. Board of Education* (1954), but local universities such as Duke resisted integration in its graduate and professional schools until 1961 and in its undergraduate schools until 1962. Rather, whites were more committed to preventing racial conflagrations that had been witnessed by other cities. To that end, they were willing to work with blacks in some limited capacities to keep the peace.

However, this conciliatory move did not translate into a committed and consistent posture toward integration in the city of Durham. In fact, Durham and the state of North Carolina actively avoided school integration well into the 1970s through their adoption of a pupil reassignment plan. Formally called the Pearsall Plan (1955), under the leadership of Governor Luther Hodges, North Carolina devised a strategy that was technically compliant with the Supreme Court decision but still acceptable to whites. The plan granted

> each local school board the authority to review and decide, each on its individual merits *other* than race, applications to reassignment in the public schools. Parents of either race had the option of applying for reassignment of their children to schools of their choice. Each school district also had the option to close its schools by a majority vote. (Anderson 1990: 432–433)

This meant segregation would continue indefinitely because white parents could simply shuffle their children as needed to avoid formal integration. Although black parents were free to make reassignment requests, they were generally denied. In the most extreme cases, parents could opt to shutter schools altogether. It was not until 1963 that Durham was compelled by federal court order to integrate its schools more rapidly. While more than one hundred black students were transferred to white schools, the city school board effectively curtailed integration by adopting a pupil assignment policy based on neighborhood zones, which, because of residential segregation, kept schools racially organized as black or white.

In this way, integration became the onus of black parents who were able to or interested in availing themselves of the lengthy transfer process. Black parents and children would not receive any relief from these practices until 1970, when Durham city schools were compelled to integrate by court order. Forced integration was "achieved by pairing black and white schools and creating attendance zones for the two high schools" (Anderson 1990: 434). Unfortunately, the court's attempts were for naught at this point because by 1970 the Durham public school system was majority black because of white flight and the proliferation of private academies that catered to this fleeing white community (Clotfelter 1976; Clotfelter et al. 2003). By 1974, the black population in the Durham city school system was over 70 percent (*Wheeler* et al. *v. The Durham City Board of Education* 379 F. Supp. 1352 (M.D. N.C. 1974)), thus rendering moot school assignment by neighborhood and transfers as ways of addressing school integration.[17]

However, it is important to note that most of the wrangling over school desegregation occurred at the city level. Durham city and county schools were separate entities; consolidation of the two systems was an issue effectively resisted by blacks and whites, albeit for different reasons, until 1992 (Fairclough 2004). Whites wanted to preserve the racial homogeneity of county schools, the county being majority white. On the other hand, blacks did not wish to see their teachers, administrators, and children compromised by integration once the systems were joined (Doddy and Edwards 1955; Fairclough 2004; Gaines 1996; Kelly 2010; Rabinowitz 1974).

By the 1970s Durham county and city were becoming "blacker." More affluent blacks were making the choice to reside in the county; at the same time, low-income housing was being developed outside of the city proper and changing the racial composition of the county (Anderson 1990). In addition, blacks residing in the city began making a number of requests for transfers from city to county schools. As a result of such racial shifting, Durham was faced with a situation where whites were placing their children in private schools while blacks were beginning to place their children in county schools. Consequently, class cleavages, which had always been there but were subsumed by the exigencies of Jim Crow, were reasserting their role alongside race as a prominent fault line in Durham.

Into the 1980s, the parties of the *Wheeler* case continued to press the matter of school desegregation. It was also during this period that a proposed merger of the city and county systems would generate more support. In 1988, Durham County Commissioners developed a Merger Issues Task Force in an effort to gauge the effectiveness of each of the school systems. This large body consisted of 40 members and 40 alternates. When the Task Force delivered its report one year later, they found the city system was plagued by dilapidated physical facilities, poor fiscal mismanagement, below average test scores, and an astronomical dropout rate (Apostoleris 2018; Cyna 2019; Eden 2001a; Schmidt 1995).

Although the Task Force would identify disparities within and between the city and county school systems, they stopped short of recommending a merger. Instead, they suggested a referendum on the issue because the Task Force itself was divided, primarily along racial lines, on how to elect the school board of a merged school system (Strom 2001).[18] By North Carolina state law, the powers to merge school districts fell to local boards of education; yet racial relations were so frayed it was nearly impossible to get all interested parties to agree on most things (Schmidt 1995). At the same time, County Commissioner Bill Bell, who would later become mayor of Durham, sought help from State Senator Jim Hunt in drafting a bill that would grant county commissioners the power to merge school districts without public vote or consent of the school boards. By unanimous vote the Durham County commissioners, both black and white, agreed they would take the lead in a merger of the school systems (Apostoleris 2018; Cyna 2019). Thus, by the time the bill was approved in 1991, the commissioners had begun devising a strategy for the merger.

Although county commissioners thought they were doing what was best for the community, this move engendered more outrage because community members felt they should have been given a voice on the issue (Herriott 2001; Schmidt 1995). The racial divisions that characterized the attitudes of the larger Durham community on the merger would eventually be seen on the Durham County Commission. Despite commissioners agreeing that a merger had to take place, the issue of how school board members would be elected remained unsettled. Blacks had a majority on the Commission and felt election districts should be drawn to ensure consistent black representation on the Board of Education. White members of the Commission wanted an at-large system, which would have harmed black representation; at this time, a majority of the registered voters in Durham were white (Eden 2001a, b). Although black members of the Commission would get their way, they needed the approval of the State Board of Education to approve the new voting plan; the State Board of Education rejected the proposal.

This impasse would eventually be settled by yet another compromise devised by Commissioner MaryAnn Black, an experienced local office holder then serving in the North Carolina State House of Representatives. When the city and county schools finally merged in 1992, the transition to a racially integrated system was anything but smooth. Almost immediately after the merger, the school system lost nearly 100 teachers and a dozen administrators from the central office, mostly from the former city schools (Eden 2001b). In addition, the newly merged system suffered from white flight as parents removed their children from the Durham school system to avoid reassignment; the 1992 school year began with 600 fewer students than the previous school year (Eden 2001b). The racial integration the merger was supposed to facilitate became harder to realize. To complicate matters further, the school system was plagued with an incompetent and inefficient transportation system that heightened concerns about the unified school system (Eden 2001b).

Although it may appear that many of the cleavages that caused blacks to seek legal curatives to the racial situation of the previous decades had passed, in post–Civil Rights Act Durham, these issues remained just below the surface of black/white relations. Although blacks and whites in Durham have disagreed on a number of racial issues, the domain of education has been the area in which these disagreements have played out most visibly (Apostoleris 2018; Cyna 2019). For example, racially balkanized voting as well as frequent verbal altercations were features of school board meetings and other related activities into the early aughts (Herriott 2001; Strom 2001).[19] One of the major causes for this racial rift was the fact that African Americans did not have a majority on the board of education but represented a majority of the population (Schmidt 1995). It was not until 2016 that Durham's board of education became majority black, a first since the school systems merged.[20] Therefore, to say that Durham has "overcome" its racial past would be an overstatement. Although outright racial discrimination and violence only make episodic appearances, the tension between white and black communities remains a defining feature of the racial landscape in the area.

The purpose of this brief history has been to provide the broad contours of the black and white racial context in which the area has been mired for centuries. While Durham is a Southern city, this narrative is one that is rather indicative of American life more generally. As the bearer of America's symbolic racial memory, the South has been a particular locus of black disenfranchisement but is not unique in that sense. An affront and challenge to black citizenship and inclusion, both nationally and locally, (Southern) white racism has proven a durable lens through which blacks have come to view their place in America's racial hierarchy (Baker and Nelson 2001; Cash 1991; Cobb 2005; DeLombard 2001; Hale 1998; Key 1996; Marx 1998; Painter 2002; Singh 2004). The story of race is a thoroughly American story despite the mythologies we have created about the liberal North and racist South. Likewise, the story of school desegregation is simply a microcosm of larger racial dynamics. Looking at cities like Chicago, New York, Los Angeles, and many others, these types of tensions characterize black and white racial relations nationally. It is not atypical to find blacks suspicious of the actions of whites, which have often left them without control of their communities and institutions regardless of where they are located (Pew Research Center 2016).

Thus, blacks recognize their citizenship and the ability to participate in the democratic process does not safeguard them against social, political, and economic exclusion. Although I have spoken extensively about education, this is still very much a story about immigration. This is because newly arriving persons are becoming a part of a rough racial terrain where the dynamics between blacks and whites are central for understanding black attitudes toward newcomers. Consequently, the uncertainty expressed regarding immigrants is as much about blacks' fraught relationship with whites as it is immigrants.

Memories, the Past and the Present

Although memories suggest a reflection on the past, they have relevance in the present. In the case of African Americans, so much of who they are as a people is about the communal nature of memories of their history. Collective memory as a concept suggests our memories are a social practice that helps groups define a sense of self. That is, memories provide a way for us to cooperatively define the narrative of our group; by providing an origin story of sorts, this act of autobiography becomes more than simply myth-making in an effort to unite one's group or raise a group's self-esteem. Rather, it becomes elevated to a political act that bonds the group such that it can agitate for its own best interests that come to be defined out of these communal narratives.[21] For example, although contemporary blacks have not experienced enslavement,[22] this history is a powerful, unifying force for black Americans who have ancestors of this period and understand this moment as connected to shaping the contours of black lives, both past and present.

Memories are a resource all groups have. These memories assist groups in determining who they were and who they are. For marginalized groups, collective memory can be a powerful mechanism in mounting effective resistance to oppression as well as deciding community interests (Dawson 1994b, 2003; Nunnally 2012; Walters 2009). Collective memory is important for black people because it gives them a context to determine their best interests as individuals and as group members (Cohen 1999; Dawson 1994a, 2001; Harris-Lacewell 2004; Nunnally 2012). Nunnally (2012) notes that community is how many blacks learn about whom to trust both interracially and intraracially. This type of social learning relies, in part, on memories of parents, community leaders, and other trusted individuals who use their experiences to guide the racial learning and trusting behaviors of later generations. In the cast of racial trust, and as suggested in the previous chapter, the history of African Americans offers important guideposts to blacks about how they can expect their group to be treated by the country. In this chapter, I return to one of my central claims, which is that white supremacy is viewed as an ongoing barrier to black inclusion in the body politic. To the extent that blacks believe structural racism to be operative in the current political climate, this influences their understanding of their place relative to immigrants. The main argument I attend to here is the ongoing significance of the black/white racial paradigm in influencing black perceptions of immigrants—in particular, their sense that recent immigrants present a potential barrier to their own full inclusion.

Using Durham as a case, this chapter focuses on the ways blacks understand the different trajectories of citizenship for their group and for others given their racial past. I argue it is collective memory that anchors blacks' past racial history to their present claims regarding their rights and privileges as Americans. Thus, this chapter provides a framework for understanding black public opinion on immigration, which is rooted in their unique experiences. To this end, I ask how the history of black struggle influences their contemporary opinions regarding immigration. How does collective memory help people articulate a clear understanding of their place in the nation's racial hierarchy? I turn now toward a discussion of the methodology of this chapter; a deeper discussion of collective memory, its uses, and importance to individual identity formation; and the everyday ways in which blacks talk about the intricacies of immigration.

Methods

To address these issues, I begin with a brief discussion of memory, its uses, and its importance to individual and group identities. By using a series of thirteen[23] interviews with African American Durham residents, I delineate several ways collective memory influences attitudes on immigration. I identify several ways that blacks talk about immigration: how race impedes blacks' abilities to be viewed as full citizens; disappointments over America's failure to live up to its promise regarding blacks; and the *perceived* failure of immigrants to understand fully the nature of white supremacy.

The way black people talk about immigration is one of the areas where we see this general distrust of whites' racial motives. The respondents for this work represented a cross-section of the local Research Triangle Park area composed of the cities of Raleigh, Durham, and Chapel Hill, North Carolina. This region, like so many around the country, has a well-documented recent history of immigration (Carter 2007; Deeb-Sossa and Mendez 2008; McClain et al. 2006, 2007; Powers 2005; Singer 2004). Primarily, this immigration is from Mexico and other parts of Latin America. Therefore, my respondents equate Latino with Mexican and immigrant in many of the interviews. Let me be clear, this book focuses on immigration writ large, not on immigration from a particular region. Yet, given the prominence of the association of "Latino" with "immigrant," particularly undocumented immigration, in national discourse on the topic, I do not believe this to be a regional phenomenon (Chavez 2013; Perea 1997; Pérez 2016; Sanchez 1997). Using a snowball sampling technique, I conducted semistructured interviews with African American Durham residents regarding their impressions of immigration. These ten women and three men represented a cross-section of the community. Although all participants hold high school diplomas, and all of them had some college, three of the people I spoke with had completed college and none had advanced degrees. Respondents were interviewed in their homes, which demonstrated a level of trust they had in me as a researcher. More importantly, I agreed to a home setting because that was where respondents would feel the most comfortable and potentially forthcoming. Given the topic of conversation, I did not want my respondents to feel inhibited by meeting in an unfamiliar space. Although this was not a random sample, this technique was best considering the circumstances. Because I was talking to people about race, especially their racial attitudes about other groups, it was fundamental to establish a rapport.

Because respondents were asked to speak to me by trusted associates, I was treated as an insider. Given the camaraderie I was able to establish with my respondents, the conversation focused not only on immigration but also evolved into a larger conversation regarding black/white racial relations that have long been emblematic of this region's racial dynamic. Although this area has become a model of "racial reconciliation," there remains an undercurrent of racial resentment that is framed not as racial hostility, which is critically important, but as uncertainty, anxiety, and a desire for acknowledgment (Carter 2007; McClain et al. 2006).

Thus, the critical intervention of this chapter is to demonstrate the continuing importance of white supremacy that has blunted the significant gains of civil rights activism. In particular, the past racial experiences of black people are so significant that "pain suffered by persons one has never met can seem to the participant . . . as present as yesterday's pain, suffered by one's relatives and friends" (Abdel-Nour 2003: 699). Thus, the collective memory of past experiences informs how blacks feel about the presence of new immigrants because, as it stands, there is no imperative to pursue an agenda of racial justice for blacks (Perea 1997).[24] Consequently, the presence of immigrants brings to the fore the myriad ways in which our founding principles of equality and openness have been elided by racist practice. Much like the foreigner-founder theorized by Honig (2001), the presence of immigrants makes blacks' questioning of the core principles of this country possible in a way that is increasingly difficult in an era of colorblindness.[25] Yet, as these "foreigners" become permanent residents, it becomes more difficult for blacks to negotiate this new racial environment that is increasingly populated by non-white newcomers. This fact alone is not an indictment of immigrants. Rather, this chapter demonstrates the difficulties of rights claims for excluded blacks because America can still proclaim itself as the proverbial "chosen land" for self (re)making, open to all—yet this waning version of the American Dream[26] remains woefully unavailable for many of its black citizens, who are allegedly better situated to take advantage of their nation's bounty by virtue of their citizenship.

Collective Memory and Black Public Opinion

The concept of collective memory is not without controversy. Too often in this country's history, black people have been told to simply "forget," "move on," "let the past be the past," because it is wrongly believed that invocations of slavery and its memory on the part of blacks render them ill-equipped to join the rest of society.[27] Because such sensibilities are undergirded by a belief "that racial subordination was largely past and that social inequalities, if any, reflected the cultural failings of minorities themselves," discussions of past racial wrongs are viewed as illegitimate deflections that make blacks incapable of taking personal responsibility for their life circumstances (Haney-Lopez 2007: 990). In short, the harm only applies to those who were actually enslaved, or those denied opportunities under Jim Crow, not their descendants. What such statements fundamentally misunderstand is the essential role history plays in our present. In the face of calls for blacks to stop talking about race, this nation has inaugurated Donald Trump as its president who routinely venerates a past that, as a matter of course, marginalized, excluded, and murdered blacks. The slogan "Make America Great Again" is a pithy phrase in a moment where blacks continue to be harassed, beaten, and murdered by police, and where white supremacy is routinely sanctioned by the White House. The America Donald Trump and his acolytes harken to and hanker for holds the WASP, straight male as its exemplar of Americanness. Thus, calls for blacks to simply forget ring hollow in a nation that routinely resurrects its racially coded past in a way that endangers black people (Abdel-Nour 2003). Moreover, such calls disregard the extent to which black in-group members feel these calls to "forget" are not only antithetical to their responsibilities as group members,[28] but are another form of oppression (Price 2009; Walters 2009). Indeed, linked fate has proven to be significant when delineating how a black political orientation is developed amid these myriad practices of exclusion (Dawson 1994a; Tate 2003).

Although we cannot draw a straight line from the period of enslavement to the present condition of blacks, it is clear that blacks themselves do not necessarily view the forward trajectory from slavery to freedom as strictly demarcated points in time. While blacks moved from slavery to freedom, their freedom was deeply impeded by the remnants of slavery and a white populace bent on maintaining relationships of dominance and dependence. For example, Jim Crow was a response to blacks' changed status as free and citizens post–Civil War. Jim Crow, and the systems of practices and laws it gave rise to, were to keep blacks in "their place." Racial segregation was not a mistake, and it was not enforced solely by the actions of corrupt individuals. Jim Crow, like the system of enslavement that preceded it, was a coordinated effort that used state, local, legal, and extralegal authorities to keep blacks in an inferior position economically, socially, and politically. This meant blacks could not own property, defend themselves, or live as they wished—as was promised by the Declaration of Independence. This practice, which continued for another 100 years after slavery, has been a severe impediment to black wealth generation, health outcomes, family structure, and neighborhood stability; we see today the implications of slavery as continued under Jim Crow (Hamilton,

Darity, Price, Sridharan, and Tippett 2015; Lui, Robles, Leondar-Wright, and Adamson 2006; Shapiro, Meschede, and Osoro 2013; White 2007). A most recent study by Perry, Rothwell, and Harbarger (2018) demonstrates that properties owned in neighborhoods that are at least half black are valued at significantly reduced prices compared to neighborhoods with little to no black representation. This is not simply a matter of poor neighborhood quality. Rather, realtors use evaluation methods that harm black neighborhoods in relation to housing of similar quality. Moreover, white homeowners on the market for homes avoid neighborhoods that are "too black" (Rusk 2001); this segregated market costs blacks an estimated $156 billion (Perry, Rothwell, and Harshbarger 2018). As a consequence, the children in these neighborhoods face a more difficult path to upward mobility because housing taxes provide the foundation for educational funding. This story is a contemporary story, not one of redlining from fifty years ago, though it is part of the same legacy. Thus homeownership, a reliable method for building intergenerational wealth, becomes a boondoggle for black folks who live in majority-black neighborhoods. This is yet another example of the ways in which American racism infiltrates all aspects of life.

In short, the same white supremacy that became the justification for slavery became the convenient justification for disallowing blacks from becoming a part of the American demos, and sees black neighborhoods systematically undervalued. Although the larger nonblack community might view enslavement, Jim Crow, and post–Civil Rights as distinct cutpoints in black life that are different from one another, by and large blacks do not (Kachun 2009; Nunnally 2012; Walters 2009). Enslavement was *the* defining institution of black lives in the United States from 1619 until its abolishment in 1865, but the racial hierarchy established in the prior 200 years did not simply vanish along with the institution. Rather, after the Reconstruction, Jim Crow stepped in to reinforce the racial boundaries set up during slavery so that white domination would continue to thrive and be supported by American social, political, and economic institutions. As Justice John Harlan stated in his opinion in *Plessy v. Ferguson* (1896): "The white race deems itself to be the dominant race in this country. And so it is, in prestige, in achievements, in education, in wealth, and in power. So, I doubt not, it will continue to be for all time if it remains true to its great heritage and holds fast to its constitutional liberty." Harlan's statement, despite being made in the context of a dissenting opinion, was no doubt the foundational logic of Jim Crow.[29] Jim Crow segregation was a

national institution, despite being portrayed as a uniquely Southern practice, which did not see its official eradication for another 100 years post-
slavery with the Civil Rights Act of 1964 and the Voting Rights Act of
1965.[30] Therefore, we can only view blacks as being truly free people in this
republic from 1965 to the present. Said in another way, black people have
been "full citizens" for only 50 years; however, by 1965 the damage had
been done. Blacks were behind on every major indicator of social progress and remain so (Massey and Denton 1993; Mettler 2005; Oliver and
Shapiro 2001; Perry et al. 2018). Therefore, by viewing the arc of black history from this vantage point, it is difficult *not* to understand how black life
is bounded by and to past circumstances, because they are not past events
but frame the racial dynamics blacks find themselves living in at present.
This is not because blacks are backward-looking victims; rather, this is a
demonstration of the power of communal or collective memory and the
vigilance required so that we do not return to that place (Kachun 2009;
Kousser 1999; Nunnally 2012; Walters 2009; Williams 1998). Recent
attempts, and successes, at rolling back black voting rights, and the racial
dog whistles of the Trump campaign (now Trump administration) are a
few ways that looking backward allows black people to be future oriented.

As Dawson (1994a) highlights in *Behind the Mule*, blacks understanding their individual path as dependent on what happens to other
blacks is a key organizing principle of black opinion. This, in part, comes
from being steeped in a tradition that recalls blacks' travails in trying
to access the levers of social progress. Collective memory, by extension,
suggests memories do not necessarily have to be individual in nature to be
real or meaningful. What collective memory proposes is that something
individuals experience privately can become part of an aggregate memory,
particularly when that event is something of great cultural significance.
This does not mean we all remember that event in the same way; what it
suggests is that the event has some resonance for the society, culture, or
group.[31]

Therefore, memory is not only about experience but also how those
memories are communicated within and between groups.[32] According to
Assman and Czaplicka (1995: 129), cultural memory is:

> . . . defined by its distance from the everyday. Distance from the
> everyday (transcendence) marks its temporal horizon. Cultural
> memory has its fixed point; its horizon does not change with the
> passing of time. These fixed points are fateful events of the past,

whose memory is maintained through cultural formation (texts, rites, monuments) and institutional communication (recitation, practice, observance).

From this vantage point, the cultural touchstones of slavery, emancipation, and civil rights become part of a collective experience that becomes accessible across time and space. In this way, blacks quite often view their past as part of their group's present, because the behaviors, institutions, and structures that have traditionally harmed blacks have not fundamentally changed. They are still facing racial segregation and have a set of lived experiences that are qualitatively different from those of whites (Haney-Lopez 2007; Massey and Denton 1993; Shapiro 2006).[33] This is not to suggest that blacks' lives have not evolved in significant ways or that there is a monolithic "black experience." Rather, the injustices faced by black people, such as disproportionate incarceration, are treated as slippages in the application of core American values, not a fundamental problem with the founding principles of this nation. Consequently, blacks who view the United States as having a tradition of ongoing oppression are less likely to believe their communal gains are indicative of some enlightenment on the part of the (white) nation as a whole. Although this oppression has transformed itself, and yielded in some instances to black demands for equality, there has yet to be true reconciliation. Thus, the ubiquitous past becomes a primary referent in explaining blacks' current circumstances.

Because the potency of memories has little to do with proximity in time, the present is highly contingent upon events of the past. Groups make and understand their place in the world as they push their memories to the fore and compete for a place in the historical register. In short, memories bear truth to the existence and experience of a people; the experience of black people is, at best, a mixed bag of triumph and failure. For example, in the 2012 presidential election, black voter turnout exceeded that of whites for the first time in American history. At the same time, numerous states instituted stricter voter identification laws in an effort to thwart so-called voter fraud, but had the effect of making it more difficult for blacks to cast ballots in future elections.[34] In the 2018 midterm elections, black voters found themselves contending with exact match laws, voter roll purges, and other measures used to suppress their votes. The individual successes of some blacks do not negate the multiple ways in which many blacks consistently live in a democracy where even something as sacrosanct as the franchise is insecure when it comes to their group. Even for those blacks who are fiscally secure, their wallets are no protection from the indignities of a society that uses their race to mark their exclusion (Alexander 2011; Bell 1993; Massey and Denton 1993; Feagin 2010).

This class dynamic has been discussed as potentially cleaving the black community into a group of haves and have-nots, but this has yet to be borne out practically or empirically. Even the educations and incomes of high-status have not dampened their commitment to black communities (Dawson 1994a; Gay 2004; Lacy 2007; Patillo-McCoy 2000). Despite affording them some privileges, the class status of black Americans does not seem to change their experiences with racial discrimination, their ability to recognize racial discrimination, or their commitment to racial justice (Bell 1993; Brown and Shaw 2002; Price 2009). In some cases it has been shown that higher-status blacks are more disenchanted with American racial politics (Feagin and Sikes 1994). This is because their opinions are driven not by their class status but by their racial identification, which is often more evident and likely to influence their daily experiences (Shelby 2005).

Hence, it matters less that all black people do not experience the same racial traumas in the same way. What does matter is that they have some awareness of their communities' racial history. This knowledge is passed intergenerationally by parents, grandparents, and other community members, as well as well as media sources that report ongoing instances of racial discrimination (Jackson 2001; Nunnally 2010, 2012). For example, recent deaths of black people, including children, at the hands of police— such as Sandra Bland, Emantic Bradford, Jr., Chavis Carter, Philando Castile, John Crawford III, Jonathan Ferrell, Freddie Gray, Akai Gurley, Botham Jean, Tamir Rice, and too many others to name[35]—who lost their lives despite being unarmed, are viewed more than skeptically. Although these people allegedly were killed for reasons other than their race, the circumstances of their deaths all strongly suggest they died because they were black. Because of this country's long history of devaluing and destroying black lives, official accounts of their deaths do not sit well. There is very little in the collective memories of black people to suggest these young people died for any reason besides their race. Thus, the racial past weighs heavily in black evaluations of these moments that some would like to characterize as having little or nothing to do with race. Although these are extreme examples, this mistrust of official authorities when dealing with black lives translates into other arenas as well, where blacks fear potential mistreatment, such as shopping (Brewster and Rusche 2012; Higgins and

Gabbidon 2009; Nunnally 2012). This sense that whites are not interested in black people is ever-present in conversations about immigration.

Memory, Discourse, and Immigration

For blacks, their strength comes from remembering and nurturing these connections from the past. As the work of Nunnally (2012) amply reveals, many learn about race from prior generations as well as a number of racially formative experiences. This may not always be in terms of details, but clear messages about racial norms are transmitted from older cohorts to younger peer groups. Likewise, Price (2009) demonstrates there are generational differences in how closely these racial norms are held. Yet, even for those who may disagree with "how to be black," the legacy of the civil rights movement, even for those born after this moment, looms large in these conversations. Not only does this moment register through images, but it is very much a part of many peoples' lives. For example, my parents and grandparents are products of the Jim Crow period. From these family members I learned that to be defiant of the prevailing racial etiquette could be extremely dangerous. My mother told me of the terror she felt as a preadolescent living in Warrenton, North Carolina, at the time of Chicago-raised Emmett Till's murder in Mississippi. Although she was still a child, she knew being black meant you did not have the opportunity to be young; geography would not protect you if you were to run afoul of a white person.[36] My awareness of race and the Jim Crow period was shaped by my parents' and grandparents' reminiscences of these moments. As Nunnally (2012) states, "socialization about race, thus, educates blacks about the social and political realities of race in America" so they can effectively negotiate the many racial situations they will encounter over their life course (p. 60). Furthermore, this socialization "suggests how 'race and place' are interwoven into the meaning, operation, experiences, and lessons of race," such that blacks not only know how to think about race but how to conduct themselves in interracial and intraracial scenarios (Nunnally 2012: 62). The sharing of experiences is a social practice that reinforces black collective memory. Therefore, through the transmission of their experiences, my family socialized me to think about race in particular ways despite being separated from the specificity of their circumstances.

Outsiders Within: Comparative Racial Progress

Throughout the interviews, one of the oft-repeated themes across subjects is the lack of confidence they have in the "system" working for them, particularly in the face of newly arrived citizens. Although my respondents are clear they are Americans, they are less sanguine in their abilities to harness this national identity for greater gains for their community. This sense of being "outsiders within" has been a usual part of black discourse from the early nineteenth century, and as I show earlier, blacks advocated for emigration as a response to American exclusion and oppression (Tillery 2011). This sentiment would continue throughout the twentieth century as black artists, political elites, and others often captured this sense of "twoness" that comes from being black in an America that routinely snubs their attempts at inclusion (DuBois [1903] 2003; Woodward 1974). Nonetheless, this sentiment is prominent among my interview respondents who frequently see their group as being outside of the American family of citizenship.

For example, when asked "Do you think that what happens to other black people matters for your life," Diane,[37] a 28-year-old phone company employee, says: "Uh because as a. . . ., you have to look at us as a whole. We are one people, and we do the best that we can to, to show more interest in, in things that's going on with our people." She suggests an understanding about the ways in which American-style racism operates to homogenize black people, but also sees racial unity as a source of strength for black people. At the same time, when black people do enter the white public sphere, there is great awareness that they are unintelligible in many ways. This sentiment was best captured by Marie, a 31-year-old administrative professional at a local medical center, relaying an interracial conversation experienced at the workplace:

> [O]ne thing in particular was one time I was at work and it was a group of ladies talking, and they were talking about one lady who had, it was three white ladies and myself, and they were talking about, um, one lady that had a heart attack. But they keep calling her "that girl," "that girl," "that girl," and I didn't know who they were talking about. And they were like, you know, the black lady and [inaudible]. And I was like oh that lady, you mean, so she's kind of older? Yeah. And then they kind of gave me that look, like ok wait

a minute, we said girl talking about her, but then they used white lady, they said white lady, but when referring to her they said girl.

What these kinds of unacknowledged slights say is that black people are not worth getting to know. So much so that the interlocutors in this particular conversation did not even refer to "that girl," who was in fact an older woman, by her proper name or any of the social deference befitting a woman of her age. Indeed, the honorific of "lady"[38] was reserved for the white women whom they, at least discursively, viewed as being worthy of respect. In fact, it was not until Marie raised the issue of age that her interlocutors perhaps recognized the social faux pas of referring to an older black woman as a "girl" rather than a "lady," which age and race would dictate as the most appropriate title outside of her given name.

These kinds of incidents were not limited to or unique among my participants. All participants, regardless of gender, could relay at least one moment where they were made to feel suspect because of their racial classification. This was especially true for male participants who had to deal with the extra burden of being men in a society that almost invariably treats youth, blackness, and maleness as being synonymous with crime (Eberhardt, Goff, Purdie, and Davies 2004; Oliver 2003; Peffley, Hurwitz, and Sniderman 1997; Quillian and Pager 2001; Steffensmeier, Ulmer, and Kramer 1998; Welch 2007). For his part, Henry, a 32-year-old musician and part-time apartment manager, discusses in quite vivid detail what it feels like to be thought of as a threat in his own community.

> Um, I'd say, um, a lot has changed, but a lot has not changed. Uh, the other day I was coming out of the gym, and my truck was parked beside a lady who was getting into her car, her vehicle. It's a public area, it's populated, there's people around, it's a big parking lot, shopping center, and . . . as soon as she rushes to get into her car, she locks the door. Um, so like I said, I'm clearly coming out of the gym, I have, you know, workout stuff on, and so in seeing that it's kind of like oh we're back at this again. Um, is it just because I'm black or because I'm a man? And you have your two children that you're oh, you know, you watch the news and say oh gosh this could happen to me or whatever. Are you just that scared? If it was a woman, would you do the same thing? Or if it was a white man would you do the same thing? So, in experiencing that and

then saying I don't care who you are, I don't care what type of black person you are, if you're black and that happens to you, or someone clutches their pocket book tighter, or someone rushes to lock their door, or whatever, then it's going to affect you. You're going to think about it and say, "Damn we're right back at this again."

Another significant part of my exchange with Henry had to do with the fact that he recognized his blackness made him someone to be feared. He wondered aloud whether this woman's reaction would have been the same had he been a white man or even a black woman. His incredulity at being considered dangerous despite obvious signs of safety (i.e., daylight, his gym clothes) is palpable as he talks further about the alienation he feels at being a lifelong resident of this community—he has resided in Durham since he was a small child—but being viewed with suspicion while carrying out the most mundane tasks. He cites the fact that he is well known in this community because "everyone knows us," referring to him and his friends who have been lifelong Durham residents, but this is not enough to stop a stranger from viewing him as a criminal. Henry views himself distinctly as an insider in Durham because of his reputation; this belonging should shield him from such indignities, but it does not, because race trumps the esteem he holds, or views himself as holding, in his community.

In fact, Henry, who describes his social network as being diverse including both black and white intimates, which he indicates by the fact they have been friends since their youth and they were welcomed in each other's homes, this incident was not uncommon. Moreover, he references the fact that he hadn't "been called a nigger in years," as evidence of racial progress, albeit small. Because he had the comparative experience of attending college in South Carolina in the 1990s, he said with confidence, "here [North Carolina], it's [racism] not that bad, but it does still exist."[39]

Although I did not follow up to inquire what "that bad" meant or looks like, this theme of comparative racial progress was a regular feature of my interviews. Thus, what often passes for progress for this group of rather young black people is the fact things are not as bad as they were under Jim Crow, which all of their parents and grandparents experienced, and which they learned of through history and socialization. This Jim Crow measure of progress was referenced multiple times by my respondents who wished to recognize that race relations are improved. However, they stopped short of saying that race no longer matters, which is evidenced by the fact they each had a story to tell about racism and how it has operated in their lives at one time or another.[40]

These brief narrative accounts demonstrate collective memory to be significant for how blacks conceptualize their relationship to the group. This work extends the literature on linked fate by demonstrating *how* the past is a key organizer of black public opinion (Dawson 1994a). Black opinions are not only about being steeped in black communities and accompanying social networks, but about the racial learning that takes place within these communities (Nunnally 2012; Walters 2009). Furthermore, much of how blacks forecast what is happening with and to their community is by looking back to understand how to evaluate present conditions and the possibility for change and improvement. These individuals are involved in communities that provide them with a way to contextualize their—and other blacks'—current circumstances. Most prevalently, my respondents express a certain understanding that they are invisible as constituent members of the American body politic. That they can be both hyper-visible and invisible in their community and workplaces suggests the ways in which the American project has left them out as members of the populace. This is not by accident; in fact, this is the way race is designed to work such that some people have the right to be afraid of a black stranger, yet that same stranger does not a priori fear this unnamed white person who is representative of the ideal citizen (Bonilla-Silva 2006; Mills 1997). According to my respondents, part of what impedes broader understandings of black people is a lack of knowledge of their struggle; this is especially true of newly arriving immigrants, whom blacks see as being ignorant of American racial history.

Black History and Immigrants

One of the prevailing themes in popular coverage of interminority relations has been the competition over resources among these communities (Dzidzienyo and Oboler 2005; Mindiola, Niemann, and Rodriguez 2003; Telles, Sawyer, and Rivera-Salgado 2011). From Texas to Florida to California, competition and conflict have come to be among the primary lenses through which to view the political relationship between blacks and other communities of color, particularly Latinos (Bobo and Johnson 2000; McClain and Karnig 1990; McClain and Tauber 1998; Oliver and Wong 2003; Waldinger 1997). Often, these conflicts are cast as haggling over finite resources and insecurity on the part of blacks, who have achieved political maturation yet are faced with an uncertain (political) future be-cause the Latino population has surpassed them in absolute numbers and continues to grow. There is no denying that the zero-sum nature of po-litical contests and outcomes has fueled much of this negativity, because there is no way to adequately share the limited political bounty (Bobo and Hutchings 1996; Meier, McClain, Polinard, and Wrinkle 2004). When minority group members come into contact with one another politically, it is generally for a definable set of possibilities (i.e., a mayoral seat, city council election, school board election). Because there can only be one mayor, one city council person from an assigned district, and the like, one group's success—assuming they have different preferences—will neces-sarily mean loss to the other group. This type of situation breeds a level of competitiveness because outcomes and resources are limited, and eve-ryone is invested in their own success. This does not mean they wish to see others fail to thrive, but it does mean every group is self-interested. Consequently, self-interest dictates one's course of action, and in the case of finite resources (i.e., city council seats) there is no way to share that resource.[41] Thus for blacks, who have only been in political offices at the local, state, and national levels since 1965, the stakes seem even higher. Therefore, one would expect some resentment to be expressed by blacks with respect to immigrants.

However, this type of hostility was not present in my interviews. Rather, I found a great deal of ambivalence on the part of blacks, who empathized with the plight of immigrants but felt immigrants did not necessarily share the same sympathies toward them. Both Diane and Marie reasoned this was because immigrants really do not know much about black people. In fact, Marie states:

> Um, because they're not, they don't, they don't learn it [inaudible] unless they're in school, I mean maybe the younger population that's in school, but the ones that are adults I don't think so.

In her statement, Marie claims the level of knowledge that immigrants would need to be sensitive to, or at least aware of, African American his-tory is unavailable unless provided through some formal setting, like school. For the adult immigrant population, the possibility for knowing more about black Americans is limited because of their absence from ed-ucational settings where this information could be gleaned. Although it is clear that African American history can be learned at any time and at any point in life, my respondents see this as a highly unlikely event—not because it is unimportant but because immigrants have other concerns. As Diane notes:

> Their [immigrants] main goal is to get a better life. A better life does not include looking back in the past and saying "what is the basis of this better life? why do we have this better life?". We [i.e. black people] are a different people, a different culture, a different skin color . . . and we can't come here, we can't prosper in our own country. Um, so I don't think they [immigrants] care . . . but since they're allowed to come over here and, you know, . . . without having to learn about our [black people] history and our culture, then it doesn't matter. They're disinterested.

However, this perceived disinterest on the part of Latinos presents consequences for the Latino and black communities. For my respondents, their black history could serve as a cautionary tale to Latinos who may not be as savvy about the ways in which race in America operates or, put more bluntly, the ways of white people. As Henry says, "for right now it doesn't matter because they're getting in, everything's good, there's no problems, everything's going smooth, but at the end of the day if somebody doesn't look into it and say oh my goodness, you know, back in the day this happened to black people, this could happen to us, we're the new black people, so this could happen to us." From multiple respondents I heard statements similar to those made by Diane and Henry. Brenda, a 25-year-old television producer, makes this statement more clearly:

> Oh, if they're thinking about taking over, the minorities, being the largest minority group, they're going to take on the issues that the minority group deals with, that's racial profiling, that's discrimination, you know, I think ultimately that all the things that are going their way because I think that the majority race is now seeing them as the new, as the new minority, the new black people. So, you know, they're going to deal, I think, with the same issues that they [i.e., black people] dealt with. And I think, uh, you know, eventually, they're going to start facing some of the same issues, I think they're going to probably start being a part of more, of the lower income, you know, welfare and things like that. So, I think, you know, all those things are going to end up affecting them.

What these quotes suggest is a sense that as Latinos become more acculturated, they will come to see their high status relative to blacks diminish as whites come to see them as more like black people. Thus, whatever positive relationships Latinos are able to cultivate now, they do so at their own risk, because my respondents view whites as being interested in exploiting people of color. My respondents seem to think that white interest in Latinos is fleeting and highly contingent on Latino's deference to white people. As Brenda's quote suggests, white charity for Latinos will wane as the novelty of Latinos wears off and they access social services, like welfare, which are consistently viewed negatively (Gilens 2000; Hancock 2004; Jordan-Zachery 2009). Once Latinos, like blacks, begin to demand access to social and/or political institutions in a way that seems to be excessive or burdensome to whites, Brenda suggests whites will terminate their support for this community. Although Latinos are enjoying this honeymoon period and relative good will from whites, they also need to be cognizant of the vagaries of white privilege. This idea is expressed in Brenda's and others' statements, which imply that whites choosing when to be supportive and when to withhold that support is indicative of their privilege. However, the capriciousness of whites has real consequences for minorities, and my respondents suggest that one way to see this is by looking at the historical record of black/white racial history.

In this way, my respondents are turning the "model minority" paradigm on its head by suggesting the black experience is *the* definitive racial experience in America. Arthur, a 27-year-old graphic artist, states definitively that Latinos are "the new niggers." For Arthur, Latinos will find their station in this country much like that of blacks as they too live in neglected neighborhoods and interact with multiple agencies and institutions that have little if any regard for their well-being. In short, Latinos will soon find themselves in the position of black people. Thus, they need to build a racial awareness that begins with an appreciation for the black experience in America.

I think these statements point to a broader view of community on the part of blacks that can apply cross-racially from blacks to other racialized minorities, like Latinos. This is not because history is necessarily uniform, but the lessons of the past regarding how blacks were treated seem to suggest something to black respondents about the future of Latino welfare. Although this may vary depending on region, it is clear that blacks share the view that what happened to them will matter to Latinos.[42] Thus, for my respondents, the racial history of blacks is a key way Latinos can forecast what will come of their group; indeed, respondents relied heavily on the past to think through the possibilities for their group in the face of newly arriving immigrants. My respondents see immigration as a way for whites to continue to deny opportunities for them. By focusing their energies on Latinos, my respondents viewed whites as wanting to avoid the rights claims of blacks. Moreover, my respondents saw their experiences as a cautionary tale for Latinos because they see America's racial ordering as exclusionary and one that will foreclose whiteness to Latinos, particularly as they become acculturated. Whatever temporary reprieve Latinos have is because they are viewed as being different enough from blacks to warrant white attentions. However, this attention is conditional on Latinos "knowing their place" and not challenging white authorities. Thus, the extent to which the "ethnic option" that Latinos currently exercise, which allows them to be of any race, will fade as their presence upsets the racial hierarchy.[43]

This is for two related reasons. First, there is the expansive notion of blackness and the constraints of whiteness. Blackness is less a coherent biological category than it is a social reality that sets up different (non-white) people for unfavorable treatment in society. Used in this way, blackness is an understanding and social location associated with ongoing, entrenched exclusion as a matter of course. At different points, the racial category *black* was a catch-all that covered all comers that were not white. For example, Asians have been placed within the category *black* because the U.S. government had no idea what to do with them, since they did not fit neatly into the racial schema (Kim 1999). Thus in the segregated South, for the purposes of education Asians found themselves functionally black (Kim 1998). Likewise, the U.S. Census tried to count "mulattoes" as a category separate from both blacks and whites in the 1850 enumeration (Nobles 2000). This experiment was quickly abandoned in the subsequent decade, and those "mulattoes" were effectively absorbed into the black racial category. What these moments show us is that race is rarely, if ever, about codifying genetic groups that we come to know as "races." Rather, these categories are functional and tell us who belongs where in the racial hierarchy. This is no less true in the present, when we can still witness a rather stable racial order where blacks, in the aggregate, remain worse off than most other Americans (Shapiro 2006; Shapiro and Oliver 2006). Consequently, the American racial order moved from being about "whites" versus. "non-whites," as white racial identity stabilized and ceased to admit new members, to one of "blacks" versus "non-blacks," where groups are categorized in the racial order relative to their distance from this bottom category (Mutua 1999). As a result, newer groups are understood as moving between these two poles, which is anchored by black racial identity. As such, my respondents see Latinos as being more akin to the black racial group than they are to whites. Not only do they feel Latinos "don't look white," but they have none of the institutional power that comes along with being prototypically white in their minds. Still, they understand that Latinos are potential defectors because they are not limited by blackness.

As a corollary, whiteness has often been defined by what it is not. As Jacobson (2001) highlights, the category *white* was rather exclusionary and was defined on negative rather than affirmative terms. The category *white* only opened up to previously excluded "lesser European stocks," like Jews and Southern Europeans, when it became politically expedient. Thus, whiteness was strictly delimited and held out as a prize for those seeking to make their way up the social ladder of America.[44] However, for whiteness to remain a prize, it had to be much more rigidly defined. This meant those who were deemed unassimilable could not and would not be incorporated into this designation. Asians are a prime example of this. Because Asians, writ large, were viewed as too distinct phenotypically and culturally, they could never be part of a white community. They were not seen as the prototypical citizen the Founders had in mind when devising the qualities it took to be an American. Indeed, Asians were viewed as a national menace the country needed to contain. This was never more apparent than the Japanese Interment during World War II. The idea that Asians could be habituated into whiteness was not a consideration of the moment. They did not "look white," and they certainly did not "act white" (Kim 1999). Because Asians were non-Christian and maintained their linguistic and culinary distinctiveness, they were viewed as too culturally distinct to assimilate into whiteness. Although this was a slippery set of criteria, it is no mistake that people of European descent eventually came to be considered white people even though there were cultural differences that made them lesser whites.[45]

In the time of demographic shifts that favor minority groups in terms of absolute numbers, it is important for blacks to consider what this will mean for their group. Of course, they know they will never be considered socially or racially "white," but they are concerned what this will mean for their Latino counterparts. If whites embrace Latinos, (as they did with Eastern and Southern Europeans) to augment their numbers, this could present a problem for blacks. This seems less likely because all Latinos may not be phenotypically able to assimilate into whiteness en masse. Of course, this presupposes Latinos desire whiteness. Given Latino population growth, the development of group consciousness, and the racial attitudes of many whites toward Latinos, assimilation and whiteness may not be all that desirable. On the other hand, it could be that whiteness will become a more exclusive category of belonging in an effort to maintain the supremacy of the group vis-à-vis the omission of non-Europeans. Another possibility is that Latinos become a middle category, a buffer category sorted somewhere between blacks at the bottom and whites at the top.[46] From Brenda's vantage point, much of this racial posturing is about white fears of becoming a minority:

> Oh I think it's just someone taking something away from them. They're so used to always having that I think it's almost like they're feeling, I don't know if they're at the point where they're feeling threatened yet, but they're at that little threshold where they want to make sure that they keep what they have and they keep their majority status. I think they want to make sure that they keep the jobs and the education and all of that. I just think they want to maintain a monopoly. And their status quo. I think that's it, that they don't want to lose their status quo.

This is speculative for sure, but my respondents do evince an understanding of whiteness that is partially biological (i.e., based on phenotype), partly numerical, but more significantly about privilege. For respondents, whiteness is about control and access. Whiteness is not simply a racial descriptor but a state of being. It is a place that is beyond the incursions of others. Thus, if whiteness is a social status, then it de facto does not apply to Latinos or any others that "don't look white" as Henry suggests below. In relaying a personal story Henry suggests how whiteness consistently insulates itself from out-groups:

> A buddy of mine at the beach who has a mortgage company, he just was talking about how he sat down and had a meeting with an Asian lady, and she just moved to South Carolina or whatever, and she was saying that she never realized how white people could be, that she really didn't like white people. And he was saying, you know, "why?" And she said because I've never been so, you know,

wrongly treated and unfairly treated by any other culture in America since she's been here. And so, it's like wow, that almost adds validity to the fact that when it comes down to it, when push comes to shove . . . you're not white. You definitely, if you're not white, you're more nigger than anything.

Part of this argument is made on quasi-biological grounds (i.e., "they don't look white") but also from a sense that "real" white people would not be treated like this by other white people. If this is the standard for measuring or establishing membership in the family of whiteness, then Latinos clearly do not meet that standard. Thus, Henry is employing a notion of an expansive blackness that incorporates all non-whites, including immigrants, to some extent. Even those minority groups viewed by whites as "better" than blacks, such as Asians, are not necessarily protected from the vagaries of racism, which seems to be thought of as a treatment that pertains to all minorities but that has been tried and perfected using the bodies of black people as practice.

> They [whites] will go to bat for themselves, of course, or whatever, and they might have their own pecking order in the back of their minds, you know, and they might wait and say "oh, he's Asian so he's not that bad," or "he's, um, Indian so he's not that bad." But ultimately, he's still a nigger. You're not white.

Despite the supposed disdain that whites might feel for immigrant groups, my respondents believe this does not stop whites from using immigrants to undercut black social, economic, and political mobility. Indeed, what seems concerning, despite their seeming skepticism at the potential for these minorities to pass fully into the category of "white," is the idea that these groups (i.e., Asians) will still be in a more favorable position than blacks because their group is the most disliked in American society.[47] Therefore, whatever provisional status may be available to other minority groups, they are not black, and that counts in the racial context of the United States.

Immigrants and Black Social Mobility

The preceding paragraphs point to the pernicious ways in which the history of race remains key to blacks' diagnosis of the current racial climate.

Blacks perceive that they remain far from the ideal of integration, and the presence of immigrants presents further challenges to their desire for greater social mobility. Although my respondents were not necessarily hostile to immigrants, they were highly suspicious of the ways in which whites seem to cater to immigrants. For example, my respondent Henry readily admitted that blacks distrust white people because of history. He says, "Why? Um, it's history basically. It's, uh, yeah, it's history based. It's Willie Lynch[48] based. It's from all of that. It's from those days." What is more, not only do blacks distrust whites, they see whites as contributing to the mobility of Latinos in ways they do not for blacks. According to Brenda:

> I see it more, because I think more white people are more compassionate toward Hispanics than they are toward blacks. So I think if anything, I've seen instances where, um, local PTAs have, you know, they've had a handful of Hispanic students in their community, and they've basically taken them on and done more for them whereas they have probably a handful of blacks in their school as well, but they're not doing the same things for them because I think it's the whole compassion issue. I don't think that they're compassionate toward them. So if anything, I could see them joining forces in smaller groups like that. I don't necessarily know of a whole, but . . .

This compassion, as she calls it, stems from the idea that immigrants are viewed as benign, hardworking people attempting to make a better life for themselves and their families despite deficits such as having less facility with the English language. Unfortunately, the compassion expressed for immigrants does not extend to black people because "they [white people] don't think of the black race as a whole as being willing to work for it. I think we're perceived as just sitting back and waiting for the government to hand us something." Therefore, because blacks are viewed as undeserving of white attention and aid, their children who may face depressed circumstances, similar to Latinos or immigrants, are not privy to the alms of whites. This sentiment is not limited to the educational sphere. My respondents perceived other ways in which whites were more willing to assist immigrants than native-born blacks. Unsurprisingly, this came up with respect to the issue of entrepreneurship.

This has been a sore spot in the black community for decades and probably reached the height of American awareness in the Los Angeles Rebellion of the early 1990s. Although the Rodney King verdict was the catalyst for days of uprising in the city, there were long-standing issues that had been just below the surface for decades preceding this moment. The death of Latasha Harlins has been cited as being as significant as the Rodney King verdict as a catalyst for the unrest in the city (Ikemoto 1993; Stevenson 2015). Blacks were frustrated by the city's lack of attention to the needs of their communities, such as failing schools, substandard or nonexistent public facilities like parks and clinics, and a lack of ownership and economic control in their own neighborhoods. This was most glaringly captured in the standoffs between armed Korean merchants and black rioters who were poised to loot and burn their businesses.[49] Although I do not seek to rehash this moment, what was key was that blacks did not feel like stakeholders in their communities because they saw newly arriving immigrants as being able to establish businesses that contributed little to their community's development and continued to deplete the economic base of their neighborhoods (Abelman and Lie 1995). What was important was the sense that businesses owned by "foreigners" were given an unjust economic advantage from the government that wanted to install them as a new breed of land barons that sought to keep blacks in a state of semi-serfdom. While for many this seemed hyperbolic, this view is not uncommon or out of step with the views of my respondents, who are separated geographically and generationally from this moment yet were able to articulate a similar point of view about their communities. Below is a sampling of what this opinion looks like in discursive practice.

> Um . . . I don't think that they have a significant problem being here. I think that they get more benefits than other people that are here. (Diane)
>
> Um, they get, they get seven years without paying taxes. Um, they're able to get more help from social services. I think that not only here in Durham, but the United States caters to foreigners before they cater to their own. (Marie)
>
> They don't want to understand us as much as we want to understand them because we want to know hey how did you get that store over there? Wow, you know, we would like to get a store. You haven't been here half as long as we have and you've already got a

store, you already got almost your own community. You have movie stores, you have clubs, so . . . (Henry)

In the U.S. and I feel like there is a sense of resentment that, that people look at them and say you know they're not even from here, and they're coming here, and they're getting more than what we have, and you know, we've been residents of Durham or wherever for this amount of time, and they're coming in and almost rising above us. And they don't even speak the language, you know, but yet still it seems like they have more. (Brenda)

Um, the only thing I would say is that, I mean as long as, as long as immigrants are coming here, I don't think that it's going to make it better for America in general if when they come here they get, you know, more opportunities than the people that are actually here. (Mohammed)

These quotes demonstrate the prevalence of the belief that the government and other actors are interested in the promotion of immigrant opportunities to the detriment of blacks. Although these alleged "tax breaks" do not exist in a real sense, the impression they do exist is integral to how these individuals understand the ways in which economics operate to disempower and disable black people. For them, the "system," which is manned by unnamed whites, is set against black progress. This harm is not necessarily caused through explicit efforts to harm blacks, but through subtle behaviors such as assisting immigrants in establishing businesses that help immigrant groups achieve economic independence and mobility at the expense of black people, who do not find the same avenues of credit open to them (Black and Strahan 2002; Blanchflower, Levine, and Zimmerman 2003).[50] After all, immigrant enterprises are located in black communities and rely on black dollars for support (Cheng and Espiritu 1989; Min 1997). Yet, blacks are not allowed to participate in such entrepreneurship because they are deemed unworthy of such efforts on the part of the government and other institutional agents. For those immigrants who are not going to achieve business ownership, it is clear there is a white preference for their labor (Maldonado 2006; Powers 2005; Tomaskovic-Devey and Roscigno 1996). In either case, the end result is further exclusion of black people from the type of commercial activities that could ensure their individual and communal viability. This is a clear indictment of white preferences and the ways in which those preferences *militate against black success,* not an indictment of immigrant achievement. Thus, blacks do not have a problem with immigrant success but with discrimination they see as preventing them access to similar resources and wealth-building potential. In each instance where these alleged tax breaks are mentioned, it is clear that immigrants do not bestow these benefits on themselves. These benefits are granted by whites, the ultimate arbiters of societal benefits. Black respondents were not mad about this, but wanted the ability to capture some of these gains for themselves. Thus, my respondents are clearly laying this inequality at the feet of white preferences, not immigrant behaviors.

The result of all of this is the idea that immigrants are favored by America because they are more easily exploited and are not viewed as having the same history of protest as black people.[51] As Maureen, a 42-year-old administrative worker states, "we feel like we still the umm like we . . . like we the step kids. Like all of a sudden, you know, it's like we low on the totem pole, but now we're even going even lower [sic]." Again, using the family metaphor, Maureen situates black people as perpetual outsiders in the blended family that is America. Literally the black sheep of the family, immigrants make more apparent how unwelcome blacks remain in the American landscape. Immigrants have not functionally changed the low status and esteem of black people, but the presence of immigrants makes it more possible to continue to deny blacks what they deem is their just due as members of the American community. In short, an immigrant presence is understood as being a way for whites to continue to ignore black needs and undercut black attempts at greater mobility.

Discussion

The main purpose of this chapter is to demonstrate the importance of history in structuring the ways in which blacks understand their present circumstances. Although blacks view themselves as thoroughly modern, it is clear that history plays a prominent role in the ways these individuals understand the lives of black people. This distinctiveness in perspective becomes clearer relative to immigrants. In short, blacks view American society as remaining adverse to their progress. This is through quotidian racial practices that mark them as lazy, criminal, and undeserving of white sympathies and efforts at greater racial equality. The result is that blacks do not see the promotion of the American Dream in their community through concrete educational and financial partnerships. Consequently, blacks see their communities being chronically underserved and watch as newly arriving immigrants excel. What becomes clear is that blacks really want the opportunity to succeed, or fail, on their own merits. They do not want special treatment; what they want are opportunities that elude them but seem readily available to immigrants, which seems unfair. Not only is this unfair, it is part of a larger pattern of neglect black people have witnessed and continue to perceive with respect to their communities over time. Hence, their analysis of their position is directly related to their collective memory of their communities' struggles with equality and inclusion.

Second, this chapter seeks to demonstrate the lack of hostility and resentment toward immigrants one might expect on the part of blacks. For their part, blacks tended to view the "system" as the root of many of their communal problems. Although there were some references to individual responsibility, the issue of immigration is viewed as something clearly out of black and immigrant hands. In this narrative, whites are the most empowered, and minorities are trying to exist within the parameters that whiteness has set for them. Racial hierarchy wrought by white supremacy is real for black people, and immigration makes this abundantly clear. Although there is a tendency to conflate immigrant with Latino, as does a general sentiment in our national conversation on the issue, the overarching theme seems to be a sense that America is an unfair place for people of color, particularly blacks. Thus, blackness becomes a way to understand how the racial politics of this America works. Immigrants help make that point more starkly, but immigrants are hardly being held responsible for the ways in which white supremacy sorts minorities in this society. Thus, what these interviews help us to see is the profound disappointment with the incomplete incorporation of black people into American society because of their race. An important undercurrent of this chapter has been what the idea of America means to blacks and how they employ national identity to make their claims to privilege in the American political landscape. The next chapter looks more concretely at how blacks utilize national attachment to form their opinion on immigration. More particularly, the following chapter examines the degree to which nativist tendencies are present in African American opinions and to what extent, if any, does this lead to hostility toward immigrant communities.

5

Conflicted Nativism

AN EMPIRICAL VIEW

WHAT DOES IT mean to be black and American? More importantly, what does it mean to be an American in the face of national trends that seem to suggest your black life does not matter? These questions are not novel considering the historical context of black lives in America. The better question is how do blacks make their American identity operative in a country where their belonging has always been contested? I argue throughout this text that immigration gives us a window into how blacks think of themselves as Americans and as black people—identities that are often in tension, if not outright conflict, with one another. In the previous chapter I delineate the dimensions of conflicted nativism. The primary idea is that blacks' national attachments are informed by their unique position in America's racial hierarchy. In practical terms, this means blacks typically do not organize around the issue of immigration, regardless of their opinions about immigrants and/or immigration policy (Carter and Pérez 2015). However, in some instances blacks do express nativist opinions, which I read as informed by their concerns regarding the meaning of immigration for *their* community. Although these opinions may be racialized, even offensive, this does not generally manifest itself in xenophobic or chauvinistic rhetoric that seeks to isolate and expurgate immigrants from the United States. On the contrary, blacks are typically more empathetic and do not espouse an essentialist view of national belonging that would mark newly arriving citizens as always outsiders.

In this chapter I test the claims of conflicted nativism while also examining other areas where attitudes about immigrants are evident: race of immigrant and immigration policy. Understanding that conflicted nativism exists is an important part of the intellectual work being done here, but it is also worthwhile to understand the extent to which, if at all, the race of the immigrant matters. This is especially true because the reports of animosities between blacks and Latinos as well as blacks and Asians have been noted in the literature (Abelman and Lie 1995; Gay 2006; Kim 2000; McClain et al. 2006b; Mindiola et al. 2003; Vaca 2004). It is my contention that despite unflattering notions regarding immigrants, these are not expressions of deep-seated racism. Rather, blacks' issue has long been the sense that their solidarity with immigrants is neither welcomed nor returned by immigrants who will be able to achieve greater social mobility because of the ways in which white supremacy operates to retard black progress. This is a subtle yet important difference in how black opinion is often characterized.

In a similar fashion, I look at the types of immigration policies blacks support. Although it has been shown that blacks have sometimes supported restrictions on immigration, this support has been conditional (Hellwig 1981). When blacks have supported the theory of restricting immigration, usually it has been because they see a diminished immigrant presence as potentially allowing them to gain some footing in the economy (Goldin 1994). But because immigration restriction has always been a racialized policy, blacks have generally not galvanized around those issues (Tichenor 1994). Furthermore, having feelings about a policy but not taking any action to pursue a set of policy demands suggests a lack of commitment to the issue. At the same time, the fact that national origins quotas were lifted at the same time blacks finally achieved the franchise says something about blacks' concern with and dedication to the idea of a more open republic. Therefore, I will also be examining the connection between attitudes about policies and policy support. It is important, however, to discuss how race-of-immigrant effects operate and what this may mean for black attitude formation.

Race and Immigration

The issue of immigration is often discussed as if there is some universal "us" versus "them" at play that defines the singular "us" as all citizens and "them" as any outsider. Of course, we know black people have often been excluded from the category of prototypical American citizen. Similarly, it would be naïve to pretend that much of the anxiety around immigrants and potential immigrants is not about *who* these people are and where they are coming from. In *Who are We?: The Challenge to America's National Identity*, Samuel Huntington posits that America is changing because of the new wave of non-European immigrants, driven largely by Mexican immigration, who, through some mix of inability, stubbornness, and proximity to their home countries do not want to become "real Americans." They resist assimilation because there is no incentive to learn and speak English, and they can essentially live in America without having to adapt to its culture at all. This is negative for native-born Americans as well as those seeking to become Americans, because the culture is being altered in ways that make it indistinguishable from our neighbors to the south. Although Huntington is one voice, he does express a common sentiment that post-1965 American arrivals are not like those of earlier centuries. To be fair, they are not; those immigrants who came to the United States after 1965 have the distinction of being the least European of all prior waves.

Although it is true that Americans worried about Germans and Irish immigrants in times past, these fears dissipated as these groups were incorporated into whiteness (Ngai 2004). Yet, the face of immigration today is largely brown. It is my sense that this is in large part driving much of the contemporary conversation about immigration, which focuses on "illegals." From American obsessions with finding potential terrorists in the wake of 9/11 to preoccupations with patrolling the Mexican border, it is undeniable that there has been far less angst about the numbers of illegal Canadians residing in our midst (Short and Magaña 2002). Although some argue their opposition to undocumented immigration is not the race of immigrant but rather the rule-breaking behavior exhibited by undocumented persons, the literature suggests otherwise (Pantoja 2006; Pérez 2016). In fact, most white Americans care very little about the movements of unauthorized immigrants who are coded as racially white.

For example, in the mid-1990s, Californians used direct democracy to pass a wave of legislation aimed at curbing illegal immigration. Propositions 187 and 227, along with the anti–affirmative action Proposition 209, were framed by proponents of these measures as being about protection of resources, but they were nothing more than thinly veiled attempts to attack Latinos. Proposition 187 was infamous for its particularly punitive policies with respect to undocumented immigrants. If passed, the Proposition would have made it illegal to educate or medically treat someone believed to be in the United States without authorization. Those without proper documentation would be barred from obtaining any kind of social services, including non-emergency medical treatment. In addition, other bureaucrats like teachers, nurses, police officers, physicians, and the like would be authorized to take on the role of quasi–immigration officials because they would be designated mandatory reporters of individuals they believed to be in the country without permission. The crux of the legislation was to make the lives of undocumented persons so uncomfortable they would rather leave the country than stay and risk discovery and deportation. Supporters of the measure claimed this was not anti-Mexican or anti-immigrant. Rather, this measure was a pro-American attempt to beat back the undeserving hordes of "illegals" coming to the United States, having "anchor babies," and taking unfairly from American taxpayers. It is unsurprising that this measure was touted as a way for California to increase revenues and prevent further economic decline.

Despite vociferous protests of Proposition 187, the measure passed with 59 percent of Californians approving it. Although the law never went into effect, its passage was a powerful testament to direct democracy under pressure. Hero and Tolbert (1996) have found direct democracy to be a favored tool of those who feel anxious locally about their national prospects. Considering the sense of racial threat white Californians were experiencing, their support for the Proposition 187 is easier to understand. It is also not a stretch to understand how and why their policy choices were not simply about race-neutral ideas of fairness and rule following. If that were the case, Proposition 227 has little defense.

Proposition 227, dubbed the English Language in Public Schools Statute, sought to end English as a Second Language (ESL) and other such programs that ease nonnative English speakers into American educational institutions by giving them a chance to learn English while also taking some instruction in their native languages. This kind of bilingual education was judged as a failure by 227 supporters, who saw bilingual education as a hindrance to the educational attainment, and ultimate assimilation, of immigrant children and as "a refusal to participate in an English-dominant society" (HoSang 2010: 210). Consequently, the programs for bilingual education were curtailed.

As was the case with Proposition 187, the Proposition 227 ballot measure was race-neutral on its face. However, in the context of California it would be disingenuous to treat these ballot measures as unrelated to the shifting population in the state, since Latinos and Asians comprised a greater share of the population. Although the law applied to all non-English languages, a majority of those with limited English proficiencies in the state spoke Spanish, followed by Chinese speakers (Parrish et al.

2006). The issue of bilingual education had many of the same hallmarks as fights regarding affirmative action. Opponents of both policies argued that such programs failed students, handicapped them by supporting their unwillingness to conform to American values, and ultimately left students unprepared. This kind of concern-trolling served to deflect attention from the thinly veiled racism of white Californians who were worried about losing their numeric, political, and social foothold in the state. It is hardly a coincidence that measures like Propositions 187, 227, and 209 came in quick succession and were all policies that disproportionately harmed minority-identified people. They were all created in a context of anxiety about what it meant to be white in an America where you were no longer going to be the numerical majority. Similar fears were shared by blacks in California, as well as other parts of the country, that saw these demographic changes as potentially disadvantaging their communities.

Blacks' fears, however, did not materialize in the types of anti-immigrant mobilizations seen in California. Even in California, a mainstay immigrant gateway where the perceived dangers of immigration are likely more imminent, blacks did not spearhead or support these types of efforts. Indeed, blacks were more likely to stay out of the political fray rather than put their electoral support behind such measures. African Americans comprised a small portion of the voting coalition that passed Proposition 187; in fact, it was more likely that proximity to other minority populations reduced black support for the measure (Morris 2000). This was largely a measure pursued and supported by an overwhelmingly white population. In fact, what happened in California is characteristic for black politics. Whether California in the 1990s or in the 2016 presidential election, blacks have demonstrated a disinterest in the electoral restriction of immigrants. Indeed, when there was a ballot measure to rescind California's sanctuary status, black voters were not persuaded by these efforts. And in Alabama, where blacks represent a larger share of the voting population, they came out against HB 56, which allowed police officers to detain individuals if they had a "reasonable suspicion" they were undocumented immigrants, and required school children to produce evidence they were authorized to be in the country. The Alabama NAACP rallied, along with the national NAACP, and campaigned to repeal the discriminatory legislation.

This sense that immigrants are not to be targets of black political agendas or policy efforts is separate from their feelings about immigration policy, which are more ambivalent. On the one hand, blacks have largely left the immigration question off their political agenda. The issue has made a periodic appearance, but it has not been a core black political issue. The Johnson-Reed Act of 1924 is a prime example.

The Johnson-Reed Act (1924) has its origins in the nativism and xenophobia of the period. This act introduced severe quotas to prevent the immigration of Southern and Eastern Europeans and effectively ushered in a total ban on Asian immigration. Filipinos were excepted because the Philippines was an American colony, and the Japanese were not explicitly banned because of the Gentleman's Agreement (1908). Moreover, the Johnson-Reed Act required a literacy test for immigrants and imposed an increased tax on them. These provisions were in place, largely unchanged, until 1965. At the time of the law's passage, the country was preoccupied with the immigration of "lesser stocks" and their potential to damage the republic. The law itself gave voice to the scientific racism that was becoming more pervasive. Despite the law being couched as an attempt to preserve the "culture" of the republic, the impetus for it rested on a perverse idea about anti-American (i.e., white) discrimination. Chief architect of the law Senator David Reed (R-PA), argued the quotas in 1921 were unfair to the American population because the quotas were based on census data that overrepresented the foreign-born. Reed, along with Alfred Johnson and John Bond Trevor, argued the quotas needed revising because by employing either the 1910 or 1920 census, the quotas would favor those immigrants from Southern and Eastern Europe to the disadvantage of "native stocks" (Ngai 2004; Trevor 1924). According to Ngai (2004), "native stock" was a term of art used to refer to those descended from the white population of the United States in 1790. All those not considered white in 1790 properly could not be considered "real" Americans. The employment of this "native stock" definition necessarily excluded Native Americans, blacks, those Europeans who immigrated after this date, Jewish people, and Asians, who were barred from becoming citizens. This understanding of what it meant to be a so-called American made eighteenth-century whiteness a prerequisite of Americanness. For the purposes of devising quotas, using this definition of "native stocks" meant Northern and Western Europeans would receive the majority of slotted positions because by this rationale, they were considered the largest contributors to American culture and identity. This meant quotas for immigrants from other regions of the world would be severely limited in order to favor these "whiter" immigrants. Therefore, it is difficult to view this act as anything other than a racially motivated attempt at white preservation.

Architects of the law argued this imbalance in sending countries created a problem for America because these newer groups were ill-prepared for the demands of popular government, did not speak English, and did not want to assimilate, as evidenced by their "resistance" to learning English and the amount of time it took them to naturalize (Trevor 1924). Although the racial overtones were apparent, those who devised the law were careful to avoid overtly racial language. In fact, the racial homogeneity the law sought was treated as a happy accident, not the result of deliberate policy attempting to socially engineer a "whiter" American society.

Another logical turn that was unanticipated was the recognition of black people into the language of citizenship. The chief architects of this law argued that blacks were the only permissible addition to the "family of citizenship" because of the 14th Amendment, which was passed in the wake of the Civil War. Although this reasoning did acknowledge black people, their African ancestry was not used in devising quotas. There were only 100 visa slots allotted to each of the African nations that were part of the 1924 immigration law. By acknowledging blacks and not their heritage, the statute made it clear black people were not part of the class of original Americans. In fact they were not really Americans, because their ancestors were not considered contributors to American population growth. Therefore, the Johnson-Reed Act acknowledges the inclusion of blacks as citizens as the only legitimate updating of American identity and treats them as evidence of the country's "openness" to non-Europeans; however, African ancestry is eschewed in devising the immigrant quota system.

While these new quotas were being promoted throughout the 1920s, W.E.B. DuBois, in an op-ed in *The Crisis,* argued that federal immigration policy was racist with a clear bias toward Europe. The Emergency Quota Act of 1921 imposed the first limits on immigration and used quotas based on national origins to determine how this finite number of visas would be distributed. Because the Emergency Quota Act relied on 1910 census data, the immigration quotas favored Southern and Eastern Europeans. The Johnson-Reed Act was devised as an improvement over the Emergency Quota Act because it would be a permanent federal act and did not rely on census data that gave too much consideration to those who were not Western European. It was believed Western Europeans were the true progenitors of America, and they deserved top billing when it came to devising immigrant quotas. For DuBois, immigration policy was morally bankrupt because it solidified in theory and practice the primacy of global whiteness. More insidious still was the fusing of American identity with whiteness. Although America is "at times heartily ashamed even of the large number of 'new' white people whom her democracy has admitted," DuBois argues, she is absolutely sanguine in her barriers to black inclusion. He states, "against Negroes she can and does take her unflinching and immovable stand," and "trains her immigrants to this despising of 'niggers' from the day of their landing" (Lewis 1995: 465).

The ways in which whiteness can be adapted to the goal of keeping black people from attaining any status in the racial hierarchy was particularly galling for DuBois. DuBois' observations on the mutable nature of white supremacy invested in its perpetuation foreshadows the attempt by Senator Reed to disavow the racist nature of the 1924 quotas. Reed sought to provide cover for the quotas by making blacks complicit in its creation, suggesting that blacks "acquiesced" to its racist provisions. As DuBois states:

> "Acquiesced" is lovely. We also "acquiesced" in slavery, the systematic rape of our women, lynching, disfranchisement and public insult. But there is a day when our acquiescence will not so naively be taken for granted.

By including the systemic racist practices aimed at blacks, DuBois undercuts the idea that blacks were somehow in cahoots with Reed or other white authorities in the exclusion of immigrants. Black people were not core constituents of white lawmakers, which makes the claim even more incredible. The idea that blacks somehow were chief beneficiaries or integral in the development of this legislation could not be claimed with any veracity. Blacks could not even convince the federal government to pass legislation making their murder by state authorities a federal crime. There was no way blacks could convince the federal government to revoke passage to potential immigration. By showing the myriad ways in which blacks were disempowered from making policy decisions in their daily lives, DuBois effectively debunks the claim that blacks were consulted in some fashion about this policy. This did not mean that blacks would not or could not see some benefits from immigration restriction. Nonetheless, as I have argued throughout, immigration was not at the top of a black political agenda then, and still is not, in any direct way.

Blacks and Contemporary Immigration

In the present political environment, black concerns about immigration may be more focused on the rhetoric coming from President Donald Trump and what the hostile racial climate means for their group. Donald Trump claims he has proposed a ban on Muslim immigrants in an attempt to stymie attacks by extremists. To bolster his claim for the need for these types of discriminatory policies, Trump has pointed to the San Bernadino and Orlando attacks and international events in France and Germany. Additionally, Trump has also called for the building of a wall along the Mexican border to prevent undocumented crossings into the United States. Although these policies have received support among his base, they have more broadly been derided as xenophobic and racist. Moreover, they are simply impractical. However, Trump is pulling from a longer history of discriminatory language and practice that has focused disproportionately on blacks and Latinos.

Trump was a recognizable figure in the "birther movement," and in 1989 he took out a full-page ad in the May 1 issue of the *New York Daily News,* along with other major news outlets in the city including, to condemn the Central Park Five, a group of black and Latino teenagers falsely accused of rape and assault of a white, female jogger, and recommended they be sentenced to death. In subsequent years when the boys, now men, were exonerated of all charges stemming from this crime, Donald Trump doubled-down on his claims of their guilt. In both cases, Trump has neither retracted his statements nor apologized for them. However, it is clear the rhetoric Trump is drawing on is part of a longer thread of white supremacy in the United States that has targeted blacks *and* immigrants variously.

Racist parlance and policies Trump proposes often have repelled black communities. Blacks understand that the same fuel that feeds white Americans' xenophobia toward immigrants also drives disdain for blacks. Philip Klinkner (2016) finds white Americans' support for Donald Trump is less about economic concerns and more motivated by an active dislike for blacks. Examining data from the American National Election Study, Klinkner found those whites who are more resentful of black Americans are more likely to support Donald Trump. Additionally, a belief that Obama is an undercover Muslim is an indicator of support for Trump. Likewise, a person who thinks the term *violent* is an accurate descriptor of Islam is more likely to support Trump. These findings have a number of implications for blacks as they relate to immigration and those who seek to appeal to nativism.

What Trump and others of his ilk fundamentally misunderstand is the engagements of black people with diasporic communities of color. The face of Islam in America is black. There is a well-known lineage of black affinities for the religion of Islam, which was popularized by Malcolm X and the Nation of Islam. Muhammad Ali and Kareem Abdul Jabbar helped to disseminate the religion in varying sectors of the black community. Although the Nation of Islam is a religious movement with a black-nationalist bent, the Nation of Islam is not representative of the many blacks who convert to traditional Islamic sects, mainly Sunni Islam. Blacks make up about 13 percent of the Muslim population in the United States with many of them converting to the religion (Pew Research Center 2017). Therefore, while Islamophobia is targeted toward those who appear "Arab," Trump's claims represent a threat to black Muslims, who frequently encounter more surveillance from state actors because of their racial designation. This rhetoric, which continues despite Muslim condemnation of religiously motivated violence, served to dampen support for the Republican candidate (Lipka 2017). A July 2016 NBC News/Wall Street Journal/Marist poll showed, Trump had zero support among black voters in the important swing states of Ohio and Pennsylvania.[1]

In many ways, the Trump phenomenon is a regurgitation of lessons blacks have learned over their centuries-long engagement with the American project. It was common for blacks to look at American stances on immigration as a proxy for where the country might stand regarding their rights (Hellwig 1987). In moments when the United States took a more restrictionist posture toward immigration, it was also not making a proactive response to the domestic terror of lynching that too many black communities were forced to endure.[2] This is partly why immigration reform should be recognized as a significant part of civil rights reforms in the 1960s. When Americans were restrictive to "outsiders," they were also restrictive toward blacks, despite their status as native-born citizens.

This sense of racial pessimism among blacks extends to other groups as well. One of the key ideas of this text is that blacks, who are displeased with their treatment in the United States, also acknowledge the difficulties other racial minority groups have in being incorporated into American society, including immigrants. In a 2018 Gallup poll, blacks are the least satisfied with their treatment in American society; among blacks, only 18% say they are satisfied with their treatment in American society. This finding holds across non-black people are also less satisfied with how blacks are treated in American society (Jones 2019).[3] At the same time, blacks are also displeased with the treatment of immigrants and Arabs. Therefore, blacks are able to acknowledge the struggles of other groups and, generally speaking, have opted not to be part of attack campaigns aimed at outsiders.

This does not mean blacks are necessarily positive toward others; it means blacks opt not to mobilize attacks on other out-groups who may be finding themselves on the wrong side of the public imagination. Furthermore, it has generally been the case that blacks feel closer to other non-white groups, including non-white immigrants, than they do native-born white Americans. This suggests the boundaries of blackness are flexible enough to express an empathy and fealty toward minorities who have similar, but different, struggles (Cohen 1999; McClain et al. 2007; Thornton, Taylor, and Chatters 2013; Thornton and Mizuno 1999). This is significant considering blacks often have had mixed interactions with immigrant communities. This indicates blacks acknowledge the difficulties of others *without* a consistent plan to support or oppose immigration. This ambivalence regarding immigration is consistent with historical trends, and the lack of political mobilization should be read as an agnosticism on the issue of immigration rather than a depth of feeling toward immigrants.

Data and Methods

To assess the expressions of conflicted nativism, I use an original survey of black (n = 1,000) and white Americans (n = 1,000).[4] Given the paucity of data available on black respondents that contain measures of racial identity and national attachment, the development of this survey was a necessity. This survey allows us to understand how racial groups interact with national attachment, immigration policy, and immigrant groups. However, because I am majorly concerned with black attitudes I only utilize the black sample. It is my sense that black opinions do not need to be measured in comparison to those of whites for them to have meaning. Although I understand the usefulness of such approaches, I am concerned with establishing what blacks believe, not showing them to be more or less prone to a certain set of ideas and behaviors than whites.

Testing Conflicted Nativism

To address these claims, I test several hypotheses. The first hypothesis is that blacks hold nativist sentiment. Given the foregoing history, this may not seem like a controversial claim. Black attitudes, however, have received less empirical attention with respect to nativism than other groups (Carter and Pérez 2015). As a result, it is necessary to test this most basic claim, as nativism is a particular expression of national attachment.

As national attachments go, nativism is a chauvinistic type of attachment that views noncitizens as interlopers. For nativists, ensuring national tranquility depends on an exclusion of outsiders and a protectionism of "national values." That said, nativism is a perverted patriotism (Carter and Pérez 2015; De Figueiredo and Elkins 2003); patriotism is a love of nation that is not dependent on the denigration of others. The signs and symbols of the nation that one attaches to are a source of national pride, not outgroup derogation. In fact, there is evidence that when blacks are patriotic they are *more* open to immigrants than their white peers (Carter and Pérez 2015). As such, I am confining my analysis to nativism because blacks have a national identity that can, at times, be derogatory toward out-groups, especially if these out-groups are viewed as endangering black social mobility.

Next, I examine how various measures of national identity influence blacks' nativist attitudes. I expect that blacks hold nativist sentiment, but I also expect nativist tendencies to be dampened by positive national identity (i.e., patriotism). This is because blacks have always exhibited a commitment to the nation, but this commitment has generally been iconoclast in that they are critical in their posture toward America (Parker 2009; Shaw 2004). Thus, blacks express their love for the nation by critiquing its failures to live up to its core principles. I anticipate seeing this type of iconoclastic patriotism at work and having a negative relationship to expressions of nativism. Likewise, for blacks who see themselves as experiencing discrimination, I expect they will be more open to immigrants than those who see themselves as experiencing less discrimination. Finally, I test the extent to which blacks demonstrate a racial preference in their attitudes toward various immigrant groups. Given earlier claims, I expect black respondents to express a greater degree of preference for immigrants than they do for whites.

Dimensions of Conflicted Nativism

To assess nativism I did a simple frequency distribution across items that capture aspects of nativism. These items ask respondents to what extent it is important to have been born in America, to be a Christian, to speak English, and to have resided in the United States for most of their life. Items were coded from 1 (strongly disagree) to 4 (strongly agree).[5] As seen in Table 5.1, a majority of black respondents feel the ability to speak English is of primary importance if one is to be an American.[6] Approximately 67 percent of blacks agree or strongly agree with this sentiment. Similarly, 45 percent of blacks feel Christianity is an important criterion of American identity. Given the high degree of religiosity in black America, particularly Christianity, this is not a surprising finding (Lincoln and Mamiya 1990; McDaniel, Noorudin, and Shortle 2011; Sahgal and Smith 2009).[7]

Blacks were less enthusiastic about the proposition that it is necessary to have lived in America for most of one's life. This is not surprising considering blacks' disinterest in defending American culture from erosion by the presence of immigrants (Diamond 1998). Blacks have historically subscribed to the belief that immigrants can become Americans and at different times, openly have embraced their immigrant brethren (Tillery 2011). In a related fashion, blacks were the least supportive of the idea that one needs to be born in America to be considered a true American. This finding supports my earlier claim that citizenship, while valued by blacks, is not necessarily what makes one an American. Blacks are and have been native-born Americans for a very long time but have not found birthright citizenship to be enough to make them Americans. Likewise, black immigrants have not found their status to offer protection from anti-black prejudice (Greer 2013). Thus, it is unsurprising blacks would be less inclined to believe birthright is what makes one an American.

Table 5.1. **Frequency of Black Respondents Who Agree with Nativist Items**

Nativism Index	Strongly Agree	Agree	N
To have been born in America	8% (58)	11% (76)	712
To be a Christian	25% (172)	20% (141)	690
To speak English	41% (275)	26% (179)	677
To have lived mostly in America	13% (91)	17% (113)	683

α =.55

Determinants of Conflicted Nativism

Although the frequency distribution establishes the fact that conflicted nativism does exist, it gives us little insight into what determines this attitude. To parse this question, I develop a conflicted nativism index using the four items in Table 5.1. The index items range from 1, or strongly disagree, to 4, strongly agree (Cronbach's α =.55). Because the index is an additive measure, the response categories range from 4, or least nativist, to a high score of 16, or most nativist. The mean score for blacks was 8.62, which suggests blacks by and large do not feel strongly about all of the items included in the nativism index. This middling response for conflicted nativism is what I expect given blacks' ambivalence; however, this ambivalence does not mean blacks do not have definite opinions about the issue of immigration.

The literature on black attitudes toward immigration have variously cited economic concerns and perceptions of discrimination as common predictors (Diamond 1998; Thornton and Mizuno 1999). To measure economic concerns, I used the item, "The job prospects of Americans are getting worse."[8] To assess their experiences with discrimination, I used the item "Which of the following groups do you think experiences the most racial discrimination." The responses were actual racial categories, which were randomized for respondents. The item was recoded as a dummy variable, where all those who felt blacks faced the most discrimination in American society were coded as 1 and all others 0.

In addition, the research on national attachments has demonstrated the importance of patriotism for creating a more welcoming environment for newcomers. Because patriotism has been measured as a type of national pride, I used measures that captured this sense of national pride. Because there were several questions tapping this tendency, I created an additive measure of pride that ranges from 3, the least proud, to 12, the proudest (Cronbach's α =.63). Blacks have exhibited their own type of national pride; however, this tendency has not been tested with respect to nativism. I expect national pride will make blacks more tolerant of immigrants because they have not been able to take full advantage of American identity. Similarly, I expect a similar negative relationship between experiences with discrimination and nativist attitudes.

To gauge group consciousness, I include a measure of linked fate.[9] I expect those blacks who view their fates as somehow being joined with other group members may have a bit more awareness about the ways in which race often disadvantages minorities. Moreover, being a strong identifier with one's racial group has not been shown to automatically lead to intolerance of others, and I expect a group like blacks to be slightly more empathetic to immigrants (Brewer 1999). In a related manner, I expect the degree to which one feels one is an exemplar of American identity will affect one's nativist orientation. This is because one's investment in an identity as American has been shown to increase negative attitudes toward immigrants. To address this issue, I used the question: "To what extent do you see yourself as a typical American?" I recoded the item so that 1 means not very typical and 4 means very typical. Finally, I anticipate that those blacks who feel "American culture is increasingly endangered" would be more nativist in their orientation. Although nativism is akin to this idea of a culture under siege, it is less clear that blacks have been invested in preserving American culture in the same way as whites (Carter and Pérez 2015). Although not shown in Table 5.2, I controlled for gender, educational attainment, political ideology and employment status.

To test these propositions, I produced a set of four iterative regression models. The intuition was that this would reveal the extent to which predictors were significant, and whether they continued to be so when they were placed up against a more robust set of variables. In Model 1, *linked fate* was the primary independent variable. Because linked fate has been noted to exercise a strong explanatory variable of black public opinion (Dawson 1994a), I expected it would exert a significant negative influence on holding nativist attitudes. Contrary to my expectations, linked fate

Table 5.2. OLS Regression Results on Nativism, Black Respondents

	Model 1	Model 2	Model 3	Model 4
Linked fate	.13	.05	-.14	.05
Pride		-.22***	-.17***	-.15***
American culture			-.39***	-.41***
Typical American				.66***
Job prospects			.021	.06
Black discrimination			-.04	-.10
Constant	8.0	10.3	9.4	9.1
Adj. R2	.04	.07	.11	.13
N = 667				

***p<.00 **p<.05 *p<.10

exhibited a slightly positive relationship to nativism. However, the effect was insignificant, which means we cannot place too much value on this finding. It is just as likely that linked fate does not matter at all. Moreover, if we look at how linked fate performs across all models, it remains insignificant and changes from a positive to a negative value with respect to nativism. Thus, I feel comfortable in rejecting linked fate's importance in predicting black attitudes toward immigration. I consider this to be a positive outcome because it suggests that being highly identified with other black people does not predispose one to anti-immigrant attitudes.

In Model 2, I was principally interested in how the notion of national pride would influence black opinion. As expected, national pride not only decreased nativist attitudes, but it did so across all models. This means that blacks subscribe to a notion of national pride that is independent of chauvinism (Carter and Pérez 2015; De Figueiredo and Elkins 2003). Consequently, being a proud American for blacks does not necessarily lead one to hold more nativist attitudes. In the case of blacks, this means a positive national identity can be open to newcomers. As such, whatever ideas blacks may have about immigrants, nativism is not driven by national pride; as national pride increases, nativism decreases.

For Model 3, I included measures that would tap into blacks' economic fears that they might lose to immigrants in the job market. Also, because these fears of loss in the employment sector seem to coincide with discriminatory behavior on the part of employers, I wanted to include an item that would proxy for this discrimination. Although this item does not ask directly about workplace discrimination, I argue that if blacks' feelings of discrimination more generally could suggest a general outlook about how they view their treatment across domains. Similarly, I wanted to include a measure that would address anxieties about the erosion of American culture. Although this measure seems to be nativist-like, it is not equivalent to nativism because one can appreciate the changes the nation is undergoing and not necessarily feel anti-immigrant as a result. Therefore, I included this measure to see to what degree, if any, blacks are preoccupied with a loss of "American culture."

None of the main independent variables proved significant in Model 3 except for national pride and American culture. As predicted, the belief that American culture was endangered does not necessarily lead one to hold more nativist sentiment. The coefficient on this variable is negative and significant. This suggests that even for those blacks who feel strongly about American culture, a nativist posture is less attractive as a way to deal with these concerns. In a similar manner, believing blacks faced the most discrimination in American society proved insignificant, but the co-efficient is negative, which is the relationship I predicted. Although job prospects proved insignificant, its positive value suggests blacks are concerned and will hold more nativist opinions if they believe they will face more difficulty in the job market.

Finally, we can examine all of the foregoing variables in concert with one another in the full model, particularly this idea of being a "typical American." While it is unclear what or who blacks think is a typical American, to the degree they hold this idea they are more likely to be nativist in orientation. This means for blacks who see themselves as exemplars of American culture, which indicates some notion of belonging, there is an increase in nativism. These four models demonstrate that black attitudes are complicated and far from settled. The findings indicate that blacks do have an identifiable attachment to the nation, but this attachment does not necessarily lead to xenophobic responses.

Attitudes Toward Immigrants

To the extent that any of this matters, it is important to take a cursory look at how blacks think about immigrants. One of the distinct features of conflicted nativism is that black attitudes are nonracial. That is, their feelings about immigrants are not necessarily wedded to the race of immigrant. Therefore, using a simple frequency distribution, I assess blacks' level of expressed warmth to Asian, African, European, and Latino immigrants. Using feeling thermometers from the Race and Nation (RAN) survey, I find that blacks' mean scores across all immigrant groups are above 50 degrees as highlighted in Table 5.3. This means blacks indicate some warmth toward all immigrant groups. Not surprisingly, blacks feel the most warmth toward African immigrants (Tillery 2011; Tillery and Chresfield 2012; Thornton and Mizuno 1999). However, it is interesting

Table 5.3. **Black Feelings of Warmth by Immigrant Group**

	African	Asian	European	Latino
Mean Thermometer Rating (in degrees)	64	59	57	58

that blacks show no clear favorites for non-African immigrants. They profess a fairly consistent level of warmth across all immigrant groups as demonstrated in Table 5.3.

The purpose of including this information was not to provide determinants of black attitudes with respect to these different groups. Instead, this demonstrates black attitudes regarding immigration are not necessarily racialized in the ways one might expect. Blacks are generally indifferent toward Asian, European, and Latino immigrants as indicated by their rather middling evaluations of the different groups. The only group they have clear warmth for are African immigrants. This makes sense if we think about the sway that Pan-Africanism has traditionally had on black communities. Although I do not test that here, there is ample historical evidence this could be at play. I will return to this result more in the discussion section.

Similarly, when blacks were asked their opinions about what racial/ethnic group they believe their group gets along best with, they chose Latinos, as seen in Table 5.4 (rank ordered by percentage).[10] However, most important is the scant number of blacks who chose Latinos; approximately 38 percent of blacks said they did not know. That the modal response was "don't know" suggests blacks have uncertainties about who they can relate to among their peers. Although Latinos were seen as chief among the groups (none of whom had a clear majority), this response is underwhelming. Nevertheless, I read this finding as indicative of the uncertainty felt by blacks about immigrants, which is the main thrust of this text.

Table 5.4. Racial Group Blacks Get Along
with Best

Don't Know	38% (n = 236)
Latinos	27% (n = 170)
Whites	14% (n = 89)
Other	9% (n = 56)
Native Americans	9% (n = 55)
Asians	3% (n = 18)
Total	100%
N	624

Immigration Policy

The substantive implications of these attitudes for immigration policy need to be addressed at this point. If blacks are ambivalent about immigration, can the same be said for their views on immigration policy? I address this question by looking at black attitudes on policies of restriction, amnesty, and open borders. These policies have been variously tried at different points in our history, such as The Naturalization Act of 1790, Chinese Exclusion Act 1882, The Emergency Immigration Act of 1921, and the Immigration Reform and Control Act in 1986. Therefore, I wanted to get a sense of how blacks feel about these issues in the present.

First, I believe it is important to understand what kind of immigration people care about. Much of the debate on immigration has really been about undocumented migrants. In fact, those who are characterized as anti-immigrant often defend themselves by saying their issue is not immigration but with rule-breaking demonstrated by undocumented immigrants. Thus, they believe persons who are in the country without documentation violate principles of fairness and lawfulness, which are considered core values (Pantoja 2006). From this perspective, legal immigration is acceptable, but illegal immigration is not. Borrowing this logic, the survey asked respondents how important they thought the issues of legal and illegal immigration are. Using separate items, approximately 85 percent of blacks think the issue of illegal immigration is very important or important; similarly, 81 percent believe legal immigration to be very important or important.[11] It does not appear that respondents draw much of a distinction between illegal and legal immigration. This is in line with findings by (Masuoka and Junn 2013) that indicate blacks are not influenced by the status of immigrants.

On the question of immigration policy, I used two items: Do you think the United States should allow unauthorized immigrants to gain citizenship if they pass background checks, pay fines, and have jobs? And do you think U.S. immigration authorities should increase their efforts to curb the flow of illegal immigration? Turning to Table 5.5, half of black respondents agreed with the idea of creating a path to citizenship for those already living in the United States without authorization. In addition, approximately 89 percent of blacks agreed with increasing border security. This makes sense, as making a pathway to citizenship is far more practical than deporting immigrants. This is especially true when considering the chaos this policy brings to families. At the same time, it stands to reason

Table 5.5. Attitudes on Immigration Policy

Percentage strongly agree/agree	Increase efforts to stop illegal immigration	Unauthorized immigrants allowed to gain citizenship	Increase wait to naturalize for legal immigrants	Decrease annual number of legal immigrants
89%	50%	43%	57%	

why blacks may not want to see increased numbers of undocumented immigrants. Therefore, it appears blacks want the government to step up their efforts, in seemingly conflicting ways, by providing access to citizenship for immigrants while preventing further encroachments by undocumented persons.

Moreover, when asked whether the government should increase wait times for legal immigrants to become naturalized citizens, blacks were strongly opposed to this idea; only 43 percent agreed with this proposal. Similarly, 57 percent of blacks subscribe to the idea that the United States should decrease the annual number of immigrants admitted to the United States. Overall, it seems blacks have very measured responses to immigration, both illegal and legal. Although they want the government to respond to this very important issue, they do not support efforts to outright ban immigrants or reduce the likelihood they could become incorporated members of the republic. This comports with what we know about blacks on immigration. Blacks recognize they have something to gain by curbing immigration, but they do not believe it fair to prevent those who are already residing in the country to have to wait longer for citizenship.

Although it appears blacks want the government to take a more active role in managing immigration, it is not clear the lengths to which they will go to achieve these ends. Opinions on policy mean little if there is no will to take action around a set of principles. Thus, if any of these ideas about immigration policy matter in any tangible way, then it is reasonable to expect blacks will pursue a political agenda around immigration. When asked whether they would add their name to a public letter concerning both documented and undocumented immigration, only 44 percent of blacks said they would address a letter to Congress on the issue of documentation. Correspondingly, 48 percent of blacks said they would send a letter to their Congress person regarding the issue of undocumented immigration.

Letter campaigns can be an effective means for registering one's public support (or opposition) to an issue and is a rather low-cost way of achieving real political ends (Brown and Brown 2003; Lee 2002). In fact, this type of political activity is one blacks are well-versed in and have practiced for hundreds of years (Brady, Verba, and Schlozman 1995; Washburn 1986). However, the fact that blacks will not engage in writing a letter to Congress on behalf of immigrants, regardless of status, suggests they simply do not care enough about the issue to do anything about it. This is historically what blacks have done with respect to immigration, and it appears they are holding fast in keeping their distance from the issue. Although we do not know exactly why blacks choose not to engage, it seems reasonable that they simply do not see immigration as part of their domain of concern, regardless of the importance they might ascribe to the issue. Taken together, it seems reasonable to suggest immigration is something blacks care about but is simply not a high priority for them.

Discussion

What this chapter has shown is that blacks have group-based interests, but these interests do not include immigration. Blacks are not concerned with the issue and may be silent on it politically. Historically, blacks have been reticent in their support for immigration because they potentially have more opportunities, economically and socially, when the numbers of immigrants are reduced. Yet, their silence on the issue of immigration should not be read as acquiescence to racist immigration policies. The Johnson-Reed Act (1924) is one such example.

The Johnson-Reed Act (1924), which enshrined immigration quotas that effectively barred immigrants who were not from Northern and Western Europe, was criticized in black circles. The criticisms of the policy had to do with the ways in which the federal government singled out non-Europeans as threats to the nation. Still, blacks had real reservations about what immigration meant for their community that extended beyond the economic. As DuBois (1929) notes, "whenever these same laborers get a chance they swat us [black people] worse than the capitalists." That immigrants adapt easily to anti-blackness is an observation made by a number of blacks (Ferreira 1999; Roediger 1999). Anti-black prejudice as a manifestation of white supremacy seems to be a hallmark of immigrant assimilation (Dixon 2006; Esses, Dovidio, Jackson, and Armstrong 2001; Gans 1979; Jacobson 1999; Omi and Winant 1994). The United States is not unique in its capacity to degrade black people; one of its achievements is the way in which anti-blackness becomes almost a prerequisite for whiteness.

For European immigrants (including those viewed as "lesser stocks") to gain entrée into racial whiteness, it was necessary they demonstrate their distinctiveness from blacks. Because they were in similar socioeconomic conditions as blacks, incorporating disdain toward blacks became a way to create the needed racial distance. To an extent then, white identity is formed by demonstrating how different one is from black people (Bashi 2004; Dyer 2008; Jacobson 1999). This has consequences for those who are deemed white in American society, but also for those who are considered black. This is because blackness is also an ill-defined category whose boundaries expand and contract depending on the political climate (Kim 1999).

Racial whiteness is demarcated by its exclusivity; on the other hand, blackness is demarcated by its extreme inclusivity. Blackness is overdetermined by the presence of African blood, even if it is in smaller proportion to European extracts. The origins of what is understood as blackness in a U.S. context has to do with the legacy of enslavement. By America's own laws, values, and investments in enslavement, the law of matrilineal descent becomes enshrined as part of the racial lexicon. To create a permanent class of enslaved people, it was necessary for slave status to be inherited. Consequently, one's status as enslaved becomes quasi-biological because it is a trait passed from mother to child. As a result of this racial logic, black blood was marked as a tainting force. There was no way one could "whiten up" regardless of how many generations passed. If one was known to be, or suspected of being black, they were always black.

Even as our country's racial geography was, and is, in flux, blackness remains curiously fixed as a signifier of the bottom of the racial hierarchy. Because of our weddedness to this notion of an all-encompassing blackness, the U.S. Census quickly abandoned any flirtation with the idea of a variegated blackness. For the 1890 census, octoroons, quadroons, and mulattoes were counted, but this idea of blood quantum for blacks was abandoned in the next census and only entertained intermittently after this period (Nobles 2000). These categories are defined by the amount of black ancestry a person has, not the amount of white ancestry. A mulatto is a person who has a black parent; a quadroon is a person who is one-quarter black, and an octoroon is a person who is one-eighth black. These definitions tell us much about the ways in which the borders of whiteness were defended. By assigning racial group membership based on black ancestors, it was impossible for communities to "whiten up." The only way a person could identify as white was to "pass," which often required relocation and severing family ties with one's black relatives. It is worth noting the "mulatto" category appeared in the 1910 and 1920 census but was finally abandoned altogether in favor of "Negro" in 1930. So powerful a notion is "blackness" for describing a condition as much as a people, various communities have been classified as racially black despite their lack of African descent (Loewen 1988; Quan 2007). For example, early Chinese settlers to Mississippi were denied entry to white schools but were shuttled to black schools (Banks 1998; JY Kim 1999). This was not because Chinese people were viewed as African descendants. Instead, their race designated them as something other than white, and whiteness could not be endangered by absorbing this immigrant population. No such reservations existed where blacks were concerned because there was no consideration for protecting black people from outsiders. Because blackness was not valued, there was nothing to preserve; therefore, as a category of people they were made to assimilate all manner of newcomers considered "unfit" for whiteness. In this way, blackness was the hyper-inclusive, catch-all racial category for everything non-white.

Unfortunately, immigrants harmed by the black/white binary often relied on a type of appeasement of whiteness, where they demonstrated their value through their positive distinctiveness from blacks. This was a strategy used by a number of immigrants throughout the late-nineteenth and into the twentieth century, who were frequently depicted as being akin to or descended from Africans. This "secondary marginalization," whereby an already subordinated group marginalizes another subordinated group to gain esteem in society, did not immediately allow immigrants access to whiteness, but it did provide them some status above blacks (Cohen 1999; Jacobson 2001).

This fear of being further marginalized is really at the core of black engagements with immigration, which this chapter demonstrates. Blacks are very aware their blackness makes them unique, in that their identity is viewed as particularly undesirable. However, the problem is that this is not merely attitude; blacks are routinely harmed by these attitudes because they are used to keep them from economic, social, and political mobility. As such, blacks are acutely aware of their racial identity and how it is denigrated in American society. I argue this leads to a sense that immigrants want the benefits of coming to America but none of the burdens of being associated with their community. This manifests as what I term a *conflicted nativist* stance.

On the one hand, blacks feel immigrants are treated poorly and face many deficits in their attempts to become Americans. On the other hand, blacks are not eager to assist immigrant groups. Blacks' attachment to the nation, as measured by their feelings of pride, does not necessarily make them more intolerant of immigrants. In fact, positive associations with the nation tempered black responses such that blacks indicating they are "more proud" are less likely to hold nativist sentiment. This is significant because it demonstrates that blacks' nativist attitudes are reduced by affirmations of their belonging in the nation, which suggests nativism is not produced by a nationalism that equates being an American with the exclusion of others.

Likewise, linked fate proved insignificant as a determinant of nativist sentiment. This non-finding is still important, because it shows black group consciousness does not necessarily make one hostile to immigrants. Similarly, the feeling that American culture is endangered did not make blacks reactionary in their response. This could be because blacks do not care much for the usual markers of "American culture," however defined. It could be the case that when individuals hear the term "American culture," they are as likely to consider the usurpation, displacement, and destruction of communities of culture as much as they think of the flag and national anthem.[12] It is difficult to say what people considered, because what constitutes "American culture" is not defined. Given blacks' iconoclasm where the United States is concerned, it would not be a leap to consider that many blacks feel American culture ought to be endangered because it truly does not belong to blacks. Whatever the reasoning, it is clear that this sense that American culture is undergoing fundamental change is not driving blacks to become more nativist in their orientation, and this is a positive outcome in the atmosphere of reactionary nationalism we are currently experiencing in the United States.

When we look at immigrant race, it is apparent that race of immigrants does not change the ways in which blacks understand the issues. Although immigration is highly racialized, it is not so for blacks. Not only do blacks report relatively warm feelings for all immigrant groups, they view themselves as getting along best with Latinos. This could be because Latinos are the group blacks are most familiar with and are viewed as being most like black people. It could also be that Latinos are as likely to be American as they are to be immigrant. Again, I cannot draw too many inferences from the available data. What is apparent is that blacks are not as stand-offish to other groups as many may have assumed. In fact, as previously stated, Table 5.4 indicates that blacks were more likely to say they "don't know" in response to what group they feel they get along best with. This seems to reinforce the underlying ambivalence blacks have regarding their own place in the American racial hierarchy. Blacks are searching for their place, and that they are unsure where they can find allies alludes to this fact.

However, blacks register more positive feelings toward African immigrants. This makes sense considering the ways in which black-ness tends to bond disparate groups of African-descended people. When black immigrants began coming to the United States between 1910 and 1940, black media outlets were largely equivocal toward them (Tillery and Chresfield 2012). Nevertheless, there existed some sensibility that foreign-born blacks were treated as "model minorities" and enjoyed rel-ative advantages over native-born blacks. This pattern is observed in the contemporary moment where the assimilation of black immigrants has been uneven at best. There is a desire to maintain that group's distinctive-ness from native-born blacks because of the stigmas attached to the latter group (Waters 1994). In some cases, black immigrants generally come to the United States and experience better socioeconomic outcomes relative to native-born blacks (Massey, Mooney, Torres, and Charles 2007; Rimer and Arenson 2004). At the same time, this "immigrant advantage" does not last, because of racial assimilation and the inability of group members to maintain distinctions from native-born blacks. What blacks are gen-erally more concerned about are the machinations of whites, who often seek to use immigrants as exemplars of blackness while shaming black Americans for not living up to that promise. Still, for all of the complexities of this intraracial relationship, black Americans and black immigrants have remained close geographically and in terms of identity (Greer 2013; Thornton, Taylor, and Chatters 2013).

Despite all of their uncertainties, blacks do want to see the federal gov-ernment manage illegal immigration and favor efforts to stop this practice. It does not matter whether the group is undocumented or documented, they want the government to provide some coherent leadership on the issue of immigration. Blacks support the idea that immigrants, both authorized and unauthorized, should be able to access citizenship. In general, blacks are opposed to the idea that legal immigrants should have to wait additional time to become naturalized citizens. In the case of unauthorized immigrants, blacks feel they should be allowed to naturalize after meeting some sort of restitution requirement in the form of fines and the like. Even though blacks feel unauthorized immigration should be curbed by the government, they do not favor a policy that would seek to return undocumented migrants to their home country. Nonetheless, 50 percent of blacks do favor the government decreasing the number of legal immigrants admitted to the country. This may be because those legal immigrants are more likely to have better skills and present more of a challenge on the job market, in which case blacks are operating purely from a self-interest position. Fewer immigrants mean less competition in the job market, which is better for their group. However, this recognition does not mean necessarily that one is hostile to immigrants because they want to see fewer of them admitted to the country. Given what we know, it does not seem hostility is a predictor of blacks' position with respect to immigration. Therefore, it seems blacks, regardless of their misgivings about immigration, maintain a fairly centrist set of positions.

In closing, black opinions are not just about what they say but what they do. To date, blacks have not mounted any campaigns against immigrants. This is because blacks fundamentally believe in a right to self-determination for all people. Although blacks certainly have opinions about immigration, the issue is not salient enough for them to do even something as low-cost as writing a letter to their congressperson regarding legal or illegal immigration. Taken together, these findings support the central idea of this text, which is that black people neither want to help nor to hurt immigrants. In short, blacks are more concerned with their own group's well-being. It is far more important for blacks to address racial inequality as a route toward more incorporation for their people, which has a way of creating a more inclusive America for all people including immigrants.

6

Beyond Immigration

BLACK PUBLIC OPINION AND AMERICAN IDENTITY
IN THE TWENTY-FIRST CENTURY

OVER THE PRECEDING chapters of the book, I have shown the context and constraints of white supremacy on the formation of black public opinion. To this end, I use immigration as a lens to understand the divergent contours of black public opinion. This is particularly important because we, as scholars and laypersons, often limit consideration of black opinion to "black issues," such as affirmative action or welfare. These are important issue areas to be sure, but there is not a lot of variation on these opinions. Moreover, because these issues have been so thoroughly "blackened" in the American mind, it is difficult to see what is new and/or interesting about black opinion formation (Hancock 2004). Immigration, however, comes with less of this perceptual baggage because, while I show black people have definite opinions about immigration, those opinions are not linear. Case in point, knowing how close black people feel to immigrants will not tell you whether black people also want to see the numbers of immigrants in the country increased. That is, black people are sympathetic to immigrants, but they are also not in favor of more open borders. And the truth is, no ethnic group favors open borders, and one's status as a member of an ethnic group tells only a partial story about opinion formation (Abrajano and Singh 2009; Branton 2007). This ambivalence is interesting and is the puzzle I have explored in this book.

In this way, then, the book is not about how individual black people feel about immigrants or immigration policy. Rather, this politics of immigration is really about a politics of belonging. Overall, the goal of this book is to offer a tool for us as analysts interested in better understanding black public opinion in the United States and *why* their opinions look the way they do. To that end, I offer my theory of conflicted nativism, which offers an accounting for how black identity creates a unique perspective on what it means to be American, and how that American identity becomes operational for black people in the domain of immigration.

Conflicted Nativism: Black Ambivalence and Immigration Politics

In the last half-century since the passage of the Voting Rights Act (1965) blacks have made tremendous strides in local, state, and federal politics. Increased mobilization efforts of blacks, as well as other racial and ethnic minorities, helped to elect Barack Obama in 2008. That same energy also had substantial influence on state and local midterm races around the United States in fall 2018, where an unprecedented number of women of color have been elected to the House of Representatives, statewide offices, local positions, and judicial seats. In this same period, an unprecedented number of immigrants from Africa, Asia, the Caribbean, and Latin America have made their presence felt in the United States. Because these communities are increasingly important, yet unstable, members of an array of political coalitions, increasing efforts to woo these voters have been documented on both the left and the right (Wong 2018). While there is much to be optimistic about in the political landscape given the political advancement of black people and the increased incorporation and visibility of immigrant populations, there is also reason to be apprehensive.

The main premise of this book is that using immigration as a cipher for understanding black public opinion gives us a way to understand their identity as Americans. I offer the theory of conflicted nativism to account for how black people internalize the lessons of white supremacy in such a way that makes them ambivalent about immigration. On the one hand, blacks believe in the right to self-determination and are more supportive of policies that allow for immigrant incorporation. On the other hand, blacks, as Americans, express reservations about the meaning of this immigration for their group and whether their group will be harmed as a result of these newcomers. By harm I mean blacks are concerned that immigrant groups' inclusion will come at their expense. Thus, my theory of conflicted nativism attempts to explain how it could be that blacks, in some instances, favor more liberal policies on immigration, but may also hold ideas about immigrant groups that seem intolerant on their face. While my theory builds on the conventional literature regarding blacks' experiences as a marginalized group, I also highlight the ways in which resistance to white supremacy, in an effort to assert their American identity, makes it possible to hold both points of view. In order for me to study black public opinion I had to include an understanding of their perceptions of how race operates to limit the social and political options for people marked non-white. Because blacks have been at the forefront of challenging these practices, historical efforts to resist inequality are part of how their group forms opinions about an issue area, and also how they choose to navigate policy—hence, why there is no evidence that blacks, in general, organize to oppose immigrants, documented or otherwise. At the same time, blacks do have an operating American identity they use to process these issues. While their orientation to American identity is different given their status as a marginalized group, they do not necessarily want to see the numbers of immigrants to the United States increased or favor a more laissez-faire immigration regime.

Therefore, my theory of conflicted nativism explains how one could be pro-immigrant in one sense and less supportive of immigration in other scenarios. Conflicted nativism argues that blacks want to be able to access, and feel they should be able to access, certain advantages as Americans over any and all immigrant groups. At the same time, they are suspicious of efforts to "root out" or "crack down" on immigrants through more aggressive police-like tactics because, as I argue throughout the text, these practices are steeped in the very same racism their group has been resisting since they have been in this country. The logic that wants to deport immigrants and separate children from their parents rests on the same foundations that allow black women, men, and children to be shot by police in the street or in their homes.

Throughout the text, my argument has been that if one wants to understand black politics in this century, and immigration by extension, one has to understand the ways in which white supremacy functions in our society. The current political climate we are living through does not bode well for black people and immigrants. Under the Obama administration, a conservative majority of the Supreme Court created the conditions to undermine the voting rights blacks and other racial and ethnic groups fought so strenuously to secure. As a result, polling places are now used as political pawns; since the Shelby County ruling in 2013, nearly a thousand polling places have been closed, mostly in black communities (Vasilogambros 2018).

At the same time, President Obama continued an ambitious schedule of deportations; this more draconian immigration regime has only ramped up under the Trump administration. While Barack Obama had a reputation for being a champion of liberal causes, he was also an advocate of Secure Communities. Secure Communities extended the reach of the federal government and made local police forces into quasi-immigration enforcement agents (Armenta 2017). This policy had particular ramifications for black immigrants who, by virtue of their skin color, were surveilled more often/ had more engagements with the law enforcement community and were more likely to be detained and deported (Palmer 2017). As such, this policy made the need for sanctuary cities more critical. Sanctuary cities are localities that refused to comply with federal immigration authorities by not requiring, or reporting, the immigration status of those they encountered for low-level offenses. These sanctuary cities, some of them located in heavily black communities like Baltimore, the District of Columbia, Jackson, New Orleans, and Philadelphia, came into being even though these issues do not appear to be of major concern for most African Americans. Why does this happen?

As I argue throughout the book there is a way in which blacks, as Americans, do not weaponize their national identity to harm others. For sure, it may be the case that black Americans are not universally flattering in their assessments/beliefs about immigrants, but that is not a requirement for doing the right thing. As in the case of border separations, that immigrants find themselves in proximity to black people, who are sympathetic to their cause but also considering their status as Americans, demonstrates the "twoness" of black opinions on immigration.

For instance, in a June 2018 Harvard/Harris Poll, blacks ranked guns, race relations, and immigration as the top issues facing the country; school shootings were a close fourth-place choice. What is more, blacks were shown to be the most favorable to deferred action on deportation for children brought by their parents to the United States without authorization. They were also most favorable to allowing those currently residing in the country without documentation to apply for citizenship, rather than deporting those individuals. At the same time, blacks did not support the idea of more lax borders, and a scant majority favor erecting a physical or electronic border with Mexico. What is more, blacks most strongly disapprove of the way in which Donald Trump has handled the issue of immigration. Using conflicted nativism, it is not incompatible to believe in creating a path to citizenship for individuals currently residing in the country without authorization *and* not wanting to see the numbers of immigrants coming to the United States increased, while being critical of the administration's poor handling of these issues.

On Being Black and American

Throughout the text, one of the chief aims has been to emphasize the ways in which black people use the issue of immigration to accentuate their incomplete incorporation into the American body politic. This theme is recurrent across time, as seen in Chapters 3 and 4, and one blacks grapple with despite their attempts, both formally and informally, to become part of the fabric of American life.

In Chapter 1, I use historical and current events to prosecute the claim that you cannot understand black public opinion if you do not have a clear understanding of blacks' unique experience in America. This history, I argue, provides the context for understanding the contours of black public opinion in the present. This is not because the lives of black people have stayed the same—there have been marked improvements since the Jim Crow period. Rather, the ways in which America has treated black Americans has been predictable despite black attempts to make gains in American society. To give you an idea, as blacks have made gains in the electoral arena there have been more attempts to circumvent their voting rights. These efforts were on full display in the 2018 midterm elections, where voter purges in key states, like Georgia and Indiana, fell disproportionately on black communities (Lopez 2018). This is not simply a hiccup in the application of the law or collateral damage to insure fraud-free elections; it is a calculated attempt to violently deny black voting rights without firing a single shot, employing a water hose, or calling out the dogs. It is the same kind of violence that allows black mothers to have their children torn from their arms for the crime of sitting on the floor. This type of violence is perpetrated by a society that does not see blacks as full citizens of the republic, but is rarely called out as such. Therefore, blacks are reasonably suspicious of whites and their politics. I argue one can see this in the domain of immigration, where blacks' opinions are strong but are not necessarily about some allegiance to the sanctity of American character. While blacks subscribe to an American identity, they utilize that identity in a distinctive fashion to critique the status of their own group. As such, their black identity operates as their superordinate identity, which they use to critique and expand the notion of what it means to be an American. In sum, black public opinion on immigration is a proxy for black feelings about whites, and for their disappointments about the continued denial of full citizenship for their community. In this way, immigration is instrumental to helping blacks articulate these unreconciled strivings.

Chapter 2 formalizes the arguments in Chapter 1 and sets forth my theory of conflicted nativism, which allows us to understand blacks' complicated relationship to their American identity. This chapter employs the lessons from the literature in political science to lay out how blacks employ their national identity in order to claim privilege in a society where their incorporation is incomplete. Yet, this identity is only superficially related to nativist attitudes and is not accompanied by strong restrictionist impulses. This is because blacks view immigration restriction as a racist enterprise targeted primarily at people of color. Blacks, therefore, view their primary problem as white supremacy, which they feel impedes their upward mobility. Immigration, then, is not the "real" issue for blacks. Consequently, blacks do not prioritize or organize around the issue of immigration restriction.

The next chapter uses historical evidence to confirm the ideas set forth in Chapter 2. In particular, Chapter 3 demonstrates blacks' deep engagement with immigration since the nineteenth century. In particular, this chapter highlights how blacks employed immigration as a strategy for liberation. Toward this end, blacks self-consciously applied terms like *immigrant* and *refugee* to their own group, given the repression they faced at the time. This chapter is significant because it demonstrates that so-called back to Africa movements were not simply black nationalist fantasies but were real efforts to define and realize a robust freedom for the first time. While the majority of free blacks chose to remain in the United States, that they engaged international immigration (in addition to domestic migration) as a tool of resistance is an underappreciated part of black political repertoires. Thus, when blacks first engaged emigration it was for their own sakes. Leaving America, and the debates that ensued, was part of a black activist tradition that sought black inclusion and political incorporation in a variety of forms (Gaines 2006). When Donald Trump was elected in 2016, #blaxit (black exit) began trending, where blacks contemplated what they would take with them if or when they divested from the United States. Of course, this was meant as a joke, but given the black tradition of immigration, there was a veneer of truth there. Indeed, most black people have not left the country, but it remains a distinct possibility for some black people. While these particular issues are not explored in Chapter 5, this chapter does help us understand the contours of black thought with respect to race and immigration in the present. In particular, the subsequent chapter uses qualitative data to uncover the complicated ways that black frame these issues.

Chapter 5 uses "everyday talk" to appreciate how black people think through race, their citizenship, and immigration. Using Durham, North Carolina, as a case study, I find blacks use their group's racial past to understand their present circumstances as members of a racial group and as individuals. In particular, my respondents are socialized to recognize the ways their blackness has come to represent a lesser status in an American context. When evaluating immigration and what it means for their group, they employ history as a way to frame what they see happening around them in the present. From their perspective, other groups are given privilege in American society, and their group's status is devalued. Through the particularities of their experience, they realize the ways in which racial hierarchy systematically hurts blacks, which has little to do with immigrants as such. The presence of immigrants is a way to highlight the inequities of blacks' status and the limits of their American citizenship in exerting privilege in society. Through discourse I find blacks do not harbor major hostility toward immigrants. Rather, their discomfort is aimed at whites who seek to exploit others in an effort to reinforce blacks' subordinate status in American society.

An additional source of corroboration comes from an analysis of original quantitative data. Chapter 5 of the text focuses on empirically testing the core claims of the book. I find blacks have some superficially nativist attitudes but are not willing to galvanize around this issue. They do not contact their elected officials or perform other political actions regarding the issue of immigration. Those blacks who view themselves as "typical Americans" exhibit more nativist attitudes, but being "proud Americans" dampens this nativist bent in their attitudes. This suggests that being a "patriot" does not necessarily mean that one will become more xenophobic toward immigrants. Moreover, blacks feel more warmly to all immigrant groups than they do to other whites, and view themselves as having more in common with Latinos. Still, blacks support the idea of more border security, but only about 40 percent are willing to write a letter to their representative regarding documented/undocumented immigration. Taken together, these findings suggest blacks have divergent attitudes about immigration without distinction to whether immigrants are in the country with or without documentation. What is more, for whatever opinions they have about immigration, they are unwilling to act upon these beliefs. Blacks are not offended by immigrants despite their somewhat nativist beliefs. In short, immigration is not a salient issue for blacks, and they do not feel as protectionist about their American identity as has been documented with whites (Branton, Cassese, Jones, and Westerland 2011; Kinder and Kam 2010; Udani and Kimball 2018).

Where Do We Go from Here?

The summer of 2018 witnessed the brutal separation of children and families along the Mexican border. While the policy was rightfully called out as a cruel interpretation of America's "zero tolerance" policy toward unauthorized border crossings, the practice of separating children and parents has been an American practice perfected over 400 years. Whether separating enslaved parents from their children in preparation for sale; Native American parents from their children to place them in boarding schools to "civilize" them; or the orphan train movement that took the children of the needy and destitute, many of them immigrants, and resettled them in orphanages across the country, America has never been sentimental about maintaining the sanctity of "family" for those deemed to be outsiders in the American body politic. The trauma of this practice was deeply felt and unfortunately all too well understood by the fractured communities still reeling from centuries of these types of processes. Despite court rulings that pronounced this practice at the Mexican border illegal and that have demanded the immediate reunification of these families, this government insists the means of family separation was justified by the end of border security.

This policy represented a full-circle moment that also made us confront another set of truths. Of the approximately 11 million undocumented people in the United States, roughly 600,000 are black; by comparison, there are nearly 800,000 Latino undocumented people (Krogstad 2017; Zong, Batalova, and Hallock 2018). What is more, black immigrants are more likely to face detention and deportation than any other group (Palmer 2017). The same criminal justice system that unjustly targets, hyper-surveils, jails, and imprisons African Americans also injures groups in proximity to them, most immediately black immigrants, but also has the potential power to hurt those marked as "un-American" or somehow suspected of being "other."

In a Quinnipiac University poll released June 2018, blacks were the most opposed to family separation and deportations of those in the country without documentation of any other group. Why this is the case I cannot say for certain, but the lessons of this text offer insights that can help us make inferences about these findings. What I have argued throughout this text is that immigration, even when it is inconvenient for black people, is about justice and doing the right thing even when it may cost their group. Not because black people are altruistic but because, as a group, they know the dangers of white supremacy. The position of blacks in American society is not simply about individual racist choices; it also the result of white supremacy. White supremacy is the set of racist practices, policies, and the unfair application of the law to groups deemed non-white. This neither means every individual white person benefits in the same way from white supremacy nor does it mean that every non-white person is poor or downtrodden. What it does mean, however, is that people racially identify as white, or near white; benefit from white supremacy whether economically, socially, politically, or psychically; and they do not have to do anything to reap these benefits (Mills 1997).

To illustrate, black people find themselves in poorer communities irrespective of their salaries, because of choices made by insurance companies and realtors' organizations that routinely undervalue their neighborhoods. This so-called "segregation tax" is not a passive relic of bygone eras but is happening right now. As a consequence of these practices, it is more difficult for black communities to build intergenerational wealth; home ownership was considered the chief way to build this kind of wealth until the subprime mortgage crisis of 2007 that was felt most acutely in black and other minority communities (Shapiro 2006). While there are black people who are legitimately below the poverty line, black people regardless of class are, and have been, kept poorer because of the cumulative nature of federal, state, and local housing statutes, tax policies, and valuation practices (Rothstein 2017). This has been a constant theme in black life, and it is deliberate whether or not the intent was racist. What happens in housing policy is but a symptom; we see similar manifestations of this type of nonracial policy with racist outcomes in the areas of criminal justice and voting rights, for example. The root cause of these outcomes is white supremacy, which is largely invisible because of the ways it has been normalized in our society.

If I have done my job, the insights gleaned from this book will help the reader to move from the particularities of immigration to understanding the broader context and applicability of black opinion formation. I argue that white supremacy is one of the necessary ways in which we must understand black public opinion. Black people are not born "black" in the biological sense, but they become black through cumulative experiences they have encountered as individuals and as a group. Interactions with whites are part and parcel of their story. Black people, by virtue of demographics and racial status, do not have the privilege of avoiding interactions with white people. What does this mean? Generally speaking, black people, even when living in all- or mostly-black enclaves, have to engage whites where they work, shop, or socialize. Even if they do not have direct experiences with whites, any television program, commercial, or other television transmission they encounter will feature a white person. Even Black Entertainment Television (BET), the favorite bugaboo of whites who believe in "reverse racism," is not a black-owned entity any longer. If black people want a car or mortgage loan, they only have 22 options if they want to give their business to a black-owned bank; the already small number of black-owned banks decreased further in the wake of the Great Recession (2007–2009). At their height, from 1888 to 1934, there were 130 black-owned banking institutions. Similarly, there are less than 50 grocery stores and farms owned by blacks. Thus, in most of life's activities from eating to entertainment, black people cannot avoid whiteness. All of this is to drive home the larger context of black opinion in this book. In sum, if you want to understand black opinion, it cannot be done in isolation from white supremacy. To the extent that black opinions are the collection of their experiences, then whiteness must be part of that conversation.

The evidence in this book focuses on historical, qualitative, and empirical data in an effort to contextualize black public opinion. While we assume we know black people, I chose to use immigration, an issue area not commonly associated with black people, and these different methodological approaches to provide a broader picture of black public opinion. In so doing, this book takes for granted that black opinions are the result of historical and contemporary forces that shape the way they see their group, outsiders, and the nation. By doing so, this book demonstrates blacks' deep engagements with the issue of immigration in an effort to understand their individual and group's investment in the American project. Immigration is part of an iterative process of defining what it means to be black in America in the twenty-first century, and how that informs how blacks formulate their opinions about the world. As a result of the evolution in blacks' lives from slavery to freedom, the meaning of American and immigrant have changed for their group. Nonetheless, the *social* meanings of blackness, Americanness, and immigrant have remained relatively steady. This is not a path-dependent argument, meaning one does not travel a straight line from the nineteenth century to the present. Rather, this book argues that one cannot understand black public opinion on immigration, or any other topic, without considering the particularities of this group's political incorporation. This is not to paint black people as saints or people without agency. Instead, this book attempts to show black people as fully human. Black people, like other people, are the sum total of their experiences as individuals and as a group. This book neither speaks for all black people nor does it attempt to explain the litany of black opinions. What it does do, however, is demonstrate the complexity of black opinions vis-á-vis their experience as Americans. By doing so, my intention is to demonstrate the myriad ways in which blacks use a range of political issues to express a particular type of American identity.

Interview Questionnaire

I would like to begin by asking you some questions about yourself. What kind of work do you do?

How long have you been doing this type of work?

Where were you born? City and state.

What brought you to this area?

How long have you lived in this area?

What year were you born?

Are most of the people you work with Black, Latino, or White?

What percentage would you say are Black, White, and Latino?

Are most of the people you interact with on your job Black, Latino, or White?

Are most of the people in your neighborhood Black, Latino, White, or is it a mixture?

What types of changes, if any, have you noticed in the racial composition of this area in the last 10 years?

How would you characterize race relations between Blacks and Whites in this area? Would you say that they're poor, excellent, fair? Why do you say that?

What do you think the relationship between Latinos and Whites is like? Would you say it's excellent, poor, or fair? Why do you say that?

How about Blacks and Latinos, what would you say that relationship is like? Why is that?

What do you think the impact of the growing Latino population will be on race relations in this area? Do you think it will be positive, negative, or no impact at all?

Why do you say that?

Do you think that Latinos in this area understand U.S. racial history of segregation and slavery? Why or why not?

Do you think White people understand that history of slavery and segregation? Why or why not?

Do you think Black people understand this history of slavery and segregation? Why or why not?

Do you agree with the statement that what happens to other Black people will have some effect on your life? Why is that?

Do you think that what happens to Black people will matter for Latinos in this area? Why is that?

What would you say are some of the most significant problems facing Black people in this area?

What would you say the significant problems facing the Latino community are?

So why do you say Black people are having problems with the issue(s) you named?

If you had to say, what group do you feel has the most in common with Black people: Latinos, Asians, Whites, Native Americans . . . ?

If you had to say, which group do you feel has the most in common with Black people: Latinos, Asians, Whites, Native Americans, or some other group? Why?

Now I want to get your ideas of what you think other groups think about Black people. Do you think that Latinos are prejudiced towards Blacks? Why do you think that is?

Do you think that Whites are prejudiced towards Blacks? Why do you think that is?

Do you think that Blacks are prejudiced towards Latinos? Why do you think that is?

I'm going to ask you about a racial group, and I want you to give me three adjectives to describe each group: Whites? Latinos? Asian Americans? Blacks? (randomize the order)

Who you think the term Latino applies to?

Do you think of Latinos as white?

Do you think of Latinos as black?

Do you think White people are competing with Blacks for work in this area? Why?

Do you think Latinos and Whites are competing for work in this area? Why?

Do you think Blacks and Latinos are competing for work in this area? Why?

Do you think that the Latino population is having a positive or negative affect on the economy? Why?

Do you think employers value Latino labor over Black labor? Why?

Do you think that Latinos in this area want to be fully included in our community? Why or why not?

Do you think that Blacks distrust Whites in this area? Why?

Do you think Black people distrust Latinos in this area? Why or why not?

Do you think White people distrust Latinos? Why or why not?

Do you think Latinos distrust Black people? Why or why not?

Do you think that Latinos distrust Whites? Why or why not?

Do you think that a political coalition is likely between Blacks and Latinos? Why or why not?

How about a political coalition between Blacks and Whites, do you think that's going to happen?

Is there anything else you want to add?

Race and Nation Survey

I. Let's begin with some statements about people's mentality in general and yourself. Please tell me whether you think these statements are true or false. [SELF-ESTEEM]

1. When in a group of people, I usually do what others want, rather than make suggestions.
   1) true 2) false 3) don't know

2. I certainly feel useless at times.
   1) true 2) false 3) don't know

II. Next, I'm going to make some statements about U.S. society. After each one, please tell me, on a scale of 1 to 4, whether you agree or disagree with it. A score of 1 means you strongly disagree, and a score of 4 means you strongly agree.
   [RANDOMIZE ORDER OF ITEMS]

3. The job prospects of Americans are getting worse.
   1) strongly disagree
   2) somewhat disagree
   3) somewhat agree
   4) strongly agree
   8) don't know

4. American culture is increasingly endangered.
   1) strongly disagree
   2) somewhat disagree
   3) somewhat agree
   4) strongly agree
   8) don't know

[RANDOMIZE ORDER OF BATTERIES DENOTED BY ROMAN NUMERALS IV—VII]

[RANDOMIZE ORDER OF RACIAL ID AND AMERICAN ID ITEMS WITHIN THE FOLLOWING BATTERY]

III. Now I have a few questions about some social groups you may identify with. These are questions about people who may be like you in their ideas and interests and feelings about things. [RACIAL ID ACCORDING TO RACE OF R].

5. How close do you feel to other [Blacks/Whites]?
   1) not close at all
   2) not very close
   3) somewhat close
   4) very close
   8) don't know

6. Do you think what happens generally to [Black/White] people in this country will have something to do with what happens in your life?
   1) strongly disagree
   2) somewhat disagree
   3) somewhat agree
   4) strongly agree
   8) don't know

7. Do you think what happens generally to [Black/White] women in this country will have something to do with what happens in your life? [REVERSE RESPONSE CATEGORIES]
   1) strongly disagree
   2) somewhat disagree
   3) somewhat agree
   4) strongly agree
   8) don't know

8. Do you think what happens generally to [Black/White] men in this country will have something to do with what happens in your life? [REVERSE RESPONSE CATEGORIES]
   1) strongly disagree
   2) somewhat disagree
   3) somewhat agree
   4) strongly agree
   8) don't know
   [AMERICAN ID]

9. How close do you feel to other Americans?
    1) not close at all
    2) not very close
    3) somewhat close
    4) very close
    8) don't know

10. To what extent do you see yourself as a typical American?
    1) very typical
    2) somewhat typical
    3) not very typical
    4) not typical at all
    8) don't know

11. When talking about Americans, how often do you say "we" instead of "they"?
    1) not often at all
    2) not very often
    3) somewhat often
    4) very often
    8) don't know

IV. Now I want to ask you about some things which may or may not make a person feel proud about the United States. After reading each statement, please tell me, on a scale of 1 to 4, whether it makes you proud. A score of 1 means the item does not make you feel proud of America at all, and a score of 4 means the item makes you feel very proud of America.
    [PATRIOTISM]

12. The way democracy works in the U.S.
    1) not proud at all
    2) not very proud
    3) somewhat proud
    4) very proud
    8) don't know

13. America's economic achievements.
    1) not proud at all
    2) not very proud
    3) somewhat proud
    4) very proud
    8) don't know

14. America's history.
    1) not proud at all
    2) not very proud
    3) somewhat proud
    4) very proud
    8) don't know

V. Now I want to ask you about your views about the United States in relation to other nations. After reading each question, please tell me, on a scale of 1 to 4, whether you agree or disagree. A score of 1 means you strongly disagree and a score of 4 means you strongly agree.
    [NATIONALISM]

15. The world would be a better place if people from other countries were more like Americans.
    1) strongly disagree
    2) somewhat disagree
    3) somewhat agree
    4) strongly agree
    8) don't know

16. Generally speaking, America is no better than most other countries.
    1) strongly disagree
    2) somewhat disagree
    3) somewhat agree
    4) strongly agree
    8) don't know

17. Generally, the more influence America has on other nations, the better off they are.
    1) strongly disagree
    2) somewhat disagree
    3) somewhat agree
    4) strongly agree
    8) don't know

VI. Now I want to ask you some questions about what it means to be an American. Some people say the following things make somebody an American. Others say these things don't necessarily make somebody an American. For each item, please tell me whether you agree or disagree that it makes somebody an American.
    [NATIVISM]

18. To have been born in America.
    1) strongly disagree
    2) somewhat disagree
    3) somewhat agree
    4) strongly agree
    8) don't know

19. To be a Christian.
    1) strongly agree
    2) somewhat agree
    3) somewhat disagree
    4) strongly disagree
    8) don't know

20. To have lived in America for most of one's life.
    1) strongly disagree
    2) somewhat disagree
    3) somewhat agree
    4) strongly agree
    8) don't know

21. To be able to speak English.
    1) strongly agree
    2) somewhat agree
    3) somewhat disagree
    4) strongly disagree
    8) don't know

VII. The following are pairs of qualities that one might try to encourage in children. As you read each one, please indicate which one you think is more important to encourage in a child.
    [AUTHORITIARIANISM]

22. If you absolutely had to choose, would you say it is more important that a child obey his parents or that he is responsible for his own actions?
    1) obey parents
    2) responsible for own actions
    3) both equally important
    4) don't know

23. Is it more important that a child has respect for his elders, or that he thinks for himself?
    1) respect elders
    2) thinks for himself
    3) both equally important
    4) don't know

24. Is it more important that a child follows his own conscience, or that he follows the rules?
    1) follow own conscience
    2) follow the rules
    3) both equally important
    4) don't know

VIII. Before moving on, please tell me how important the following things are to you. [ATTITUDE IMPORTANCE—MODERATORS]

25. How important to you is it to identify with other [Black Americans/Whites] [ACCORDING TO RACE OF R]?
    1) not important at all
    2) not very important
    3) somewhat important
    4) very important
    8) don't know

26. How important to you is it to identify with other Americans?
    1) very important
    2) somewhat important
    3) not very important
    4) not important at all
    8) don't know

27. How important to you is it to feel proud of the United States?
    1) not important at all
    2) not very important
    3) somewhat important
    4) very important
    8) don't know

28. How important to you is it for the United States to be a better nation than other countries?
    1) very important
    2) somewhat important
    3) not very important
    4) not important at all
    8) don't know

29. How important to you is it to have been born in America?
    1) not important at all
    2) not very important
    3) somewhat important
    4) very important
    8) don't know

30. How important to you is the issue of legal immigration?
    1) very important
    2) somewhat important
    3) not very important
    4) not important at all
    8) don't know

31. How important to you is the issue of illegal immigration?
    1) Not important at all
    2) Not very important
    3) Somewhat important
    4) Very important

IX. Now I have some questions about your views regarding discrimination in the United States.

32. How often are you personally a victim of racial discrimination in your life?
    1) Not often at all
    2) Not very often
    3) Somewhat often
    4) Very often

33. Which of the following groups do you think experiences the most racial discrimination?
    [ROTATE ORDER]
    1) Blacks
    2) Whites

3) Latinos
4) Asians
5) Native Americans
6) Other
7) Don't know

34. In your opinion, [INSERT R'S RACIAL GROUP] get along best with:
[insert all groups from previous question except for R'S group]

X. The following is a question about the government in Washington, D.C. Please fill in the answer in the blank provided. Many people don't know the answer to this question, so if you don't know, just leave it blank and move on.

35. How long is the term of office for a U.S. Senator?

XI. Now I want to ask you a different set of questions. [Legal Experiment]
Control: No Information Provided
Treatment 2—Legal Latino: Our country is often thought of as nation of immigrants, which explains why so many legal immigrants continue to come to our nation. Currently, many of these legal immigrants are Latino. Some Americans believe that there are already too many legal Latino immigrants in our nation. These individuals believe that we should reduce the number of legal Latino immigrants to avoid overcrowding in our local schools and neighborhoods. Other Americans, though, believe that the current level of legal Latino immigration is just fine and should not be tinkered with. These Americans believe that we should continue to allow the same number of legal Latino immigrants as we have in the past.
Treatment 2—Legal Asian: Our country is often thought of as nation of immigrants, which explains why so many legal immigrants continue to come to our nation. Currently, many of these legal immigrants are Asian. Some Americans believe that there are already too many legal Asian immigrants in our nation. These individuals believe that we should reduce the number of legal Asian immigrants to avoid overcrowding in our local schools and neighborhoods. Other Americans, though, believe that the current level of legal Asian immigration is just fine and should not be tinkered with. These Americans believe that we should continue to allow the same number of legal Asian immigrants as we have in the past.
Treatment 3—Legal African: Our country is often thought of as nation of immigrants, which explains why so many legal immigrants continue to come to our nation. Currently, many of these legal immigrants are African. Some Americans believe that there are already too many legal African immigrants in our nation. These individuals believe that we should reduce the number of legal African immigrants to avoid overcrowding in our local schools and neighborhoods. Other Americans, though, believe that the current level of legal African immigration is just fine and

should not be tinkered with. These Americans believe that we should continue to allow the same number of legal African immigrants as we have in the past.

36. Do you think the United States should increase the number of years legal immigrants wait to become eligible for citizenship?
   1) strongly agree
   2) somewhat agree
   3) somewhat disagree
   4) strongly disagree
   8) don't know

37. Do you think the United States should decrease the annual number of legal immigrants?
   1) strongly disagree
   2) somewhat disagree
   3) somewhat agree
   4) strongly agree
   8) don't know

38. You can make your voice heard on the issue of legal immigration by joining other people in signing a public letter to Congress urging them to pay more attention to this political issue. The letter will only include your name, city and state of residence, and your stated support for Congress to decrease the annual number of legal immigrants admitted each year to the United States.
   Do you want to add your name to this public letter to Congress concerning legal immigration?
   1) Yes
   2) No

XII. Now I want to ask you a question about a prominent political figure and what their role in government is. Please fill in the answer in the blank provided. If you don't know the answer to this question, just leave it blank and move on.

39. What job or political office does John Roberts now hold?

XIII. Now I want to ask you a different set of questions [ILLEGAL EXPERIMENT].
   Control: No Information Provided
   Treatment 1—Illegal Latino: A large number of Latino immigrants have found it relatively easy to enter our country undetected. This ease of movement has permitted many of these undocumented Latino immigrants to settle and find jobs in our nation. Some Americans believe that undocumented immigration is beneficial to our economy because it supplies labor that employers demand. Other Americans

believe, however, that the unchecked flow of illegal immigrants into our country leads to more problems than benefits, such as an increase in crime.

Treatment 2—Illegal Asian: A large number of Asian immigrants have found it relatively easy to enter our country undetected. This ease of movement has permitted many of these undocumented Asian immigrants to settle and find jobs in our nation. Some Americans believe that undocumented immigration is beneficial to our economy because it supplies labor that employers demand. Other Americans believe, however, that the unchecked flow of illegal immigrants into our country leads to more problems than benefits, such as an increase in crime.

40. Do you think the U.S. should allow unauthorized immigrants to gain citizenship if they pass background checks, pay fines, and have jobs?
    1) strongly agree
    2) somewhat agree
    3) somewhat disagree
    4) strongly disagree
    8) don't know

41. Do you think U.S. immigration authorities should increase their efforts to curb the flow of illegal immigration?
    1) strongly disagree
    2) somewhat disagree
    3) somewhat agree
    4) strongly agree
    8) don't know

42. Make your voice heard on the issue of illegal immigration by joining other people in signing a public letter to Congress urging them to pay more careful attention to this political issue. The letter will only include your name, city and state of residence, and your stated support for Congress to prevent undocumented immigrants from gaining citizenship, even if they pass background checks, pay fines and have jobs.
    Do you want to add your name to this public letter to Congress concerning undocumented immigration?
    1) Yes
    2) No

XIV. Now I'd like to get your feelings toward some political figures and social groups that have been in the news these days. Using what is called a feeling thermometer, I want you to rate how you feel toward each group or individual. Ratings between 0 and 49 mean that you feel unfavorable or cool toward the group or individual. Ratings from 51 to 100 mean that you feel favorable or warm toward the group or individual. You can rate the group or individual at the 50 degree mark if you don't feel warm or cool toward them.

[RANDOMIZE ORDER OF ITEMS]

43. Democrats
     o to 49 = unfavorable toward them; 50 = neutral; 51 to 100 = favorable toward them

44. Republicans
     o to 49 = unfavorable toward them; 50 = neutral; 51 to 100 = favorable toward them

45. Latino Immigrants
     o to 49 = unfavorable toward them; 50 = neutral; 51 to 100 = favorable toward them

46. Barack Obama
     o to 49 = unfavorable toward them; 50 = neutral; 51 to 100 = favorable toward them

47. Asian Immigrants
     o to 49 = unfavorable toward them; 50 = neutral; 51 to 100 = favorable toward them

48. White Immigrants
     o to 49 = unfavorable toward them; 50 = neutral; 51 to 100 = favorable toward them

49. John McCain
     o to 49 = unfavorable toward them; 50 = neutral; 51 to 100 = favorable toward them

50. African Immigrants
     o to 49 = unfavorable toward them; 50 = neutral; 51 to 100 = favorable toward them

[SURVEY SHOULD SAMPLE U.S. BORN AFRICAN AMERICANS AND WHITE AMERICANS, 18 AND OVER].

[SURVEY DOESN'T CONTAIN POLIMETRIX'S STANDARD DEMOGRAPHIC ITEMS]

Notes

1. The term *controlling image* was originally coined by Patricia Hill Collins to explain the outsider status of black women. Collins' term assists in our understanding of the myriad ways in which those in power use stereotypes of black women to define the cultural value of this marginalized group. The power of these images resides in their ability to render black bodies as outside the boundaries of belonging and mark them as perpetual outsiders. The degree to which a group can differentiate itself from black women will make them more acceptable in the racial hierarchy. Thus, black women's "stand at the margins of society" normalize systems of oppression because, as an excluded group, they "emphasize the significance of belonging" (Collins 2000, p. 70).

2. Officer Loehmann was deemed emotionally unfit to be a police officer in a previous position. This information was not disclosed to the Cleveland police department, and, subsequent to the shooting of Tamir Rice, he was fired for not having disclosed this information in his employment application. While Tamir Rice was shot in a matter of seconds upon the officers' arrival at the scene, a grand jury declined to prosecute. Subsequent to Tamir Rice's shooting, Officer Loehmann had been hired as a part-time police officer in Bellaire, Ohio; following a public outcry he withdrew his application for employment. Officer Frank Garmback, who accompanied Loehmann to the Rice scene, had been the subject of an excessive-force lawsuit for placing a citizen in an unlawful chokehold, but had been allowed to continue in his role as a police officer. Officer Betty Shelby was charged and tried for Terrence Crutcher's murder but was acquitted. Upon her acquittal, she received back pay from the Tulsa police department. She is currently employed by the Rogers County Sheriff's Department.

3. The prevalence of cellphones has enabled the video capture of whites calling police on black people, including children, for such activities as canvassing a political

district, babysitting, taking naps in dormitory study lounges, selling lemonade, leaving an AirBnB, going to the pool in their communities, returning home, moving into their homes, sitting in coffee shops, sitting in their cars, cutting the grass, accessing homes they have purchased, grilling at a public park, attempting to use a store coupon, and other everyday acts.

4. Liberia was the focal point of many of these discussions. Established in 1820 by the American Colonization Society, Liberia was constructed to be a haven for freed slaves. However, it was largely unsuccessful at attracting black people and was criticized by a number of thinkers as a scheme by whites to rid themselves of the "Negro problem" and ease their own consciences rather than being an altruistic attempt to assist blacks. Additionally, those blacks who did migrate to Liberia were not necessarily more progressive in their attitudes and treatment of native Liberians than their white counterparts. The rift between Americo-Liberians, descendants of the black American settlers, and native Liberians was accentuated during the First Liberian Civil War in 1980. Still, there were writers like Martin Delany and Henry Highland Garnet who suggested blacks take themselves to various islands of the Caribbean as well as Latin America in an effort to achieve success and thwart white attempts to harm their social progress.

5. It is also true that some immigrants are able to access whiteness, or approximate the white ideal, where blacks cannot. Blacks light enough to "pass" are a notable exception, but this is a rare circumstance that is widely unavailable to the larger group. This is significant because access to a white racial identity brings with it a degree of cultural currency in this country. For most groups, being able to cross into whiteness was a bridge to social mobility (Erie 1978; Jacobson 2001). By gaining a more favorable position in the racial matrix, immigrants once considered nonwhite were able to gather social and economic capital despite their newcomer status. Blacks were barred from many of these programs and remained unable to access the rights and privileges associated with white identity (Perlmann 1989; Pinderhughes 1987).

6. In 2005, former Mexican president Vicente Fox said, in Spanish, "There is no doubt that Mexicans, filled with dignity, willingness and ability to work, are doing jobs that not even Blacks want to do there in the United States." Although the statement was widely rebuked, the sentiment President Fox expressed is not uncommon; the stereotype that Mexicans, as well as other immigrants, are hard-working, is relatively prevalent (Esses, Jackson, and Armstrong 1998; McClain et al. 2006; Waldinger 1997; Waters 1994). This is especially true when immigrants are juxtaposed to American-born blacks, who are more likely to be characterized as "lazy" rather than industrious (Alexander, Brewer, and Livingston 2005; Peffley, Hurwitz, and Sniderman 1997; Weber, Lavine, Huddy, and Federico 2014). However, what this concept ignores is how jobs are structured by employers so they can attract workers they deem to be easily exploited (Saucedo 2006).

7. Sigelman and Tuch (1997) have shown that blacks are well aware of the stereotypes that exist about them. Torres and Charles (2004), like Steele (1997), find that blacks internalize these negative ideas, and these (meta)stereotypes have implications for various kinds of interracial interactions, educational performance, and self-esteem.

8. Naming conventions have also been found to be a significant hurdle for blacks to access employment regardless of their skill set. Bertrand and Mullainathan (2004) confirmed that applicants with more "black sounding" names were the least likely candidates to receive callbacks. The authors' findings suggest employers make determinations regarding individuals' social class based on their names.

9. Anti-Catholic bias was an additional layer of the discrimination faced by these immigrant groups. Some reasoned that because of the organization of the Church, Catholic immigrants would be more inclined to follow the directives of the Vatican rather than act of their own free will. This resulted in wild theories that United States democracy was threatened if these immigrant groups were granted the full rights of participatory citizenship.

10. I use the terms *whiteness* and *blackness* to correspond to the social positions these racialized identities have come to signify in American life. Thus, these designations are not about color per se, but about how individuals who are differentially identified with these designations are sorted in the American racial order.

11. Sociologist Eduardo Bonilla-Silva uses the term *near white* to refer to those groups who embraced whiteness, or white racial identity, because it is the embodiment of power in this country, by distancing themselves from darker racial identities (i.e., black identity in the United States).

12. Black codes were enacted across the nation after the end of the Civil War to circumscribe black life. They varied in degree of severity, but prevented blacks from voting, serving on juries, legally possessing firearms, and providing testimony against whites in a court of law, to name a few. More pernicious, these codes devised harsher penalties for "black crimes" like theft of livestock or public drunkenness and criminalized unemployment through the use of loitering or vagrancy statutes. By criminalizing these relatively harmless crimes, states could essentially reinforce slave labor.

13. After the 2008 election of President Barack Obama, many in the media declared the United States to be "post-racial" because he was able to garner the support of white voters. Some viewed this as an indication that the United States had overcome its tortured racial past and evolved into a society that no longer harbors racial resentment. Yet, this declaration was made without any meaningful societal conversation about race, and, given the current racial climate, it seems the alleged post-racial moment was just that, because there has been nothing to suggest that Americans are any less attentive to race now than they were in prior generations.

14. Revisions of U.S. immigration policy in 1965 provided a path of entry for non-European immigrants for the first time. Caribbean immigrants are among the first sojourners of this period, arriving almost immediately after the 1965 changes, and by the 1980s there is a sharp increase in immigrants from various parts of Africa, Asia, and Latin America.

15. A Google search of "Latinos dominate Blacks" returned 11.5 million unique results. Though not scientific, this gives the reader some sense of how pervasive is this characterization of American demographics.

16. As of 2000, Latinos are the largest minority group in the United States. Although administratively enumerated as an ethnic and not a racial group, Latinos are nonetheless touted as the largest minority group, composing roughly 15 percent of the American population. Blacks are the second largest minority at 13 percent of the population, followed by Asians at roughly 6 percent and Native Americans at 2 percent.

17. In 2012, both Asian American and Latino communities increased their participation in the electorate and became a more integral part of the Obama political coalition than had been appreciated prior to this time. For a more detailed look at the Asian American and Latino electorates, refer to "Inside the 2012 Latino Electorate," by Mark Hugo Lopez and Ana Gonzalez-Barrera of the Pew Research Center (http://www.pewhispanic.org/files/2013/05/the-latino-electorate_2013-06.pdf) and the Post-Election Survey of the Asian American and Pacific Islander Voters in 2012 commissioned by the National Asian American Survey (http://www.naasurvey.com/resources/Presentations/2012-aapipes-national.pdf).

18. The daily incursions into black life—from the mundane, such as anti-black hair policies, to the spectacular, such as mass incarceration—suggest to scholars and laypersons alike that black people have yet to transcend race in such a way where their life chances are not adversely effected by their racial group membership.

19. Although the works of McClain et al. (2006, 2009) and others (Hernández-León and Zúñiga 2000; Marrow 2005) have started to look outside of traditional urban centers, there remains a bias in the literature that focuses on urban areas because these remain spaces of concentrated minority representation.

20. It is also important to note that such behaviors can be expected in situations of zero-sum competition. By definition, zero-sum situations incentivize competition because a win for one person/group represents a loss for another. Because zero-sum competition can only have one winner and the resources are finite (i.e., city council seats) there is no way to share cooperatively. Thus, competition is a predictable and necessary outcome, not a representation of some ethical failing by any person or group.

21. A notable exception was the Harold Washington campaign of Chicago in the early 1980s. Washington vigorously pursued the Latino community of that city—composed primarily of Puerto Ricans—and thus had campaign literature in the Spanish language explaining voting rights of U.S. citizens. Such measures

taken by Washington worked, and he was elected Chicago's first nonwhite mayor (Muñoz Jr. and Henry 1986) For a more complete discussion of this case and the election of Mayor David Dinkins in New York City, see John J. Betancur and Douglas C. Gills (2000) *The Collaborative City: Opportunities and Struggles for Blacks and Latinos in American Cities.*

CHAPTER 2

1. Although this party was only active from about 1843–1856, they organized, mainly in northern industrial areas, around Irish Catholic exclusion. They were able to harness the energy of this anti-immigrant fervor for electoral gain. Campaigning on fear of the "Catholic menace," they presented themselves as an alternative to the Democrats, a number of whom were Irish Catholics (Hanagan 1998). Although this movement was short-lived, they were able to win several elections in the 1850s. Their biggest achievement was control of the Massachusetts legislature and governorship in 1855 (Higham 1976). In various cities, such as Philadelphia and New York, campaign promises to hire native-born American workers were extremely popular and helped the American Republican Party win city offices. Although this organization was episodic, the sentiments of the organization and its appeal to native-born white Americans continued to resonate.

2. This controversial organization was founded in the late 2000s to stem the flow of immigrants from Mexico to the United States. Located primarily in the southwest, this organization and others like it have cropped up throughout the country.

3. Alternatively, the border control issue has also been framed as a safety concern because porous borders suggest to would-be terrorists that America is ripe for another attack.

4. For a more detailed discussion of this particular case, see Barbara M. Posadas (1982) "The Hierarchy of Color and Psychological Adjustment in an Industrial Environment: Filipinos, the Pullman Company and the Brotherhood of Sleeping Car Porters," *Labor History* 23(3): 349–73.

5. This sensibility that blacks are entitled to a certain consideration in racial matters because they are the archetypal minority in the United States would exist despite the fact immigrants naturalize and subsequent generations become birthright citizens. The fact immigrants naturalize and become some version of Americans supports the sense that blacks are unfairly penalized for their race, while those believed to be descended from immigrants are deemed more valuable because they have a culture that understands and practices hard work, thrift, and other symbols of the Protestant work ethic.

6. Mexican exclusion would not come until significantly later; however, it followed many of the same contours as Asian exclusion. For a more detailed discussion, please refer to Clare Sheridan (2002), "Contested Citizenship: National Identity and the Mexican Immigration Debates of the 1920s," *Journal of American Ethnic*

History 21(3): 3–35 and Ariela J. Gross (2003), "Texas Mexicans and the Politics of Whiteness," *Law and History Review* 21(1): 195–205.

7. The 1924 act placed quotas on immigration from Eastern and Southern Europe, Asia and India, the Caribbean, and Africa. One of the key provisions of the act was to disallow individuals from immigrating to the country if they could not become citizens. This had the effect of preventing Japanese, Indians, and other Asians from entering the country because at the time, they were not allowed to naturalize.

8. The idea of a fit citizenry is one where those who are considered part of the body politic are those viewed as having the qualities that make for a functional society. In general, the fit citizen was one who was self-possessed and able to put aside their individual needs for the greater good. Such a person was ruled by reason rather than passion; therefore, he or she practices self-governance in a way that makes the survival of a democracy possible, because this individual is concerned with doing the best thing for the most of us. Consequently, because of prevailing norms and practices, the only individuals thought to hold the requisite characteristics for citizenship were white, male, Protestant, wealthy, and educated.

9. When Senator Joe Lieberman was selected to be Al Gore's running mate in 2000, his religion became a central part of the conversation because many speculated on how Lieberman would be able to complete the duties of his position as an orthodox Jew who observes the Sabbath on Fridays. Likewise, Representative Keith Ellison (D-MN) has been heavily scrutinized as the first Muslim elected to Congress in 2007. Moreover, one of the chief oppositions to President Barack Obama was the idea that he was an undercover Muslim.

10. The relationship between acculturation and assimilation is similar to that of patriotism and nativism. Acculturation is the process of becoming familiar with the identity and practices of one's new nation. However, assimilation connotes a replacement of one's national, cultural, and ethnic identities with that of the home country such that vestiges of one's native culture are no longer perceptible. In either case, the drive is to belong in the new nation, but the acculturation approach attempts to do so while retaining cultural markers from one's native community, and assimilation seeks to obliterate those connections in order to be absorbed by the new, receiving context.

11. Dred Scott was an enslaved person who lived for two years in free territory with his owner. In Missouri, Dred Scott sued for his freedom declaring that because slavery was illegal in that territory, he was being held illegally. The Court took the case one step further and suggested Congress had overstepped its authority when they passed the Missouri Compromise in 1820. The Missouri Compromise was an attempt to contain slavery as the United States expanded westward; the idea was to permit slavery in those territories where it already existed but not to allow the expansion of this system, as Congress sought to strike a balance between slave and free states.

12. Native Americans were also named in the majority opinion, where the Court suggested that Native Americans were "foreigners not living under our Government." Thus, Native Americans, according to the Dred Scott decision, would be treated as immigrants and allowed to naturalize if they wanted to live among whites.

13. Part of the defense of this reading of the Declaration of Independence and U.S. Constitution, according to Chief Justice Taney, is the idea that the Framers were too learned to have made the mistake of including enslaved Africans in the clause, "all men are created equal," because the inclusion of blacks in the family of humankind would have been contradictory. On the contrary, as Justice Taney argued, these were great men who understood what they were writing, and some of them held slaves. Therefore, they necessarily separated black people from ideas of citizenship because black people's incapacity for civilization doomed them to a lifetime of slavery. The Founders, being aware of this, properly understood them as belongings.

14. The residency requirement was extended to five years and fourteen years in subsequent revisions of the law in 1795 and 1798, respectively. The right to naturalize was broadened to Africans in 1870, Native Americans in 1924, and Chinese were allowed to naturalize in 1943 after the official Chinese exclusion policy was repealed.

15. Even though Proposition 187 passed, it was effectively killed after being challenged on appeal. Morris (2000) found that interminority conflict did not predict black support of Proposition 187. In fact, Morris found that blacks were more likely to support the ballot measure as their personal finances improved. Thus, black support for Proposition 187 seemed to be more a function of socioeconomic status rather than racial animus. Nevertheless, 47 percent of California's black voters supported the measure (Cummings and Lambert 1997). However, the state NAACP and other organizations were firmly opposed to the act.

16. Douglass' sympathy for the Irish people was subsequent to a visit he made to the country in 1845. It was there he witnessed the Irish famine, as well as their struggle for independence—two themes that resonated with his abolitionist activities. Because citizenship was not legally granted to blacks at this time, Douglass went to Ireland as a man without a country. Therefore, he traveled to volatile Ireland without the protection of the U.S. government (Ferreira 1999). There is a mural portraying Frederick Douglass in Belfast, Ireland, where he is regarded as a hero for the voice he gave to the Irish cause in their battles with Great Britain.

17. I bracket the term *citizen* because blacks, both slave and free, were not technically American citizens at this point; citizenship was not granted to blacks until 1868. However, blacks frequently applied this appellation to themselves despite this legal formality.

18. The Reconstruction period (1865–1877) was a brief moment where blacks saw their political fortunes change. With the federal government occupying the South after the Civil War, blacks were able to successfully engage the political system and elect the first representatives to state governments across the South. However, these early successes were quickly lost upon the federal government's departure from the region. Still, the Reconstruction was not a panacea. For example, the Georgia State Legislature ejected over twenty black, duly elected officeholders in 1868. Bishop Henry McNeal Turner, a member of the African Methodist Episcopal clergy and a Civil War chaplain, was among those removed from office. His address, "On the Eligibility of Colored Members to Seats in the Georgia Legislature," offers a great reflection on this period and the state policies used to undermine black gains made during Reconstruction.

19. It should be noted that this piece was run eight times verbatim in *The Appeal* from January 1921 to March 1921. It appeared bi-weekly in January, weekly in February, and bi-weekly in 1921. Why this particular piece ran this often is unclear, but it does suggest the urgency some blacks felt with respect to the issue and the desire to have a government that would protect their interests through tighter restrictions on immigration.

20. The fact that black critics of white America, particularly journalists, did so under the threat of death has to be kept in mind. Public critics of white supremacy spoke out at great peril. Ida B. Wells-Barnett was forced to flee Memphis for her writings on lynching, and her newspaper was destroyed. Similarly, the Wilmington, NC, Race Riot of 1898 began partly because Alex Manly, the editor of the black newspaper the *Daily Record*, condemned lynching by writing that white women willingly entered into interracial relationships with black men. Manly was forced to escape Wilmington because there was a bounty offered for his death, and the *Daily Record*'s offices were destroyed, as were original issues of the newspaper. The *Daily Record* never recovered, and Alex Manly never returned to North Carolina. Moreover, because of the riot, a number of Wilmington's black residents fled the city. Race riots like that in Wilmington occurred in Springfield, IL (1908), East St. Louis, IL (1917), Tulsa, OK (1921), and Rosewood, FL (1923). Thus, given the racial climate of this time, any type of perceived opposition to white supremacy was dealt with by extreme shows of force. In fact, simply being black was a crime that could result in punishment. Mary Frances Berry, in her piece "Reckless Eyeballing: The Matt Ingram Case and the Denial of African American Sexual Freedom," (2008) discusses the ways in which black bodies are criminalized.

21. Rayford Logan defined "the Nadir" as a period where black efforts to gain equality were fiercely resisted, legally and extra-legally. For example, the *Plessy v. Ferguson* (1896) decision affirmed the constitutionality of Jim Crow, lynching of black people increased, and the general retreat away from black civil rights was fairly widespread. Although Logan stopped his analysis, scholars have extended his

original periodization and argue "the Nadir" lasted until around 1940, where white supremacist behavior nationally was at its peak.

22. It should be noted that these were very masculinist conceptions of national belonging (Estes 2005). Although black women were as much a part of the black struggle, voting rights were not fully extended to black women until the Voting Rights Act of 1965. The right to vote was not granted to women until 1920 by the 19th Amendment, and to blacks not until 1965, doubly excluding black women.

23. This is not to suggest that European immigrants were not racialized. Nor is it to suggest that blacks were unaware of the ways in which whites used employed immigrants from other parts of the world, such as Asia, to undermine their efforts at employment equity, higher wages, better working conditions, and the like. What it does suggest is that blacks were far more empathetic to the motivations of immigrants of all stripes for coming to the United States, but not to the ways in which these immigrants were mobilized to retard black upward mobility.

24. Immigration is far from the only issue to have a dampening effect on black optimism. Events such as Hurricane Katrina, the murder of Trayvon Martin, the rollback of voting rights provisions and statewide voter intimidation initiatives, high unemployment, rampant incarceration, as well as a host of other issues, also matter. Although these issues are not the focus of this text, I wish to acknowledge their import as it pertains to the development and crystallization of black public opinion.

25. Groups like Choose Black America and the African American Leadership Council are exceptions. Although these groups are fronted by blacks, they cannot claim to represent black interests. In particular, Choose Black America was founded by the Federation of American Immigration Reform (FAIR), a larger, majority white, anti-immigrant organization, which discredits their claims to speaking for a general black population. Likewise, the AALC is highly critical of established black organizations such as the Congressional Black Caucus and the NAACP for being too lenient on immigration in ways that hurt black Americans. The Black American Leadership Alliance, founded in 2013, is another ardently anti-immigrant group, has organized rallies in opposition to immigration, and is opposed to any type of amnesty for undocumented persons. Despite the sensationalism surrounding these groups, they are far from mainstream organizations and do not represent the prevailing attitudes of blacks with respect to immigration as borne out by numerous public opinion polls. These groups are in no discernible way connected to black America. For example, the Pew Research Center (2006) shows that blacks generally hold positive views with respect to immigrants despite their concerns about economic competition from Latino immigrants. This mirrors work by Thornton and Mizuno (1999), which shows that blacks typically have warmer feelings toward immigrants than they do toward whites. Additionally, both the NAACP and The National Urban League

have issued statements supporting comprehensive immigration reform. This is significant because, as long-standing organizations focused on the betterment of black lives, these agencies recognize the import of immigration reform for black progress. As Marc Morial, president of the National Urban League, noted, it is important to have temporary work visas for immigrants provided there is also job training particularly for blacks and Latino citizens, so that their job prospects are not harmed by the presence of immigrants.

26. Marcus Garvey's Universal Negro Improvement Association (UNIA) focused strongly on the resettlement of black people in their ancestral homeland of Africa. Garvey's attempts to finance this action through the ill-fated Black Star Line would be the impetus for his prosecution and subsequent incarceration in federal prison, after which he was deported to London.

27. A form of this black nationalist tradition of self-determination was still around in the later twentieth century as blacks experimented with alternative living practices in this country. For example, Soul City, North Carolina, was established in 1969 as one of the first model city programs in the country. The idea was to make a racially harmonious community that would serve the educational, social, health, and recreational needs of the area's largely black rural community. Similarly, the Republic of New Africa was conceived by the Black Government Conference as a self-sustaining nation to serve the needs of black Americans. The country would be composed of majority-black states of the former Confederacy (Mississippi, Louisiana, Georgia, Alabama, and South Carolina) and would secede from the United States. The belief was that as long as blacks continued to live within the confines of a white-identified country they could never hope for true self-determination. The MOVE Organization based in Philadelphia, Pennsylvania, was another attempt by blacks to lead self-sustaining lives. Founded in 1972, MOVE was a small organization whose members lived communally, eschewed technology, and maintained a vegan lifestyle. Most of the members of MOVE were killed when the Philadelphia Police Department bombed their home in 1985. Eleven people, including several children, were killed by the bombing. Ramona and Birdie Africa were the only two survivors.

28. This has changed somewhat in the current political environment because immigration has become a much more prominent national issue. A July 2013 Gallup poll cites immigration as an important issue, but is not as salient as unemployment.

CHAPTER 3

1. This is not to suggest a majority of free blacks lived in the North. Free blacks, like the enslaved, lived primarily in the South. Still, they often lived in larger cities away from rural areas where they may have been enslaved. As Ira Berlin notes in *Slaves without Masters* (1975), women composed the majority of free blacks in

the South because men had a tendency to leave the region. Moreover, free blacks tended to be older than the enslaved population because they may have had to accrue the funds to buy their freedom, or their owners manumitted them when they became less valuable. Please consult Berlin for a more detailed discussion of the free black population.

2. Colonization has typically been used to refer to the process of inhabiting other lands for the purposes of empire building. In the case of blacks it was more akin to setting up an expatriate community, which is not typically done for the purposes of expanding national territories and influence.

3. The term *refugee* is typically used to refer to those persons who have fled their country because of conflict or various forms of persecution. An internally displaced person is similar, with the important distinction of not having crossed an international boundary. Legalities aside, I employ the terms that blacks used to describe their status during this period.

4. According to the United Nations, a stateless person is one without nationality or citizenship. Blacks prior to 1868 were *de jure* stateless people. They were essentially unclaimed by the United States as citizens; in fact, the primary legal definition for black people until this point was that of property. Thus, because of their primary status as enslaved—or at least that had been the beginning of their narrative in what would become the United States—they struggled with identifying their place in the American body politic because the country was so thoroughly bifurcated by color as slave (read as racially black) and free (read as racially white). Consequently, because race had become shorthand for who belonged and who did not, being a free black person did not confer citizenship. Black non-citizenship was affirmed by the Supreme Court decision in *Dred Scott v. Sandford* (1857). This is not to suggest that this was a settled matter, because the fact the Supreme Court entertained a suit filed by a black person can be read as acknowledgment that blacks were in some small measure a part of the American landscape, even though the standing of Dred Scott to bring the case was at issue. Nevertheless, the fact that black citizenship had to be conferred by Constitutional amendment, despite the colorblind language employed in the Constitution, suggests blacks were not citizens as properly understood by the Founders, as highlighted by Justice Taney in his decision. If nothing else, these seeming contradictions provide limited evidence of the uncertainty regarding blacks and their status as members of the republic. For a more detailed discussion of stateless persons, refer to the United Nations High Commissioner on Refugees (http://www.unhcr.org/4cb2fe326.html).

5. In 1934, as he resigned from the NAACP, DuBois delivered a speech entitled "A Negro Nation within a Nation," wherein he reasoned that because of the indefatigable nature of white supremacy, integration would be thwarted at every turn. Because of the social segregation, blacks represented a quasi-nation within the United States because they had their own religious, educational, and economic

institutions. Therefore, blacks had to take care to nurture these institutions and use their significant educational and financial resources for the betterment of their own communities, because the majority of whites were invested in maintaining black exclusion from the public sphere. Black communities had to be invested in and focused on their own survival, and perhaps turn away from their integrationist hopes in the moment in favor of strengthening the black community.

6. The term *emigration* is usually employed when talking about the moves made on the part of black Americans because their movements were part of an exodus; essentially, they were moving out of the country. *Immigration* is employed to talk about people moving into a new homeland. The term chosen is largely about perspective: because of the liminal space occupied by blacks, they were both emigrants and immigrants at different points in time. Moreover, where they use the term *emigrant* I have preserved that usage.

7. Paul Cuffee was a wealthy, free man from Massachusetts. A devout Quaker of Ghanaian origin, Cuffee left Philadelphia in 1810 on an expedition to present-day Sierra Leone to investigate the possibility of black resettlement in the country. Although he remained committed to emigration, he worked outside the auspices of organizations like the ACS because of the endemic racism of these groups. For a more detailed discussion of Paul Cuffee and his work, see Lamont D. Thomas (1988), *Paul Cuffee: Black Entrepreneur and Pan Africanist* (Urbana and Chicago: University of Illinois Press).

8. In 1787 the British established a settlement in Sierra Leone, West Africa, for black Loyalists who had to leave the colonies at the conclusion of the American Revolution.

9. Gabriel, popularly referred to as Gabriel Prosser, was a skilled blacksmith hired out by his master. Historian Doug Egerton posits that Gabriel was probably inspired, in part, by the Haitian Revolution (1791), which established Haiti as the first independent black republic in the western hemisphere. This rebellion was supposed to take place in Richmond with the main aim of negotiating an end to slavery in the state of Virginia. The rebellion was thwarted as other enslaved persons told of the plan. Although the rebellion did not occur, the state subsequently more carefully tracked the movements of enslaved persons and was less hospitable to free blacks. In 1806, the state of Virginia passed a law requiring free blacks manumitted on or after May 1, 1806, to leave the state within a year or risk (re)enslavement; those who wished to stay in Virginia had to petition the state government for permission. In many ways, this law turned blacks into forced immigrants because the only alternative was voluntary enslavement (Maris-Wolf 2015). Conditions for blacks would only worsen in 1831 after Nat Turner's Rebellion in Southampton County, Virginia. At this time, the state of Virginia and other southern states prohibited blacks from gathering for religious purposes without white supervision, banned all manner of education and literacy, and restricted black gun ownership.

10. Because of the demand for free labor, the black populations of South Carolina, Virginia, Georgia, and Mississippi outnumbered whites. For extensive maps of the slave population, see the Schomburg Center for Research in Black Culture's project on Black Migration (http://www.inmotionaame.org/gallery/ ?migration=3&topic=7&type=map).

11. Henry Clay served the state of Kentucky as senator and representative in the U.S. Congress. He is best known for negotiating several compromises around the issue of slavery—most notably the Missouri Compromise (1820) and the Compromise of 1850, which effectively quelled sectional conflicts by allowing the institution of slavery to remain unchallenged.

12. Randolph was a U.S. congressman from Virginia who defended the institution of enslavement because his livelihood depended on the free labor of Africans. Upon his death, those he enslaved were manumitted and resettled in Ohio.

13. All of these states had passed or attempted to pass resolutions barring the settlement of free blacks within their borders. Pennsylvania also attempted such legislation in 1813.

14. Nevertheless, the ACS was founded with the idea of improving race relations by supporting the removal of blacks and sending them to Sierra Leone and Liberia. The founding of the society brought together a number of strange bedfellows. Abolitionist Quakers and members of the slave-owning elite formed the ACS with the belief that blacks' chances for advancement would be better if they existed in a society where their skin color was not a barrier to progress. While both groups supported the move, they did so for varied reasons. Those with abolitionist leanings did not see color prejudice receding and reasoned blacks would be better off in the land of their origin. They viewed sending blacks to Africa as a form of penance for the destruction slavery had caused the continent of Africa. Moreover, those blacks who were repatriated would be able to "civilize" their African counterparts via Christianity and education. A byproduct of Africa's development would be an end to the slave trade. If slaveholders knew they could free their property and send them away, they could feel more secure and thus be more inclined to manumit slaves. The manumitted would then go to Africa and help her develop her gifts. They reasoned that if the continent were adequately developed, she would have more to offer the world than her human cargo. Slaveholders were concerned that the presence of free blacks would increase the chance of rebellion, which is why some supported the ACS. Some believed if blacks remained anywhere in the United States they might make "common cause with the Indians and border nations, and furnish an asylum for fugitives and runaway slaves" (Sherwood 1917: 222). Thus, the importance of disconnecting free blacks from their enslaved counterparts outweighed the costs associated with their removal and relocation. The removal of free blacks from the United States was the ultimate goal of the ACS, and this was their chief concern. Their message was tailored to fit whatever region they were trying to

persuade to join their cause. This helped the ACS gain traction in white circles, but they were unable to convince a majority of blacks to buy into their ideas. Blacks would not separate the ACS's goals from its myriad messages—all of which portrayed blacks as the source of the trouble. For a more detailed discussion see Forbes (1990: 210–223) and Sherwood (1917: 209–228).

15. In 1819, the federal government pledged $100,000 to the ACS. The first ship to Liberia left in 1820 and transported two whites and 88 black emigrants. These first sojourners died of yellow fever and other tropical diseases. At this time, there were approximately 2 million blacks in the United States; around 200,000 of those were free blacks.

16. Between 1816 and 1830, approximately 2,600 blacks were resettled in Liberia.

17. This meant the franchise would need to be extended to poor whites if elite whites were going to protect their social dominance. Thus, the vote was given grudgingly by elite whites who did not think highly of the uneducated mob the Founders warned against in the Federalist Papers. Nevertheless, elite whites recognized that an uncontrolled class of angry whites would not serve their ends well. As such, the first grandfather clauses were passed in 1898 following the demise of Reconstruction (1876); these laws enfranchised poor white men who heretofore had been summarily excluded from the voting rolls. By linking the right to vote with the status of one's grandfather in 1867, white elites could still use slavery as the basis for white solidarity without extending any material gains to poor whites. By relying on racial appeals that harkened back to America's slave-owning past, white elites gave poor white men some false sense of superiority without any corresponding change in status. This extension of racial coverture helped galvanize whites in their opposition to black attempts at social equality. Yet the only interests being served by such attempts were those of white elites, who would continue to occupy higher stations because aspirational whiteness would be enough to feed the needs of their white brethren for another century, or longer, depending on how one reads the political winds.

18. Some of the leaders of this meeting were James Forten, Russell Parrott, Rev. Absalom Jones, Rev. Richard Allen, Robert Douglass, Francis Perkins, and Robert Gordon.

19. This, however, did not mean all blacks gave up on colonization completely. Martin Delany, for example, argued that accepting white resources was a misguided reliance on their altruism. If blacks were to be truly independent they would need to emigrate with their own funds.

20. At the same time Garnet was the president of the Africa Colonization Society, he was working under the aegis of the Haytian [*sic*] Emigration Bureau, which hired him to encourage blacks to settle the island nation. Trumpeting Haiti's distinction as the first free black country in the western hemisphere after defeating France, Garnet wrote in the *Anglo-African* (1860), "Hayti needs population to develope [*sic*] her agricultural and mineral resources and to fortify and defend her against

the invasion of the slave power of the western world" (Garnet 2004: 32). Framing emigration as a way to fend off slavery, Garnet was attempting to induce those blacks who held the nation in such esteem to emigrate there. His argument was not that Africa was less important, but that it did not need the population as urgently as Haiti.

21. Martin R. Delany was born free in West Virginia. He was an ardent nationalist and had his first introduction to colonization through the First Negro Convention held in Philadelphia in 1831. Although he remained dedicated to emigration throughout his life, he remained in the United States to fight the emancipation of enslaved blacks in the Union Army and because of personal obligations.

CHAPTER 4

1. Preclearance was a provision of section 4(b) of the Voting Rights Act that made covered jurisdictions seek preapproval from the Department of Justice to make any changes to the time, manner, and location of elections. This section was essentially gutted by the Supreme Court in *Shelby County v. Holder* (2013). The majority opinion of the Court held that preclearance is unconstitutional because the coverage formula was based on data that was over 40 years old. This made it possible for state election officials to circumvent voter protections, and ushered in a wave of voter identification measures, exact match laws, and shortening of early voting periods that had proved a boon for minority voters in previous elections. The abandonment of this provision of the Voting Rights Act has had the (unintended) consequence of legalizing, or at least countenancing, voter suppression efforts in more than half the states in the union. For a more detailed discussion of voter suppression in the aftermath of *Shelby County v. Holder* see Blacksher, James, and Lani Guinier. "Free at Last: Rejecting Equal Sovereignty and Restoring the Constitutional Right to Vote: Shelby County v. Holder." *Harvard Law & Policy Review* 8 (2014): 39.

2. North Carolina has been ground zero for many of the recent fights around the retrenchment of voting rights for blacks in the state. Started by Rev. William Barber, head of the North Carolina NAACP, the Moral Mondays protests began in 2012 when Republican Governor Pat McCrory and the Republican majority legislation made moves to restrict voting rights as well as passage of a more conservative agenda that endangered the environment and various social programs. Since the beginning of this social justice movement, its model of civil disobedience has spread to other states around the country.

3. Atlanta, GA, is most akin to Durham, NC, in this respect. The black community of Durham began in the 1880s, and the black businesses of that city got their start in the late nineteenth and early twentieth centuries—earlier than other cities with large, black middle-class populations. Although lacking much of its former reverence, Durham was an extremely popular destination for blacks seeking better

fortunes. In its prime, Durham was held in great esteem by scholars (DuBois 1912; Frazier [1957] 1997) and laypersons alike, having a reputation as "Black Wall Street" because of the presence of North Carolina Mutual and Mechanics and Farmers Bank, which ultimately stimulated the growth of other black-owned businesses along Parrish Street.

4. North Carolina Mutual and Life Insurance Company was founded by John Merrick—barber to tobacco executive Washington Duke and multiple–business owner—and Dr. Aaron M. Moore, Durham's first black physician. Later, Charles Clinton (C.C.) Spaulding was brought in during the company's reorganization. Overall, there were seven men associated with the founding of the company, including Dr. James E. Shepard, founder of NCCU, and W.G. Pearson, local businessman and business associate of John Merrick.

5. The Mechanics and Farmers Bank was chartered by a collective of black businessmen in the city of Durham. These included R. B. Fitzgerald, J. A. Dodson, J. R. Hawkins, John Merrick, Aaron M. Moore, W. G. Pearson, James E. Shepard, G. W. Stephens, and Stanford L. Warren.

6. C.C. Spaulding was a well-respected Durham businessman. The son of an ex-slave, Spaulding was the president of five companies. He founded three insurance companies, a bank, and a property company.

7. It should be noted that blacks did live in other parts of the city; however, Hayti was the flagship neighborhood that anchored most of black life in Durham until it was greatly disabled by the building of North Carolina Highway 147. For a more detailed discussion of Hayti and other black Durham neighborhoods, consult Andre Vann and Beverly W. Jones, *Durham's Hayti* (1999), and Pauli Murray's (1999) biography *Proud Shoes*.

8. However, entrepreneurship was not a guarantee of blacks' safety. North Carolina Mutual and Life Insurance Company built fireproof headquarters presumably because of the very real possibility of arson at the hands of white criminals (Brown and Valk 2004). Moreover, the company also provided some residential space for female employees who may have been harassed by white landlords for their association with the company as well as facing sexual harassment by white men because of their unprotected status as black women (Brown and Valk 2004).

9. The North Carolina College for Negroes was renamed the North Carolina Central University in 1969 after undergoing several name changes. Founded by Dr. James E. Shepard and chartered in 1909 as a religious training school, the university opened in 1910 and later became a teacher's college for blacks with the help of Mrs. Russell Sage (Anderson 1990). By 1925 the school was expanded to a liberal arts college, and by the 1940s it began to incorporate graduate training. By the 1970s North Carolina Central University was a regional university joining the Consolidated University of North Carolina system.

10. According to Gershenhorn, at the time of the Hocutt case North Carolina had more college and normal school students than any other segregated state (2001: 283).

11. Hocutt was unable to include a certified transcript with his application because James Shepard refused to send the transcript to UNC. UNC would not accept an unofficial transcript sent directly by Hocutt (Anderson 1990). Although this technical detail did not matter much, it should be noted UNC's pharmacy program was an undergraduate program, thus it was argued by Hocutt's legal team that a college transcript was not needed.

12. Shepard was still reeling from a public relations fiasco in 1930 where he supported John J. Parker, a Supreme Court nominee put forward by Herbert Hoover. The black community stood against Shepard because Parker was very vocal in his denial of black voting rights. As such, in 1933 at the time of the Hocutt case, Shepard could not afford another public dust-up with the black community. Although the Depression heightened Shepard's anxiety about continued funding for NCCN from whites, he depended on the black community for the conferral of legitimacy and authority as a leader. Because the majority of blacks were in favor of Hocutt's efforts, Shepard and Spaulding were very careful in how they approached this case.

13. All parties, including the national NAACP, agreed an appeal in the Hocutt case was a lost cause given the state's racial climate and the fact that Hocutt was not a strong student. Still, they opted not to refile the case rather than to bump Hocutt as the lead plaintiff, citing Hocutt's bravery in participating in the case. Alas, the case was never appealed, and Hocutt never became a pharmacist. Hocutt relocated to New York City where he worked for the transit authority.

14. For a more detailed history of the founding and legacy of the North Carolina Central University College of Law, please refer to "So Far" (http://law.nccu.edu/wordpress/img/uploads/2010/09/so-far-2009.pdf).

15. By 1953 activism had reached new heights in Durham; there had been a race riot in the Hayti neighborhood, and a 16-year-old girl was fined for refusing to go to the back of the bus (both events occurred in 1943). Also, by 1944 two black police officers were added to the Durham police force. Moreover, the prosperity of Durham's black community was recognized nationally by a feature in *Ebony* magazine.

16. It should be noted that because Durham had such a high number of black registered voters at the passage of the Voting Rights Act (1965), this county was not covered by the Act. The same is true of Wake and Orange counties. Given the disastrous Supreme Court decision in *Shelby County v. Holder* (2013), key provisions of the VRA, such as preclearance, have been struck down, and now approximately 40 counties are no longer covered by Section 5 of the VRA.

17. These cases consolidated after initially being filed in 1960 for the dismantling of segregation in the Durham County and city school systems. This case effectively

pushed Durham city and county to form a unitary school district. This case would be revisited several times as the plaintiffs continually sought further relief, especially in light of Supreme Court rulings such as *Green v. School Board of New Kent County* (1968). This ruling found the freedom of choice plans being used by the different Durham administrative school units to address segregation to be inadequate to disassemble school segregation. However, the *Wheeler* case would not be settled well into the 1970s, with other administrative matters surrounding the case not settled until the early 1980s.

18. The Merger Issues Task Force was followed by the Merger Vision Task Force, which reviewed the initial report and recommended a merger of the school systems (Apostoleris 2018).

19. In 2002 the local NAACP, under the leadership of Curtis Gatewood, filed complaints with the Department of Education charging that Superintendent Ann Denlinger, a white woman, violated the policy on site-based decision-making committees when she fired the principal of Hillside High School, a historically black high school, replacing him without the input of this committee. The complaint claimed that Denlinger had destabilized the learning environment of Hillside High School because of her constant administrative changes (Cyna 2019; Herriott 2001). Moreover, Denlinger aroused further anger when she required 24 Hillside employees to reapply for their positions (Abram 2002; WRAL 2002b). Another investigation was launched by the Office of Civil Rights in 1998 after the Durham Committee for the Affairs of Black People charged that black students were being unfairly suspended and placed in remedial and special education classes. The Office of Civil Rights came to the conclusion that these charges were unfounded subsequent to an 18-month investigation. Another lawsuit was heard in 2007 regarding the targeting of black students for suspension (WRAL 2007). This case was subsequently dismissed.

20. According to Durham Public Schools, black students are 44.7% of the public school students; 30.7% are Hispanic/Latino; and 18.8% are white. For more information on the demographic breakdown, please refer to durham.schoolwires.net//site/Default.aspx?PageID=324. As of the 2016, blacks make up approximately 37% of the city's 254,620 residents; the remainder of the city is 42 percent non-Hispanic White, 4 percent Asian, and 14 percent Latino (of any race). For a more detailed breakdown of Durham city and county by race, please see the U.S. Census.

21. Communal narratives, also called creation stories, are ubiquitous. In some cases these are based on genetics, others around culture or geography. Regardless of their orientation, these narratives are considered constitutive of group identity and provide the "roots" of a group's ongoing connection, thereby guarding against potential cultural dislocation. In sum, these narratives provide a fairly stable basis for the existence of a group and its members that is considered necessary and valuable.

22. Although there were free blacks, the institution of slavery necessarily bounded their freedom because of their racial identity as black people. Thus, the free black experience was different, but nonetheless connected to those enslaved. In fact, free blacks were very active in the abolition movement, and in many cities, like Philadelphia, they organized mutual aid societies and other efforts to assist escaped slaves and those relocating to free states (Hershberg 1971). For a more thorough discussion of free blacks and their activism, see Leon Litwack's *North of Slavery: The Negro in the Free States* (2009) and Horton and Horton's *In Hope of Liberty: Culture, Community and Protest among Northern Free Blacks, 1700–1860* (1996).

23. Although thirteen is not a large number, it has been demonstrated that for non-probabilistic samples, themes are made apparent in as early as six interviews. Moreover, "saturation," the point at which the researcher ceases to discover new information by the inclusion of additional participants, is reached in approximately twelve interviews (Guest, Bunce, and Johnson 2006). Although I can hardly determine causation from the number of interviews I have, this is not the purpose of these interviews. I use the interviews to provide an understanding of the ways blacks talk about immigration, which is the crux of public opinion. Everyday talk has been shown to provide the best evidence for what black people think (Harris-Lacewell 2004; Price 2009; Sawyer 2005). Surveys are a way to measure certain ideas, but they are limited by the imagination and resources of their creators. The interview is another tool that can give us important insights, albeit in a different fashion and with more nuance.

24. This is to suggest that in a moment where there is a black president, yet the Supreme Court has been steadily eroding the force of the Voting Rights Act, it would seem that greater equality for black people is on the wane. Indeed, it has been argued by Perea (1997) and others (Bell 1993; Von Eschen 1997) that black people only received greater social inclusion when it became important for the United States' interests, as in the Cold War. Another important part of these moments was the organizing activities of black people (Parker 2009; Von Eschen 1997).

25. In *Democracy and the Foreigner* (2001), Honig argues that immigrants are symbols of renewal. Immigrants reaffirm our beliefs in the nation and its principles at times when we are undergoing great challenge. For example, Honig explains that stories of immigrants' successes at a time of economic distress, such as during economic recession, function to renew the belief of the less successful native-born in upward mobility, despite rampant unemployment. In this way, immigrants allow us to remain hopeful about our future economic progress despite indicators that would suggest otherwise. By renewing our collective faith in the bedrock principles of hard work and economic success, the core principles of capitalism that structure such negative outcomes remain unchallenged.

26. In her text, *Facing Up to the American Dream*, Jennifer Hochschild describes the "American Dream" as an ideology that suggests and "individual can attain success and virtue through strenuous effort." Those groups who are not successful are viewed as somehow deficient because they are seen as having poor cultural values that do not support social progress. This is a particularly pernicious myth that has plagued black communities for decades but became more crystallized with the infamous Moynihan Report that blamed a "pathological" black culture for upholding a "culture of poverty" antithetical to American virtues of hard work, thrift, and delayed gratification (Nunnally and Carter 2012). Hochschild finds the most likely culprit of this lack of success as the nation's failure to provide enough access to those institutions we know create the kind of success the American Dream espouses.

27. In 2013, a Tea Party operative by the name of Glynis Racine sent a Twitter message that read "White Irish slavers were treated worse than any other race in the US. When is the last time you heard an Irishman bitching & moaning about how the world owes them a living?" The offending message, though it does not mention black people by name, attempts to shame black people into leaving the legacy of slavery behind, which she reads as both historically inaccurate because some Irish people were enslaved, and as "bitching & moaning" by blacks who are simply holding onto the legacy of enslavement in an effort to receive a handout, presumably from the government. Although the offending tweet was quickly removed, her follow-up message read, "Slavery is a black mark on American history, but it's time to move on." Again, imploring those who commemorate slavery as woefully stuck "back there" and unable to move on, failing to acknowledge that neither she nor any other person can tell black people when it's "time to move on," and that people do not want to leave the legacy of slavery behind because that would be, in many ways, leaving themselves behind. To read more about this incident, coverage can be found here: http://www.huffingtonpost.com/2013/12/18/tea-party-racist-tweet_n_4467221.html. More recently, the fight to remove, or preserve, Confederate statues curiously mirrored many of these same conversations—except whites reacted violently to the removal of these monuments to white supremacy. In Charlottesville, VA, protests by white supremacist groups and their sympathizers resulted in the death of Heather Heyer, other injured persons, and property damage.

28. Although there are no strict rules for responsible group membership, there have been ongoing discussions within the black community about what it means to be a member of the racial group. Many of these conversations were not simply about political preferences but also about individual behaviors and how they reflect on the esteem of the group (Cohen 1999; Gaines 1996; Griffin 2000; Kelly 2010; White 2007; Wolcott 1997). Often called the *politics of respectability*, early efforts on the part of blacks adhered to these principles, which preached moral rectitude and good values as the key to group success. Although this has

shifted over time, it is clear there is something called a black community self-identified racial group that members value. Further, this identity has real political implications, as authors as diverse as Dawson (2001), Greer (2013), Harris, Sinclair-Chapman, and McKenzie (2006), Harris-Perry (2011), Nunnally (2012), Parker (2009), and Price (2009) have demonstrated. Although prosecuting racial group interests is one of the outcomes of responsible group membership, group solidarity can have differential outcomes for different group members. For example, group members of nonconforming sexualities, women, and/or poor may not have their interests acknowledged, if represented at all, and many deny their individual needs so as to not besmirch the identity of the larger group, especially when that group, like blacks, has a stigmatized public identity (Nunnally and Carter 2012; Carter and Pérez 2015; Cohen 1997, 1999).

29. Justice Harlan was the sole dissenter to the Supreme Court's "separate but equal" logic in the *Plessy v. Ferguson* case. Nevertheless, although Harlan frames his dissent based on a reading of the U.S. Constitution as a colorblind document, he clearly has a view of racial hierarchy that places white citizens as top-tiered citizens. He does not view whites as in any danger because of their numerical superiority; he does see the potential for white supremacy to be threatened by fomenting distrust among the black population because of this ruling, which suggests blacks do not have enough self-control to sit in train cars alongside whites. In short, according to Harlan, allowing blacks to avail themselves of public facilities will not bring about the equality of races in all spheres. For a complete reading of Harlan's decision, see *Plessy v. Ferguson* 163 U.S. 537, 229 (1896). To see a legal analysis of the Harlan dissent, see Haney-Lopez (2007), "A Nation of Minorities": Race, Ethnicity, and Reactionary Colorblindness, *Stanford Law Review* 59(4): 985–1063.

30. Although the Supreme Court decision in *Brown v. Board of Education* (1954) is often cited as the dissolution of segregation because it overturned the "separate but equal" rule of the *Plessy v. Ferguson* case, these practices would continue well into the 1960s because states were able to maneuver around these dictates, and the "all deliberate speed" clause of the Brown decision was sufficiently vague that states could avoid acting on the directive immediately.

31. There are many events that individuals may not experience personally or in a profound way (because of distance or lack of interest), but they can form some recollection of it because of the significance of that event. For example, September 11, 2001, had a significant impact on many Americans who were separated from the primary zones of attack. However, because the event was framed as an attack on "us" (i.e., America) and it was covered as the most significant terrorist attack on the nation, over and above the Oklahoma City bombing, that moment has a special place in American collective memory and identity. In contradistinction to September 11 is the enslavement period. Although this period is arguably one of the most traumatic for this country, and not only for black people, this

trauma is not framed or experienced as an "American tragedy." Despite the institution of slavery being the catalyst for the Civil War, this nation is far more
comfortable venerating these battles than the lives of black people who were the
lynchpin of this historical moment. Although I do not wish for black people to
be caricatured as enslaved persons for the purposes of recreating the past, this
nation has not had a full discussion on slavery or race. The attempts to do so
often have been thwarted or never fully realized. The Clinton Forum on Race
circa 1992 was heralded as this moment, but the report from this moment was
largely ignored, and none of the measures the working group suggested were
ever addressed. For a more detailed discussion about the psychology of memory,
see Pennebaker, Rim, and Paez 2013).

32. There are different terminologies used by scholars of memory, such as "collective," "social," and "cultural." These differences are largely about disciplinary
approach rather than disagreement about the important social considerations in
memory creation, production, and perpetuation. Although I do not attempt to
adjudicate these issues here, for the sake of clarity I refer to "collective memory"
throughout this chapter, yet retain the authors' language when discussing their
theories.

33. Unlike September 11, the trauma of enslavement and the Jim Crow period are
collectively ignored, if not outright denied, because the so-called black experience is viewed in many ways as separate and apart from the American experience. Instead, America is characterized as being part of a legacy of resistance
from Great Britain, the Founding, and the documents of this founding moment.
However, Abdel-Nour argues that national responsibility is ours by virtue of our
national identity. Thus, for us to claim the triumphs of the Founding we also
have to accept responsibility for the terrors of this time, such as enslavement. As
he states, "an Individual incurs a national responsibility for actions performed
by others (dead or alive) when she actively associates herself in a very specific
way with these actions" despite the length of time that has passed (Abdel-Nour
2003: 694). Yet, the responsibility for the egregious treatment of blacks in the
recent past is not something the United States has managed well. For example,
there has yet to be more than a tepid acknowledgement of responsibility for the
harm caused to blacks in specific cases of terrorism, like the Wilmington, NC
Race Riots of 1898 and the Tulsa, OK Race Riots of 1921.

34. Voter identification laws have either been enacted or have been placed on the
legislative agenda in 30 states. These laws typically increase the identification
necessary to register to vote. They have been criticized as thinly veiled measures
to discourage voters of color who are not as likely to have the various forms of
identification required by these new state laws (i.e., social security cards, birth
certificates, state-issued photo identification) and the least likely to feel politically efficacious and turn out. Further, some critics argue that by requiring state-
issued photo identification and/or birth certificates, which are not provided for

free, these laws would have the effect of making people pay for the privilege to vote, which is illegal (Gaskins and Iyer 2012). Thus, these laws do not and are not devised to stop virtually nonexistent voter fraud. They are in place to prevent chronic nonvoters from even attempting to participate through intimidation. In October 2013, a North Carolina Republican operative, Don Yelton, admitted on "The Daily Show" that these laws were meant to hurt black voters and deprive Democrats of their votes.

35. Emantic Bradford, Jr. was shot in the back three times on Thanksgiving 2018 after being misidentified as a mall shooter. Twenty-one-year-old Chavis Carter was found shot in the head inside an Arkansas police cruiser in summer 2012. Mr. Carter was in the company of two white men when they were pulled over for suspicious activity. However, he was the only person detained by the police. Although Mr. Carter died while in police custody, no formal charges were brought against the officers. An unarmed Jonathan Farrell was shot ten times by a police officer that he was running toward for help after a traumatic car accident. The officer who killed the recent college graduate has been charged with voluntary manslaughter. In 2014, John Crawford was killed by a police officer inside of an Ohio Walmart holding a BB gun sold by the store. In 2015, Freddie Gray died while in police custody due to spinal cord injuries. Six officers were charged in his death but were either acquitted or not prosecuted. In 2018, Botham Jean was shot and killed in his home by Dallas office Amber Guyger who wrongfully entered Mr. Jean's home. She is currently awaiting trial on the charge of manslaughter.

36. My mother, like my father, both graduated from segregated high schools and attended historically black colleges despite the passage of *Brown v. Board of Education* (1954). In fact, many of the public accommodations in my mother's hometown that would have had to be integrated, such as schools and movie theaters, were either privatized or shuttered. The trend toward creating private schools that were de facto "white only" institutions to circumvent school desegregation has been well documented (Clotfelter 1976; Ryan 2004; Walder and Cleveland 1971). To date, there is not a movie theater in Warrenton, NC.

37. Names of respondents have been changed to protect their anonymity.

38. The term "lady" was highly contested because it was a term used exclusively for upper class, respectable white women (Barnard 1993; Feimster 2009; Sharpley-Whiting 1995). Therefore, calling a black adult a "boy" or "girl" was not viewed as impolitic among whites. It would have been unfathomable to bestow a title of respect on a black person, especially by a white person. In a similar fashion, the practice of calling black adults either "Uncle" or "Aunt" was another way to avoid having to show deference by using the titles Mr. or Mrs. In his seminal book, *The Miseducation of the Negro*, Carter G. Woodson argues some white men would go so far as to not wear hats when in the presence of blacks so as to not have to remove or tip it to a black woman, as was customary.

39. South Carolina was the target of an NAACP boycott in the late 1990s because of the state's insistence on flying the Confederate flag over the statehouse, which it had done since 1962. The media attention and boycott embarrassed the state and cost it significant tourist revenues. As a result, the South Carolina legislature retired the Confederate flag from the statehouse in 2000. However, the flag was moved to a prominent place in front of the Capitol next to a monument honoring Confederate soldiers. It was not until 2015, subsequent to the brutal Charleston, SC church shootings by white gunman Dylann Roof, which left nine black parishioners dead at Emanuel A.M.E. Church, that Gov. Nikki Haley, a Republican, signed a bill to discontinue the use of the Confederate flag altogether. For a more significant discussion of the Confederate flag and its history, see Woliver, Ledford, and Dolan (2001).

40. Post-racial language has pervaded the conversation of contemporary race relations since the first election of Barack Obama in 2008. Because white voters turned out to vote for Obama in numbers not anticipated and never seen before for a black candidate, some suggested we were getting to a place where race mattered less than it had in prior generations. This myth of a post-racial world has quickly been debunked by multiple scholars and journalists who demonstrate the bifurcation of the nation along racial lines despite the election of Obama (Bonilla-Silva 2010; Mukherjee 2016; Ohl and Potter 2013; Tabak 2010). In fact, some argue the election of a black president and increasing prominence of minorities have left us more polarized than ever before, because whites have reacted negatively to their declining dominance in U.S. society and elected Donald Trump.

41. This is not to suggest members of different racial groups are opposed to supporting representatives from other racial groups. However, it has been shown that those who are high identifiers with their group are more apt to desire a same-race representative. Furthermore, it has been shown in some instances that the election of different-raced individuals will not necessarily mean other groups will be harmed. For example, Meier et al. (2004) find that in situations where there are more minority administrators, minority students tend to do better. This suggests minority representation, from any group, can be a boon for all minority students.

42. Although it is clear that other groups besides Latinos are recognized as immigrants (i.e., Asians), the presence of immigrants from other regions is not discussed primarily because of the questions I asked and the many ways in which black ethnics are obscured on the landscape because they are largely subsumed by the larger category of blackness, given the ways in which race operates in this country (Greer 2013; Rogers 2006). Moreover, although the southern region of the United States is being dominated by Latino immigration, the conversation in this space mirrors the conversation happening at the national level, which overlooks immigrants from Africa and the Caribbean.

43. According to the Office of Management and Budget that administers the U.S. Census, Latino is not a racial category. Rather, Latino is an ethnic category whose members can be of any race. This means Latinos are not technically counted as a race. Nevertheless, the majority of Latinos in the United States choose the "white" racial category. For a more detailed rationale, see "Overview of Race and Hispanic Origin: 2010" by Karen R. Humes, Nicholas A. Jones, and Robert R. Ramirez (http://www.census.gov/prod/cen2010/briefs/c2010br-02.pdf).

44. The extent to which Latinos will remain better off is hard to forecast. Nevertheless, Sears and Savalei (2006) argue that Latinos exhibit a high degree of group consciousness, but this tendency weakens over time as group members become more acculturated. To the extent that blacks continue to experience racial discrimination, this will continue to condition their political consciousness. Consequently, Sears and Savalei suggest the color line will continue to discipline blacks in ways that it does not other minorities, including Latinos.

45. Religion was a major concern with Southern and Eastern European immigrants, as well. Anti-Catholicism and anti-Semitism were prevalent in the United States. However, because of their skin color, in most cases, these European groups were passable as racially "white." However, this racial logic excluded Asian people as potential inheritors of whiteness. For example, in the Bhagat Singh Thind (1923) case the Supreme Court ruled that for the purposes of naturalization, Indian persons did not meet the criteria of racial whiteness despite the fact they were understood as "Aryan." Moreover, it was also believed that other Asian people had a permissive culture rife with drug abuse and a desire to have access to white women (Lui 2009).

46. This notion of a middle tier of racial categorization with respect to Latinos has been explored by Dávila (2008) and O'Brien (2008). The basic argument is that a white supremacist racial hierarchy is self-interested in its own preservation. To do so, some racial categories are selected to act as buffers between privileged whites and relatively lower-status groups by providing these middle-status groups with some benefits. This prevents organized opposition from lower-status groups, because those in the middle statuses are relatively better off and more content with their racial place in the hierarchy.

47. This statement has to be qualified with respect to Arab Americans and those deemed "Arab-looking," such as South Asians post-9/11 who found themselves under scrutiny and in some cases physically assaulted because they were deemed "Muslim" and therefore terrorists (Sekhon 2003). The "us" versus "them" discourse changed the ways in which people viewed those with darker skin who may have been viewed with some degree of favorability prior to this moment (Kinder and Kam 2010).

48. This is a reference to an unauthenticated speech allegedly delivered by a white man named Willie Lynch in the eighteenth century. Entitled "The Making of a Slave," and variously referred to as the "Willie Lynch Letter," this document

advocates keeping black people enslaved by controlling their minds and sowing seeds of dissension within the group by pitting them against each other using devices such as skin color and the like. The idea was to prevent blacks from gaining liberation by enslaving their minds, thereby preventing intragroup unity. Still, the content of this piece retains some cultural significance in black communities and is shorthand for a type of thinking that is antithetical to racial unity and black mobility.

49. It is important to note that many constituencies of the Los Angeles community where the riots took place were looting. Yet, it is the image of the black rioter cum looter in a protracted battle with Korean merchants that received the majority of media coverage. For a discussion of this dynamic, see the works of Abelman and Lie (1995), Johnson, Jones, Farrell, and Oliver (1993) and Ikemoto (1993).

50. It is worth noting that many of these small businesses, particularly Korean- and Chinese-owned companies, rely on social networks for start-up funds (Bates 1997).

51. This is clearly not the case. For example, Latinos were at the forefront of civil rights protests, particularly in the western United States, and Asian Americans have been represented, albeit in a more limited capacity, in these same struggles (Donato 1996; Iijima 1997; Maeda 2005; Tamayo 1995). Still, it has been shown that blacks are viewed as angry troublemakers (Hugenberg and Bodenhausen 2003; Powers 2005; Russell-Brown 2009).

CHAPTER 5

1. It is worth noting the Philadelphia metropolitan area has one of the largest Muslim populations in the country, with a significant portion of that being composed of black adherents.

2. Concurrent with attempts to revise immigration law, the Dyer Bill (1922), a federal anti-lynching bill, passed in the House of Representatives and filibustered in the Senate despite enjoying significant senatorial support. Successive attempts to pass federal anti-lynching legislation failed throughout the 1950s.

3. These data were gathered June 7–July 1 prior to the deaths of Alton Sterling and Philando Castile, as well as the police shootings in Dallas, TX and Baton Rouge, LA.

4. The Race and Nation (RAN) survey was co-authored with Efren O. Pérez and was fielded by YouGov/Polimetrix (YGP) from June 17–29, 2010. YouGov/Polimetrix administered the survey online and generated the survey samples through an opt-in respondent panel.

5. For complete question wording, please see Appendix C items 17–20. Items that were reverse ordered on the survey were recoded according to this schema in the analysis.

6. Don't know/Refused responses were dropped from this analysis.
7. McDaniel et al. (2011) find that although churches have been a great political resource for blacks, some religious denominations, like Evangelical Protestants, are less tolerant of immigrants because of a particular interpretation they call Christian nationalism. Christian nationalists view the nation's success as dependent on adherence to Christian principles. Although I do not study that idea, I think it is an important caveat about the ways in which church identity and religiosity can influence the opinions of congregants, in this case blacks, in ways that may seem at cross purposes with a broader, social justice agenda.
8. All items were coded from 1-strongly disagree to 4-strongly agree.
9. I used the standard linked fate measure as devised by Dawson, Brown and Jackson in the National Black Politics Study and popularized by Dawson's (1994) work on linked fate in *Behind the Mule.* The question asks "Do you think what happens generally to [black/white] people in this country will have something to do with what happens in your life?" Responses ranged from 1, strongly disagree, to 4, strongly agree. Respondents were matched with their chosen racial group, such that blacks were only asked about linked fate with other blacks and whites were asked about linked fate with other whites.
10. Respondents were asked about their group only. Therefore, the racial group was changed depending on a respondent's self-identification.
11. To see complete question wording, see questions 30 and 31 in Appendix C.
12. The national anthem is not without controversy. The third stanza of the national anthem derides enslaved blacks who fought with the British at the Battle of Fort McHenry to gain their freed. This stanza of the Star-Spangled Banner is virtually scrubbed from the historical record because it is not a part of the official anthem that is performed. In addition, NFL player, Colin Kaepernick has refused to stand for the national anthem in protest of the murders of blacks by police.

Bibliography

Abdel-Nour, Farid. "National Responsibility." *Political Theory* 31, no. 5 (2003): 693–719. https://doi.org/10.1177/0090591703252156.

Abelmann, Nancy, and John Lie. *Blue Dreams: Korean Americans and the Los Angeles Riots*. Cambridge: Harvard University Press, 1995.

Abram, Ben. "A Student's-Eye View of Hillside High." *IndyWeek*. August 14, 2002.

Adelman, Robert M. "Neighborhood Opportunities, Race, and Class: The Black Middle Class and Residential Segregation." *City & Community* 3, no. 1 (March 1, 2004): 43–63. https://doi.org/10.1111/j.1535-6841.2004.00066.x.

Adelman, Robert M., and Stewart E. Tolnay. "Occupational Status of Immigrants and African Americans at the Beginning and End of the Great Migration." *Sociological Perspectives* 46, no. 2 (June 1, 2003): 179–206. https://doi.org/10.1525/sop.2003.46.2.179.

Ainslie, Ricardo C., and Kalina Brabeck. "Race Murder and Community Trauma: Psychoanalysis and Ethnography in Exploring the Impact of the Killing of James Byrd in Jasper, Texas." *Journal for the Psychoanalysis of Culture and Society* 8, no. 1 (April 8, 2003): 42–50. https://doi.org/10.1353/psy.2003.0002.

Akpan, Monday B. "Black Imperialism: Americo-Liberian Rule Over the African Peoples of Liberia, 1841–1964." *Canadian Journal of African Studies* 7, no. 2 (1973): 217–236.

Alba, Richard D., John R. Logan, and Kyle Crowder. "White Ethnic Neighborhoods and Assimilation: The Greater New York Region, 1980–1990." *Social Forces* 75, no. 3 (March 1, 1997): 883–912. https://doi.org/10.1093/sf/75.3.883.

Alderman, Derek H. "A Street Fit for a King: Naming Places and Commemoration in the American South." *The Professional Geographer* 52, no. 4 (November 1, 2000): 672–684. https://doi.org/10.1111/0033-0124.00256.

Alex-Assensoh, Yvette Marie, and Lawrence J. Hanks. *Black and Multiracial Politics in America*. New York: NYU Press, 2000.

Alexander, Michelle. "The New Jim Crow." *Ohio State Journal of Criminal Law* 9, no. 1 (2011): 7–26.

Alexander, Michelle G., Marilynn B. Brewer, and Robert W. Livingston. "Putting Stereotype in Context: Image Theory and Interethnic Stereotypes." *Personality and Social Psychology Bulletin* 31, no. 6 (2005): 781–794. https://doi.org/10.1177/0146167204271550.

Allen, Richard L., Michael C. Dawson, and Ronald E. Brown. "A Schema-Based Approach to Modeling an African-American Racial Belief System." *American Political Science Review* 83, no. 2 (June 1989): 421–441. https://doi.org/10.2307/1962398.

Allport, Gordon Willard. *The Nature of Prejudice.* Boston: Addison-Wesley, 1954.

Alvarez, R. Michael, and Tara L. Butterfield. "The Resurgence of Nativism in California? The Case of Proposition 187 and Illegal Immigration." *Social Science Quarterly* 81, no. 1 (2000): 167–179.

Anbinder, Tyler. "'Boss' Tweed: Nativist." *Journal of the Early Republic* 15, no. 1 (1995): 109–116. https://doi.org/10.2307/3124385.

Anbinder, Tyler. *Nativism and Slavery: The Northern Know Nothings and the Politics of the 1850's.* New York: Oxford University Press, 1992.

Ancheta, Angelo N. *Race, Rights, and the Asian American Experience.* New Jersey: Rutgers University Press, 1998.

Anderson, Carol. *White Rage: The Unspoken Truth of Our Racial Divide.* New York: Bloomsbury Publishing, 2016.

Anderson, Jean Bradley. *Durham County: A History of Durham County, North Carolina.* Durham: Duke University Press, 1990.

Andreas, Peter. "The Escalation of U.S. Immigration Control in the Post-NAFTA Era." *Political Science Quarterly* 113, no. 4 (December 1, 1998): 591–615. https://doi.org/10.2307/2658246.

Andrews, Kenneth T. *Freedom Is a Constant Struggle: The Mississippi Civil Rights Movement and Its Legacy.* Chicago: University of Chicago Press, 2004.

Andrews, Kenneth T. "The Impacts of Social Movements on the Political Process: The Civil Rights Movement and Black Electoral Politics in Mississippi." *American Sociological Review* 62, no. 5 (1997): 800–819. https://doi.org/10.2307/2657361.

Aponte, Robert, and Marcelo Siles. "Latinos in the Heartland: The Browning of the Midwest." JSRI Research Report. East Lansing: The Julian Samora Research Institute. Michigan State University, November 1994. https://eric.ed.gov/?id=ED414104.

Apostoleris, Ana Maria. "The Effects of Integration on Durham City High Schools." *Journal of Southern Legal History* 25 (2018): 139–204.

Aptheker, Herbert, ed. *A Documentary History of the Negro People in the United States.* Tenth. Vol. 1. Secaucus, NJ: The Citadel Press, 1973.

Armenta, Amada. *Protect, Serve, and Deport: The Rise of Policing as Immigration Enforcement.* Oakland: University of California Press, 2017.

Arrow, Kenneth J. "What Has Economics to Say about Racial Discrimination?" *Journal of Economic Perspectives* 12, no. 2 (June 1998): 91–100. https://doi.org/10.1257/jep.12.2.91.

Assman, Jan, and John Czaplicka. "Collective Memory and Cultural Identity." *New German Critique* 65, no. Spring-Summer 1995 (1995): 125–133. https://doi.org/10.2307/488538.

Austin, Algernon. "The Unfinished March: An Overview." Washington, DC: Economic Policy Institute, June 18, 2013. https://www.epi.org/files/2013/EPI-The-Unfinished-March-An-Overview.pdf.

Avila, Eric. *Popular Culture in the Age of White Flight: Fear and Fantasy in Suburban Los Angeles.* Berkeley and Los Angeles: University of California Press, 2004.

Baker, Houston A., and Dana D. Nelson. "Preface: Violence, the Body and 'The South.'" *American Literature* 73, no. 2 (June 1, 2001): 231–244.

Balfour, Katharine Lawrence, and Lawrie Balfour. *The Evidence of Things Not Said: James Baldwin and the Promise of American Democracy.* Ithaca: Cornell University Press, 2001.

Banks, Antoine J. *Anger and Racial Politics: The Emotional Foundation of Racial Attitudes in America.* New York and Cambridge: Cambridge University Press, 2014.

Banks, Antoine J., Ismail K White, and Brian D. McKenzie. "Black Politics: How Anger Influences the Political Actions Black Pursue to Reduce Racial Inequality." *Political Behavior* (2018): 1–27. https://doi.org/10.1007/s11109-018-9477-1.

Bankston, Carl L. "Immigrants in the New South: An Introduction." *Sociological Spectrum* 23, no. 2 (April 1, 2003): 123–128. https://doi.org/10.1080/02732170309216.

Barker, Lucius J. "Black Americans and the Politics of Inclusion." *PS: Political Science & Politics* 16, no. 3 (1983): 500–507. https://doi.org/10.1017/S1049096500015626.

Barker, Lucius Jefferson, Mack H. Jones, and Katherine Tate. *African Americans and the American Political System.* New Jersey: Prentice Hall, 1999.

Barker, Lucius Jefferson, and Ronald W. Walters. *Jesse Jackson's 1984 Presidential Campaign: Challenge and Change in American Politics.* Champaign: University of Illinois Press, 1989.

Barnard, Amii Larkin. "The Application of Critical Race Feminism to the Anti-Lynching Movement: Black Women's Fight Against Race and Gender Ideology." *UCLA Women's Law Journal* 3 (1993): 1–38.

Baron, Harold M. "The Demand for Black Labor: Historical Notes on the Political Economy of Racism." In *Workers' Struggles, Past and Present: A "Radical America" Reader,* edited by James Green, 25–61. Philadelphia: Temple University Press, 1983.

Baron, Reuben M., and David A. Kenny. "The Moderator–Mediator Variable Distinction in Social Psychological Research: Conceptual, Strategic, and Statistical Considerations." *Journal of Personality and Social Psychology* 51, no. 6 (December 1, 1986): 1173–1182.

Barrett, James R., and David R. Roediger. "Inbetween Peoples: Race, Nationality and the New Immigrant Working Class." In *American Exceptionalism?*, edited by Rick Halpern and Jonathan Morris, 181–220. London: Palgrave Macmillan, 1997.

Bashi, Vilna. "Globalized Anti-Blackness: Transnationalizing Western Immigration Law, Policy, and Practice." *Ethnic and Racial Studies* 27, no. 4 (July 1, 2004): 584–606. https://doi.org/10.1080/0149198704200216726.

Bashi, Vilna. "Racial Categories Matter Because Racial Hierarchies Matter: A Commentary." *Ethnic and Racial Studies* 21, no. 5 (1998): 959–969. https://doi.org/10.1080/014198798329748.

Bates, Timothy. "Financing Small Business Creation: The Case of Chinese and Korean Immigrant Entrepreneurs." *Journal of Business Venturing* 12, no. 2 (1997): 109–124.

Bayertz, Kurt, ed. *Solidarity*. Philosophical Studies in Contemporary Culture. New York: Springer Netherlands, 1999.

Bell, Derrick. *Faces at the Bottom of the Well: The Permanence of Racism*. New York, NY: Basic Books, 1993.

Berbrier, Mitch. "The Victim Ideology of White Supremacists and White Separatists in the United States." *Sociological Focus* 33, no. 2 (2000): 175–191.

Bergesen, Albert, and Max Herman. "Immigration, Race, and Riot: The 1992 Los Angeles Uprising." *American Sociological Review* 63, no. 1 (1998): 39–54. https://doi.org/10.2307/2657476.

Berlin, Ira. *Slaves Without Masters: The Free Negro in the Antebellum South*. New York: Pantheon, 1975.

Berlin, Ira. *Many Thousands Gone: The First Two Centuries of Slavery in North America*. Cambridge: Harvard University Press, 2000.

Berlin, Ira, Joseph Patrick Reidy, and Leslie S. Rowland. *Freedom's Soldiers: The Black Military Experience in the Civil War*. Cambridge, UK; New York: Cambridge University Press, 1998.

Bernasconi, Robert. "The Constitution of the People: Frederick Douglass and the Dred Scott Decision." *Cardozo Law Review* 13 (1991): 1281–1296.

Berthoff, Rowland T. "Southern Attitudes Toward Immigration, 1865–1914." *The Journal of Southern History* 17, no. 3 (1951): 328–360. https://doi.org/10.2307/2198190.

Bertrand, Marianne, and Sendhil Mullainathan. "Are Emily and Greg More Employable Than Lakisha and Jamal? A Field Experiment on Labor Market Discrimination." *American Economic Review* 94, no. 4 (September 2004): 991–1013. https://doi.org/10.1257/0002828042002561.

Betancur, John. *The Collaborative City: Opportunities and Struggles for Blacks and Latinos in U.S. Cities*. Abingdon: Taylor & Francis, 2000.

Betancur, John J. "Framing the Discussion of African American-Latino Relations: A Review and Analysis." In *Neither Enemies nor Friends: Latinos, Blacks, Afro-Latinos,* edited by Anani Dzidzienyo and Suzanne Oboler, 159–172. New York: Palgrave Macmillan US, 2005. https://doi.org/10.1057/9781403982636_8.

Black, Christopher Allan. "Frederick Douglass, Daniel O'Connell, and the Transatlantic Failure of Irish American Abolitionism." *Making Connections: Interdisciplinary Approaches to Cultural Diversity* 12, no. 1 (2010): 17–25. https://doi.org/10.5555/maco.12.1.c3m53n21u2436707.

Black, Earl, and Merle Black. *The Rise of Southern Republicans.* Cambridge: Harvard University Press, 2003.

Black, Isabella. "American Labour and Chinese Immigration." *Past & Present*, no. 25 (1963): 59–76.

Black, Sandra E., and Philip E. Strahan. "Entrepreneurship and Bank Credit Availability." *The Journal of Finance* 57, no. 6 (2002): 2807–2833.

Blacksher, James, and Lani Guinier. "Free at Last: Rejecting Equal Sovereignty and Restoring the Constitutional Right to Vote *Shelby County v. Holder.*" *Harvard Law & Policy Review* 8, no. 1 (2014): 39–70.

Blalock, Hubert M. *Toward a Theory of Minority-Group Relations.* New York, NY: John Wiley & Sons Inc, 1967.

Blanchflower, David G., Phillip B. Levine, and David J. Zimmerman. "Discrimination in the Small-Business Credit Market." *Review of Economics and Statistics* 85, no. 4 (2003): 930–943. https://doi.org/10.1162/003465303772815835.

Blassingame, John W. *The Slave Community: Plantation Life in the Antebellum South.* New York: Oxford University Press, 1979.

Blumenthal, Henry. "Woodrow Wilson and the Race Question." *The Journal of Negro History* 48, no. 1 (January 1, 1963): 1–21. https://doi.org/10.2307/2716642.

Blumer, Herbert. "Race Prejudice as a Sense of Group Position." *The Pacific Sociological Review* 1, no. 1 (1958): 3–7.

Bobo, Lawrence. "Attitudes Toward the Black Political Movement: Trends, Meaning, and Effects on Racial Policy Preferences." *Social Psychology Quarterly* 51, no. 4 (1988): 287–302. https://doi.org/10.2307/2786757.

Bobo, Lawrence. "Race, Public Opinion, and the Social Sphere." *The Public Opinion Quarterly* 61, no. 1 (1997): 1–15.

Bobo, Lawrence, and Franklin D. Gilliam. "Race, Sociopolitical Participation, and Black Empowerment." *American Political Science Review* 84, no. 2 (June 1990): 377–393. https://doi.org/10.2307/1963525.

Bobo, Lawrence, and Vincent L. Hutchings. "Perceptions of Racial Group Competition: Extending Blumer's Theory of Group Position to a Multiracial Social Context." *American Sociological Review* 61, no. 6 (1996): 951–972. https://doi.org/10.2307/2096302.

Bobo, Lawrence D., and Devon Johnson. "Racial Attitudes in a Prismatic Metropolis: Mapping Identity, Stereotypes, Competition, and Views on Affirmative Action." In *Prismatic Metropolis: Inequality in Los Angeles,* edited by

Lawrence D. Bobo, Melvin L. Oliver, James H. Johnson, Jr., and Abel Valenzuela, Jr., 81–167. New York: Russell Sage Foundation, 2000.

Bogan, Vicki, and William Darity Jr. "Culture and Entrepreneurship? African American and Immigrant Self-Employment in the United States." *The Journal of Socio-Economics* 37, no. 5 (2008): 1999–2019.

Boger, John Charles, and Gary Orfield. *School Resegregation: Must the South Turn Back?* Chapel Hill: University of North Carolina Press, 2005.

Bonacich, Edna. "A Theory of Middleman Minorities." *American Sociological Review* 38, no. 5 (1973): 583–594.

Bonilla-Silva, Eduardo. "From Bi-Racial to Tri-Racial: Towards a New System of Racial Stratification in the USA." *Ethnic and Racial Studies* 27, no. 6 (November 1, 2004): 931–950. https://doi.org/10.1080/0141987042000268530.

Bonilla-Silva, Eduardo. *Racism without Racists: Color-Blind Racism and the Persistence of Racial Inequality in the United States.* 2nd ed. Lanham: Rowman & Littlefield Publishers, 2006.

Bonilla-Silva, Eduardo. "The Structure of Racism in Color-Blind, 'Post-Racial' America." *American Behavioral Scientist* 59, no. 11 (2015): 1358–1376. https://doi.org/10.1177/0002764215586826.

Bonnett, Alastair. "Who Was White? The Disappearance of Non-European White Identities and the Formation of European Racial Whiteness." *Ethnic and Racial Studies* 21, no. 6 (1998): 1029–1055. https://doi.org/10.1080/01419879808565651.

Borjas, George J. "Yes, Immigration Hurts American Workers." *Politico Magazine*, October 2016.

Borjas, George J., Jeffrey Grogger, and Gordon H. Hanson. "Immigration and African-American Employment Opportunities: The Response of Wages, Employment, and Incarceration to Labor Supply Shocks." NBER Working Paper Series, no. w12518. Cambridge, MA: National Bureau of Economic Research, 2006. http://www.nber.org/papers/w12518.

Borstelmann, Thomas. *The Cold War and the Color Line.* Cambridge: Harvard University Press, 2009.

Boswell, Terry E. "A Split Labor Market Analysis of Discrimination Against Chinese Immigrants, 1850–1882." *American Sociological Review* 51, no. 3 (1986): 352–371. https://doi.org/10.2307/2095307.

Bound, John, and Richard B. Freeman. "What Went Wrong? The Erosion of Relative Earnings and Employment Among Young Black Men in the 1980s." *The Quarterly Journal of Economics* 107, no. 1 (1992): 201–232. https://doi.org/10.2307/2118327.

Boyd, Robert L. "Race, Labor Market Disadvantage, and Survivalist Entrepreneurship: Black Women in the Urban North During the Great Depression." *Sociological Forum* 15, no. 4 (December 1, 2000): 647–670. https://doi.org/10.1023/A:1007563016120.

Brader, Ted, Nicholas A. Valentino, and Elizabeth Suhay. "What Triggers Public Opposition to Immigration? Anxiety, Group Cues, and Immigration Threat." *American Journal of Political Science* 52, no. 4 (2008): 959–978. https://doi.org/10.1111/j.1540-5907.2008.00353.x.

Brady, Henry E., Sidney Verba, and Kay Lehman Schlozman. "Beyond SES: A Resource Model of Political Participation." *American Political Science Review* 89, no. 2 (1995): 271–294. https://doi.org/10.2307/2082425.

Branton, Regina. "Latino Attitudes toward Various Areas of Public Policy: The Importance of Acculturation." *Political Research Quarterly* 60, no. 2 (2007): 293–303.

Branton, Regina, Erin C. Cassese, and Chad Westerland. "All along the Watchtower: Acculturation Fear, Anti-Latino Affect, and Immigration." *The Journal of Politics* 73, no. 3 (2011): 664–679. https://doi.org/10.1017/S0022381611000375.

Bratton, Kathleen A., and Kerry L. Haynie. "Agenda Setting and Legislative Success in State Legislatures: The Effects of Gender and Race." *The Journal of Politics* 61, no. 3 (1999): 658–679. https://doi.org/10.2307/2647822.

Brechin, Gray. "Conserving the Race: Natural Aristocracies, Eugenics, and the U.S. Conservation Movement." *Antipode* 28, no. 3 (July 1, 1996): 229–245. https://doi.org/10.1111/j.1467-8330.1996.tb00461.x.

Brenkman, John. "The Citizen Myth." *Transition*, no. 60 (1993): 138–144. https://doi:10.2307/2934923.

Brewer, Marilynn. "The Psychology of Prejudice: Ingroup Love and Outgroup Hate?" *Journal of Social Issues* 55, no. 3 (1999): 429–444.

Brewster, Zachary W., and Sarah Nell Rusche. "Quantitative Evidence of the Continuing Significance of Race: Tableside Racism in Full-Service Restaurants." *Journal of Black Studies* 43, no. 4 (2012): 359–384. https://doi.org/10.1177/0021934711433310.

Briggs, Jr., Vernon M. "The Economic Well-Being of Black Americans: The Overarching Influence of U.S. Immigration Policies." *The Review of Black Political Economy* 31, no. 1–2 (2003): 15–42. https://doi.org/10.1007/s12114-003-1002-y

Brisbane, Robert H. *Black Vanguard.* Pennsylvania: Judson Press, 1970.

Brock, Lisa. "Questioning the Diaspora: Hegemony, Black Intellectuals and Doing International History from Below." *African Issues* 24, no. 2 (1996): 9–12. https://doi.org/10.1017/S1548450500005059.

Broder, John M. "Latino Victor in Los Angeles Overcomes Division." *The New York Times*, May 19, 2005, sec. U.S. https://www.nytimes.com/2005/05/19/us/latino-victor-in-los-angeles-overcomes-division.html.

Brooks, Joanna. "The Early American Public Sphere and the Emergence of a Black Print Counterpublic." *The William and Mary Quarterly* 62, no. 1 (2005): 67–92. https://doi.org/10.2307/3491622

Brotz, Howard, ed. *African-American Social and Political Thought 1850–1920.* New Brunswick: Transaction Publishers, 1991.

Brown, Elsa Barkley. "Negotiating and Transforming the Public Sphere: African American Political Life in the Transition from Slavery to Freedom." *Public Culture* 7, no. 1 (January 1, 1994): 107–146. https://doi.org/10.1215/08992363-7-1-107.

Brown, Elsa Barkley. "Womanist Consciousness: Maggie Lena Walker and the Independent Order of Saint Luke." *Signs* 14, no. 3 (1989): 610–633.

Brown, Leslie, and Anne Valk. "Black Durham Behind the Veil: A Case Study." *OAH Magazine of History* 18, no. 2 (January 1, 2004): 23–27. https://doi.org/10.1093/maghis/18.2.23.

Brown, M. Christopher. "Good Intentions: Collegiate Desegregation and Transdemographic Enrollments." *Review of Higher Education* 25, no. 3 (2002): 263–280.

Brown, R. Khari, and Ronald E. Brown. "Faith and Works: Church-Based Social Capital Resources and African American Political Activism." *Social Forces* 82, no. 2 (2003): 617–641. https://doi.org/10.1353/sof.2004.0005.

Brown, Robert A., and Todd C. Shaw. "Separate Nations: Two Attitudinal Dimensions of Black Nationalism." *The Journal of Politics* 64, no. 1 (2002): 22–44. https://doi.org/10.1111/1468-2508.00116.

Browne, Irene. *Latinas and African American Women at Work: Race, Gender, and Economic Inequality*. New York: Russell Sage Foundation, 1999.

Browning, Rufus P., and Dale Rogers Marshall. "Is Anything Enough?" *PS: Political Science & Politics* 19, no. 3 (1986): 635–640. https://doi.org/10.1017/S1049096500018205.

Browning, Rufus P., Dale Rogers Marshall, and David H. Tabb. *Racial Politics in American Cities*. New York: Pearson, 2002.

Brush, Paula Stewart. "Problematizing the Race Consciousness of Women of Color." *Signs: Journal of Women in Culture and Society* 27, no. 1 (October 1, 2001): 171–198. https://doi.org/10.1086/495676.

Brush, Paula Stewart. "The Influence of Social Movements on Articulations of Race and Gender in Black Women's Autobiographies." *Gender & Society* 13, no. 1 (February 1, 1999): 120–137. https://doi.org/10.1177/089124399013001007.

Bryce-Laporte, Roy Simon. "Black Immigrants: The Experience of Invisibility and Inequality." *Journal of Black Studies* 3, no. 1 (1972): 29–56.

Buckley, Gail Lumet. *American Patriots: The Story of Blacks in the Military from the Revolution to Desert Storm*. New York: Crown, 2001.

Bullock, Charles S. "The Election of Blacks in the South: Preconditions and Consequences." *American Journal of Political Science* 19, no. 4 (1975): 727–739. https://doi.org/10.2307/2110724.

Bunche, Ralph J. "The Negro in the Political Life of the United States." *The Journal of Negro Education* 10, no. 3 (1941): 567–584. https://doi.org/10.2307/2292760.

Burin, Eric. *Slavery and the Peculiar Solution: A History of the American Colonization Society*. Gainesville: University Press of Florida, 2005.

Burns, Peter, and James G. Gimpel. "Economic Insecurity, Prejudicial Stereotypes, and Public Opinion on Immigration." *Political Science Quarterly* 115, no. 2 (2000): 201–225. https://doi.org/10.2307/2657900.

Bynum, Victoria E. *Unruly Women: The Politics of Social and Sexual Control in the Old South*. Chapel Hill: The University of North Carolina Press, 1992.

Cantú, Lionel. "The Peripheralization of Rural America: A Case Study of Latino Migrants in America's Heartland." *Sociological Perspectives* 38, no. 3 (September 1, 1995): 399–414. https://doi.org/10.2307/1389434.

Carmichael, Stokely, and Charles V. Hamilton. *Black Power: The Politics of Liberation in America*. New York: Vintage Books, 1967.

Carr, James H., and Nadinee K. Kutty, eds. *Segregation: The Rising Costs for America*. New York and London: Routledge, 2008.

Carter, Niambi M. "The Black/White Paradigm Revisited: African Americans, Immigration, Race and Nation in Durham, NC." PhD Dissertation, Duke University, 2007.

Carter, Niambi M. "Intimacy without Consent: Lynching as Sexual Violence." *Politics & Gender* 8, no. 3 (2012): 414–421.

Carter, Niambi M. "The Curious Case of Judge Aaron: Race, the Law, and the Protection of White Supremacy." *Politics, Groups, and Identities* 1, no. 3 (2013): 370–379.

Carter, Niambi M., and Pearl Ford Dowe. "The Racial Exceptionalism of Barack Obama." *Journal of African American Studies* 19, no. 2 (June 2015): 105–119. https://doi.org/10.1007/s12111-015-9298-9.

Carter, Niambi M., and Efrén O. Pérez. "Race and Nation: How Racial Hierarchy Shapes National Attachments." *Political Psychology* 37, no. 4 (2015): 497–513.

Cash, William J. *The Mind of the South*. New York: Vintage Books, 1991.

Chambers, Jr., Henry L. "Slavery, Free Blacks, and Citizenship." *Rutgers Law Journal* 43, no. 3 (Fall/Winter 2013): 487–514. https://heinonline.org/HOL/P?h=hein.journals/rutlj43&i=506.

Chang, Edward T, and Jeannette Diaz-Veizades. *Ethnic Peace in the American City: Building Community in Los Angeles and Beyond*. New York: NYU Press, 1999.

Chavez, Leo R. *The Latino Threat: Constructing Immigrants, Citizens, and the Nation*. 2nd ed. Stanford: Stanford University Press, 2013.

Chay, Kenneth Y. "The Impact of Federal Civil Rights Policy on Black Economic Progress: Evidence from the Equal Employment Opportunity Act of 1972." *ILR Review* 51, no. 4 (July 1, 1998): 608–632. https://doi.org/10.1177/001979399805100404.

Cheng, Lucie, and Yen Espiritu. "Korean Businesses in Black and Hispanic Neighborhoods: A Study of Intergroup Relations." *Sociological Perspectives* 32, no. 4 (December 1, 1989): 521–534. https://doi.org/10.2307/1389136.

Cheng, Lucie, and Philip Q Yang. "Asians: The 'Model Minority' Deconstructed." In *Ethnic Los Angeles*, edited by Roger Waldinger and Mehdi Bozorgmehr, 315–344.

New York: Russell Sage Foundation, 1996. https://www.jstor.org/stable/10.7758/9781610445474.

Chideya, Farai. *The Color of Our Future*. New York: William Morrow and Company, 2000.

Cho, Sumi. "Korean Americans vs. African Americans: Conflict and Construction." In *Reading Rodney King/Reading Urban Uprising*, edited by Robert Gooding-Williams, 196–214. New York: Routledge, 1993. http://via.library.depaul.edu/law-faculty-pubs/1561.

Citrin, Jack, Ernst B. Haas, Christopher Muste, and Beth Reingold. "Is American Nationalism Changing? Implications for Foreign Policy." *International Studies Quarterly* 38, no. 1 (1994): 1–31. https://doi.org/10.2307/2600870.

Citrin, Jack, Cara Wong, and Brian Duff. "The Meaning of American National Identity." In *Social Identity, Intergroup Conflict, and Conflict Reduction*, edited by Richard D. Ashmore, Lee Jussim, and David Wilder, 71–100. New York: Oxford University Press, 2001.

Clarke, Kristen. "The Congressional Record Underlying the 2006 Voting Rights Act: How Much Discrimination Can the Constitution Tolerate." *Harvard Civil Rights-Civil Liberties Law Review* 43, no. 2 (Summer 2008): 385–434.

Clawson, Rosalee A., Elizabeth R. Kegler, and Eric N. Waltenburg. "Supreme Court Legitimacy and Group-Centric Forces: Black Support for Capital Punishment and Affirmative Action." *Political Behavior* 25, no. 4 (December 1, 2003): 289–311. https://doi.org/10.1023/B:POBE.0000004060.38932.54.

Clawson, Rosalee A., and Zoe M. Oxley. *Public Opinion: Democratic Ideals, Democratic Practice*. 2nd ed. Washington, DC: CQ Press, 2012.

Clegg III, Claude Andrew. *The Price of Liberty: African Americans and the Making of Liberia*. Chapel Hill: The Univ of North Carolina Press, 2004.

Clemens, Michael. "International Harvest: A Case Study of How Foreign Workers Help American Farms Grow Crops—and the Economy." Partnership for a New America and the Center for Global Development, May 2013. https://www.cgdev.org/sites/default/files/international-harvest.pdf.

Clotfelter, Charles T. "School Desegregation, 'Tipping,' and Private School Enrollment." *The Journal of Human Resources* 11, no. 1 (1976): 28–50. https://doi.org/10.2307/145072.

Clotfelter, Charles T., Helen F. Ladd, and Jacob L. Vigdor. "Segregation and Resegregation in North Carolina's Public School Classrooms." *The North Carolina Law Review* 81, no. 4 (2003): 1463–1512.

Coates, Ta-Nehisi. *Between the World and Me*. New York: Random House, 2015.

Cobb, James C. *Away Down South: A History of Southern Identity*. New York: Oxford University Press, 2005.

Cohen, Cathy J. "Punks, Bulldaggers, and Welfare Queens: The Radical Potential of Queer Politics?" *GLQ: A Journal of Lesbian and Gay Studies* 3, no. 4 (1997): 437–465. https://doi.org/10.1215/10642684-3-4-437.

Cohen, Cathy J. *The Boundaries of Blackness: AIDS and the Breakdown of Black Politics*. Chicago: University of Chicago Press, 1999. http://catdir.loc.gov/catdir/enhancements/fy0608/98031088-t.html.

Cohen, Harlan Grant. "The (Un)Favorable Judgment of History: Deportation Hearings, the Palmer Raids, and the Meaning of History Note." *New York University Law Review* 78 (2003): 1431–1474.

Cole, Elizabeth R., and Safiya R. Omari. "Race, Class and the Dilemmas of Upward Mobility for African Americans." *Journal of Social Issues* 59, no. 4 (2003): 785–802. https://doi.org/10.1046/j.0022-4537.2003.00090.x.

Collins, Patricia Hill. *Black Feminist Thought: Knowledge, Consciousness, and the Politics of Empowerment*. London: HarperCollins, 2000.

Collins, Patricia Hill. "Like One of the Family: Race, Ethnicity, and the Paradox of US National Identity." *Ethnic and Racial Studies* 24, no. 1 (January 1, 2001): 3–28. https://doi.org/10.1080/014198701750052479.

Collins, Patricia Hill. *Black Sexual Politics: African Americans, Gender, and the New Racism*. New York: Routledge, 2004. http://catdir.loc.gov/catdir/toc/ecip0410/2003022841.html.

Collins, Wiiliam J. "When the Tide Turned: Immigration and the Delay of the Great Black Migration." *The Journal of Economic History* 57, no. 3 (September 1997): 607–632. https://doi.org/10.1017/S0022050700019069.

Conley, Dalton. "Getting into the Black: Race, Wealth, and Public Policy." *Political Science Quarterly* 114, no. 4 (December 1, 1999): 595–612. https://doi.org/10.2307/2657785.

Crenshaw, Kimberlé. "Mapping the Margins: Intersectionality, Identity Politics, and Violence against Women of Color." *Stanford Law Review* 43, no. 6 (1991): 1241–1299. https://doi.org/10.2307/1229039.

Crenshaw, Kimberlé Williams. "Race, Reform, and Retrenchment: Transformation and Legitimation in Antidiscrimination Law." *Harvard Law Review* 101 (1987): 1331–1387.

Cummings, Scott, and Thomas Lambert. "Anti-Hispanic and Anti-Asian Sentiments among African Americans." *Social Science Quarterly* 78, no. 2 (1997): 338–353.

Currah, Paisley. "Searching for Immutability: Homosexuality, Race, and Rights Discourse." In *A Simple Matter of Justice? Theorizing Lesbian and Gay Politics*, edited by Angelia Wilson, 51–90. London: Cassell, 1995.

Cyna, Esther. "Equalizing Resources vs. Retaining Black Political Power: Paradoxes of an Urban-Suburban School District Merger in Durham, North Carolina, 1958–1996." *History of Education Quarterly* 59, no. 1 (2019): 35–64. https://doi.org/10.1017/heq.2018.50.

Darity, William A. "Employment Discrimination, Segregation, and Health." *American Journal of Public Health* 93, no. 2 (February 1, 2003): 226–231. https://doi.org/10.2105/AJPH.93.2.226.

Dávila, Arlene. *Latino Spin: Public Image and the Whitewashing of Race*. New York: NYU Press, 2008.

Davis, F. James. *Who Is Black?: One Nation's Definition*. University Park: Pennsylvania State University Press, 1991.

Dawson, Michael C. *Behind the Mule: Race and Class in African-American Politics*. Princeton, NJ: Princeton University Press, 1994a. http://catdir.loc.gov/catdir/toc/prin031/93044088.html.

Dawson, Michael C. "A Black Counterpublic?: Economic Earthquakes, Racial Agenda(s), and Black Politics." *Public Culture* 7, no. 1 (January 1, 1994b): 195–223. https://doi.org/10.1215/08992363-7-1-195.

Dawson, Michael C. *Black Visions: The Roots of Contemporary African-American Political Ideologies*. Chicago: University of Chicago Press, 2001. http://catdir.loc.gov/catdir/toc/uchi051/2001003294.html.

Dawson, Michael C. "Globalization, the Racial Divide, and the New Citizenship." In *The New Majority: Toward a Popular Progressive Politics*, edited by Stanley B. Greenberg and Theda Skocpol, 264–278. New Haven: Yale University Press, 1997.

De Figueiredo, Rui J. P., and Zachary Elkins. "Are Patriots Bigots? An Inquiry into the Vices of In-Group Pride." *American Journal of Political Science* 47, no. 1 (February 5, 2003): 171–188. https://doi.org/10.1111/1540-5907.00012.

De La Garza, Rodolfo O. "Latino Politics: A Futuristic View." *Pursuing Power: Latinos and the Political System*, 1997, 448–456.

Deeb-Sossa, Natalia, and Jennifer Bickham Mendez. "Enforcing Borders in the Nuevo South: Gender and Migration in Williamsburg, Virginia and the Research Triangle, North Carolina." *Gender & Society* 22, no. 5 (2008): 613–638. https://doi.org/10.1177/0891243208321380

Delgado, Richard. "Rodrigo's Fifteenth Chronicle: Racial Mixture, Latino-Critical Scholarship, and the Black-White Binary," *Texas Law Review* 75, no.5 (1997): 1181–1202.

DeLombard, Jeannine. "'Eye-Witness to the Cruelty': Southern Violence and Northern Testimony in Frederick Douglass's 1845 Narrative." *American Literature* 73, no. 2 (2001): 245–275.

DeNavas-Walt, Carmen, Bernadette D. Proctor, and Jessica C. Smith. "Income, Poverty, and Health Insurance Coverage in the United States: 2009." *Current Population Reports*, P60-238 (2010): 1–85.

Devos, Thierry, and Mahzarin R. Banaji. "American=white?" *Journal of Personality and Social Psychology* 88, no. 3 (2005): 447–66. https://doi.org/10.1037/0022-3514.88.3.447.

Diamond, Jeff. "African-American Attitudes towards United States Immigration Policy." *International Migration Review* 32, no. 2 (1998): 451–470.

DiAngelo, Robin. *White Fragility: Why It's So Hard for White People to Talk about Racism*. Boston: Beacon Press, 2018.

Diaz-Veizades, Jeannette, and Edward T. Chang. "Building Cross-cultural Coalitions: A Case-study of the Black-Korean Alliance and the Latino-Black Roundtable." *Ethnic and Racial Studies* 19, no. 3 (1996): 680–700.

Dittmer, John. *Local People: The Struggle for Civil Rights in Mississippi*. Vol. 82. Champaign: University of Illinois Press, 1994.

Dixon, Jeffrey C. "The Ties That Bind and Those That Don't: Toward Reconciling Group Threat and Contact Theories of Prejudice." *Social Forces* 84, no. 4 (2006): 2179–2204. https://doi.org/10.1353/sof.2006.0085.

Doane, Ashley W., and Eduardo Bonilla-Silva. *White out: The Continuing Significance of Racism*. New York: Psychology Press, 2003.

Doddy, Hurley H., and G. Franklin Edwards. "Apprehensions of Negro Teachers Concerning Desegregation in South Carolina." *The Journal of Negro Education* 24, no. 1 (1955): 26–43.

Doherty, Carroll. "Attitudes toward Immigration: In Black and White." Washington, DC: Pew Research Center, April 25, 2006.

Donato, Ruben. "The Irony of Year-Round Schools: Mexican Migrant Resistance in a California Community During the Civil Rights Era." *Educational Administration Quarterly* 32, no. 2 (1996): 181–208.

Donnelly, Robert A. "Immigrants and Health Agency: Public Safety, Health, and Latino Immigrants in North Carolina." Center for Comparative Immigration Studies: University of California San Diego, 2017. https://escholarship.org/uc/item/4mt541ph.

Dooley, Brian. *Black and Green: The Fight for Civil Rights in Northern Ireland & Black America*. London: Pluto Press, 1998.

Douglass, Frederick. *Life and Times of Frederick Douglass. New Revised ed.* Boston: DeWolfe & Fiske Co., 1892.

Douglass, Frederick. "African Civilization Society." In *Douglass' Monthly*, Volumes 1-3, 1859–1861. New York: Negro Universities Press, 1969. https://hdl.handle.net/2027/inu.30000007703154.

Downey, Liam. "Spatial Measurement, Geography, and Urban Racial Inequality." *Social Forces* 81, no. 3 (2003): 937–952.

Drake, Susan B., and Karen J. Miksch. "Immigrant Tax Issues and the Earned Income Tax Credit." *71 Interpreter Releases* 8 (1994): 275.

Dray, Philip. *At the Hands of Persons Unknown: The Lynching of Black America*. New York: Modern Library, 2007.

Du Bois, W. E. B. "Close Ranks." *The Crisis* 16, no. 3 (1918): 111.

Du Bois, W. E. B. "The Shape of Fear." Credo. June 1926. Mums312-b208-i038. Special Collections and University Archives, University of Massachusetts Amherst Libraries. http://credo.library.umass.edu/view/full/mums312-b208-i038.

Du Bois, W. E. B. "Immigration Quota." *The Crisis* 36–37 (August 1929): 278.

Dudziak, Mary. *Cold War Civil Rights: Race and the Image of American Democracy*. Princeton: Princeton University Press, 2003.

Dudziak, Mary L. "Brown as a Cold War Case." *The Journal of American History* 91, no. 1 (2004): 32–42. https://doi.org/10.2307/3659611

Dugger, Julie M. "Black Ireland's Race: Thomas Carlyle and the Young Ireland Movement." *Victorian Studies* 48, no. 3 (2006): 461–485.

Duncan, Otis Dudley, and Stanley Lieberson. "Ethnic Segregation and Assimilation." *American Journal of Sociology* 64, no. 4 (1959): 364–374.

Durand, Jorge, Douglas S. Massey, and Fernando Charvet. "The Changing Geography of Mexican Immigration to the United States: 1910–1996." *Social Science Quarterly* 81, no. 1 (2000): 1–15.

Dyer, Richard. "The Matter of Whiteness." In *White Privilege: Essential Readings on the Other Side of Racism*, 3rd ed., edited by Paula S. Rothenberg, 9–14. New York: Worth Publishers, 2008.

Dyste, Connie. "Proposition 63: The California English Language Amendment." *Applied Linguistics* 10, no. 3 (1989): 313–330.

Dzidzienyo, Anani, and Suzanne Oboler, eds. *Neither Enemies Nor Friends: Latinos, Blacks, Afro-Latinos*. New York: Palgrave Macmillan, 2005.

Eberhardt, Jennifer L., Phillip Atiba Goff, Valerie J. Purdie, and Paul G. Davies. "Seeing Black: Race, Crime, and Visual Processing." *Journal of Personality and Social Psychology* 87, no. 6 (2004): 876–893. http://dx.doi.org/10.1037/0022-3514.87.6.876.

Edelman, Lauren B. "Legal Ambiguity and Symbolic Structures: Organizational Mediation of Civil Rights Law." *American Journal of Sociology* 97, no. 6 (1992): 1531–1576.

Eden, Rebecca E. "A Lesson in Change." *Durham Herald Sun*. August 19, 2001a.

Eden, Rebecca E. "Dropping Diversity in Schools." *Durham Herald Sun*. August 22, 2001b.

Edwards, Laura F. "Enslaved Women and the Law: Paradoxes of Subordination in the Post-Revolutionary Carolinas." *Slavery and Abolition* 26, no. 2 (2005): 305–323.

Effland, Anne, and Kathleen Kassel. "Hispanics in Rural America: The Influence of Immigration and Language on Economic Well-Being." In *Racial/Ethnic Minorities in Rural Areas: Progress and Stagnation, 1980-1990, Report no. AER-731*, edited by Linda L. Swanson, 87–99. Washington, DC: Economic Research Service, 1996.

Eisinger, Peter K. "The Conditions of Protest Behavior in American Cities." *American Political Science Review* 67, no. 1 (1973): 11–28.

Elliott, Aprele. "Ella Baker: Free Agent in the Civil Rights Movement." *Journal of Black Studies* 26, no. 5 (1996): 593–603.

Erie, Steven P. "Politics, the Public Sector, and Irish Social Mobility: San Francisco, 1870–1900." *Western Political Quarterly* 31, no. 2 (1978): 274–289.

Espenshade, Thomas J., and Charles A. Calhoun. "An Analysis of Public Opinion toward Undocumented Immigration." *Population Research and Policy Review* 12, no. 3 (1993): 189–224. https://doi.org/10.1007/BF01074385.

Espenshade, Thomas J., and Katherine Hempstead. "Contemporary American Attitudes toward US Immigration." *International Migration Review* 30, no. 2 (1996): 535–570.

Esses, Victoria M., John F. Dovidio, Lynne M. Jackson, and Tamara L. Armstong. "The Immigration Dilemma: The Role of Perceived Group Competition, Ethnic Prejudice, and National Identity." *Journal of Social Issues* 57, no. 3 (2001): 389–412. https://doi.org/10.1111/0022-4537.00220.

Esses, Victoria M., Lynne M. Jackson, and Tamara L. Armstong. "Intergroup Competition and Attitudes toward Immigrants and Immigration: An Instrumental Model of Group Conflict." *Journal of Social Issues* 54, no. 4 (1998): 699–724. https://doi.org/10.1111/j.1540-4560.1998.tb01244.x.

Estes, Steve. *I Am a Man!: Race, Manhood, and the Civil Rights Movement.* Chapel Hill: University of North Carolina Press, 2005.

Fairclough, Adam. "The Costs of Brown: Black Teachers and School Integration." *The Journal of American History* 91, no. 1 (2004): 43–55.

Fairlie, Robert W., and William A. Sundstrom. "The Emergence, Persistence, and Recent Widening of the Racial Unemployment Gap." *ILR Review* 52, no. 2 (1999): 252–270.

Fairlie, Robert W., and William A. Sundstrom. "The Racial Unemployment Gap in Long-Run Perspective." *The American Economic Review* 87, no. 2 (1997): 306–310.

Falcon, Angelo. "Black and Latino Politics in New York City." *Latinos in the Political System*, 1988, 171–194.

Farley, Reynolds. "The Quality of Life for Black Americans Twenty Years after the Civil Rights Revolution." *The Milbank Quarterly* 65, no. 1 (1987): 9–34.

Farley, Reynolds, and William H. Frey. "Changes in the Segregation of Whites from Blacks during the 1980s: Small Steps toward a More Integrated Society." *American Sociological Review*, 1994, 23–45.

Feagin, Joe R. *Racist America: Roots, Current Realities, and Future Reparations.* 2nd ed. New York: Routledge, 2010.

Feagin, Joe R., and Melvin P. Sikes. *Living with Racism: The Black Middle-Class Experience.* Boston: Beacon Press, 1994.

Feimster, Crystal N. *Southern Horrors: Women and the Politics of Rape and Lynching.* Cambridge, MA: Harvard University Press, 2009.

Ferreira, Patricia. "All But 'A Black Skin and Wooly Hair': Frederick Douglass's Witness of the Irish Famine." *American Studies International* 37, no. 2 (1999): 69–83.

Feshbach, Seymour. "Nationalism, Patriotism, and Aggression." In *Aggressive Behavior*, edited by L. Rowell Huesmann, 275–291. The Plenum Series in Social/Clinical Psychology. Boston: Springer, 1994.

Fields, Barbara J. "Ideology and Race in American History." In *Region, Race, and Reconstruction: Essays in Honor of C. Vann Woodward*, edited by Morgan Kousser and James McPherson, 143–177. New York: Oxford University Press, 1982.

Fitzhugh, George. *Cannibals All! Or, Slaves without Masters*. Cambridge: Harvard University Press, 2009.

Fix, Michael, Wendy Zimmermann, and Jeffrey S. Passel. *The Integration of Immigrant Families in the United States*. Washington, DC: The Urban Institute, July 2001.

Fleming, Walter L. "Immigration to the Southern States." *Political Science Quarterly* 20, no. 2 (1905): 276–297.

Fogg-Davis, Hawley G. "Theorizing Black Lesbians within Black Feminism: A Critique of Same-Race Street Harassment." *Politics & Gender* 2, no. 1 (2006): 57–76.

Fong, Timothy P. "Why Ted Dang Lost: An Analysis of the 1994 Mayoral Race in Oakland, California." *Journal of Asian American Studies* 1, no. 2 (1998): 153–171.

Forbes, Ella. "African American Resistance to Colonization." *Journal of Black Studies* 21, no. 2 (1990): 210–223.

Foster, Holly, and John Hagan. "The Mass Incarceration of Parents in America: Issues of Race/Ethnicity, Collateral Damage to Children, and Prisoner Reentry." *The ANNALS of the American Academy of Political and Social Science* 623, no. 1 (April 15, 2009): 179–194. https://doi.org/10.1177/0002716208331123.

Fraga, Luis R., and Gary M. Segura. "Culture Clash? Contesting Notions of American Identity and the Effects of Latin American Immigration." *Perspectives on Politics* 4, no. 2 (2006): 279–287.

Frank, Reanne, Ilana Redstone Akresh, and Bo Lu. "Latino Immigration and the US Racial Order: How and Where Do They Fit In?" *American Sociological Review* 75, no. 3 (2010): 378–401. https://doi.org/10.1177/0003122410372216.

Frankenberg, Ruth. *Displacing Whiteness: Essays in Social and Cultural Criticism*. Durham: Duke University Press, 1997. http://site.ebrary.com/id/10207637.

Franklin, John Hope. "The New Negro History." *The Journal of Negro History* 42, no. 2 (1957): 89–97.

Franklin, John Hope. *The Free Negro in North Carolina, 1790–1860*. Chapel Hill: University of North Carolina Press, 1995.

Franklin, John Hope. "New Black Migration Patterns in the United States: Are They Affected by Recent Immigration?" In *Immigration and Opportunity: Race, Ethnicity, and Employment in the United States*, edited by Frank Bean and Stephanie Bell-Rose, 311–344. New York: Russell Sage Foundation, 1999.

Franklin, John Hope. *From Slavery to Freedom: A History of African Americans*. New York: A.A Knopf, 2000.

Franklin, Vincent P. *Black Self-Determination: A Cultural History of African-American Resistance*. 2nd ed. Brooklyn: Lawrence Hill Books, 1992.

Frazier, E. Franklin. *Black Bourgeoisie: The Book That Brought the Shock of Self-Revelation to Middle Class Blacks in America*. New York: Free Press, 1997.

Fredrickson, George M. "A Man but Not a Brother: Abraham Lincoln and Racial Equality." *The Journal of Southern History* 41, no. 1 (February 1975): 39–58. https://doi.org/10.2307/2206706.

Frey, William H. "Black Migration to the South Reaches Record Highs in 1990s." *Population Today* 26, no. 2 (1998): 1–3.

Frey, William H. "Melting Pot Suburbs: A Census 2000 Study of Suburban Diversity." Census 2000 Series. Washington, DC: Brookings Institution, 2001. https://www.brookings.edu/wp-content/uploads/2016/06/frey.pdf.

Frey, William H. *Immigration and Domestic Migration in US Metro Areas: 2000 and 1990 Census Findings by Education and Race.* University of Michigan, Population Studies Center, 2005.

Frey, William H. "The New Great Migration: Black Americans' Return to the South, 1965–2000." Washington, DC: Brookings Institution, 2004. https://www.brookings.edu/research/the-new-great-migration-black-americans-return-to-the-south-1965-2000/.

Frey, William H. "New Black Migration Patterns in the United States: Are They Affected by Recent Immigration?" In *Immigration and Opportunity: Race, Ethnicity, and Employment in the United States*, edited by Frank Bean and Stephanie Bell-Rose, 311–344. New York: Russell Sage Foundation, 1999.

Frey, William H., and Kao-Lee Liaw. "Interstate Migration of Hispanics, Asians and Blacks: Cultural Constraints and Middle Class Flight." Population Studies Center Report. Ann Arbor: University of Michigan, 2005.

Fryer Jr, Roland G., and Steven D. Levitt. "The Causes and Consequences of Distinctively Black Names." *The Quarterly Journal of Economics* 119, no. 3 (2004): 767–805.

Frymer, Paul. "Acting When Elected Officials Won't: Federal Courts and Civil Rights Enforcement in US Labor Unions, 1935–85." *American Political Science Review* 97, no. 3 (2003): 483–499.

Frymer, Paul. *Uneasy Alliances: Race and Party Competition in America.* Princeton: Princeton University Press, 2010.

Gaines, Kevin Kelly. *Uplifting the Race: Black Leadership, Politics, and Culture in the Twentieth Century.* Chapel Hill: The University of North Carolina Press, 1996.

Gaines, Kevin Kelly. *African Americans in Ghana: Black Expatriates and the Civil Rights Era.* Chapel Hill: The University of North Carolina Press, 2006.

Gallicchio, Marc S. *The African American Encounter with Japan and China: Black Internationalism in Asia, 1895–1945.* Chapel Hill: The University of North Carolina Press, 2000.

Gans, Herbert J. "Symbolic Ethnicity: The Future of Ethnic Groups and Cultures in America." *Ethnic and Racial Studies* 2, no. 1 (1979): 1–20.

Garnet, Henry Highland. "No Change—A Word to My Friends and Foes." In *Freedom's Journey: African American Voices of the Civil War*, edited by Donald Yacovone, 32–33. Chicago: Lawrence Hill Books, 2004.

Garrison, William Lloyd. *Thoughts on African Colonization: Or an Impartial Exhibition of the Doctrines, Principles, and Purposes of the American Colonization Society.*

Together with the Resolutions, Addresses, and Remonstrances of the Free People of Color. Boston: Garrison and Knapp, 1832.

Gaskins, Keesha, and Sundeep Iyer. *The Challenge of Obtaining Voter Identification*. New York: Brennan Center for Justice at New York University School of Law, 2012.

Gasman, Marybeth. *The Changing Face of Historically Black Colleges and Universities*. Center for Minority Serving Institutions: University of Pennsylvania, Philadelphia, 2013. https://saportareport.com/wp-content/uploads/2013/05/Changing_Face_HBCUs.pdf.

Gay, Claudine. "Spirals of Trust: The Effect of Descriptive Representation on the Relationship between Citizens and Their Government." *American Journal of Political Science* 46, no. 4 (October 2002): 717–732. https://doi.org/10.2307/3088429.

Gay, Claudine. "Putting Race in Context: Identifying the Environmental Determinants of Black Racial Attitudes." *American Political Science Review* 98, no. 4 (2004): 547–562. https://doi.org/10.1017/S0003055404041346

Gay, Claudine. "Seeing Difference: The Effect of Economic Disparity on Black Attitudes toward Latinos." *American Journal of Political Science* 50, no. 4 (October 2006): 982–997. https://doi.org/10.1111/j.1540-5907.2006.00228.x.

Georgakas, Dan, and Marvin Surkin. *Detroit, I Do Mind Dying: A Study in Urban Revolution*. New York: St. Martin's Press, 1975.

Gershenhorn, Jerry. "Hocutt v. Wilson and Race Relations in Durham, North Carolina, During the 1930s." *The North Carolina Historical Review* 78, no. 3 (2001): 275–308.

Gerstle, Gary. *Working-Class Americanism: The Politics of Labor in a Textile City, 1914–1960*. Interdisciplinary Perspectives on Modern History. New Jersey: Princeton University Press, 2002.

Giddings, Paula. *When and Where I Enter: The Impact of Black Women on Race and Sex in America*. New York: William Morrow, 1996. http://catdir.loc.gov/catdir/description/hc043/96019349.html.

Gilens, Martin. *Why Americans Hate Welfare: Race, Media, and the Politics of Antipoverty Policy*. Chicago: University of Chicago Press, 2000.

Giles, Micheal W., and Kaenan Hertz. "Racial Threat and Partisan Identification." *American Political Science Review* 88, no. 2 (1994): 317–326.

Gill, Tiffany M. "Civic Beauty: Beauty Culturists and the Politics of African American Female Entrepreneurship, 1900–1965." *Enterprise & Society* 5, no. 4 (2004): 583–593.

Gilroy, Paul. *"There Ain't No Black in the Union Jack": The Cultural Politics of Race and Nation*. Chicago: University of Chicago Press, 1991. http://catdir.loc.gov/catdir/toc/uchio51/91027129.html.

Gilroy, Paul. *The Black Atlantic: Modernity and Double Consciousness*. Cambridge, MA: Harvard University Press, 1993. http://www.gbv.de/dms/bowker/toc/9780674076068.pdf.

Gleeson, David T. *The Irish in the South, 1815–1877*. Chapel Hill: University of North Carolina Press, 2001. http://www.h-net.org/review/hrev-aoc6t4-aa.

Goldberg, Barry. "Black Resistance in the Age of Jim Crow." *New Politics* 7, no. 3 (1999): 71–82.

Goldin, Claudia. "The Political Economy of Immigration Restriction in the United States, 1890-1921." In *The Regulated Economy: A Historical Approach to Political Economy*, edited by Claudia Goldin and Gary D. Libecap, 223–258. Chicago: University of Chicago Press, 1994.

Goldstein, Eric L. "The Unstable Other: Locating the Jew in Progressive-Era American Racial Discourse." *American Jewish History* 89, no. 4 (2001): 383–409.

Gong, Gwendolyn. "The Changing Use of Deference among the Mississippi Chinese." *English Today* 19, no. 3 (2003): 50–56.

Gooding-Williams, Robert., ed. *Reading Rodney King/Reading Urban Uprising*. New York: Routledge, 1993. http://catdir.loc.gov/catdir/enhancements/fy0651/92043381-d.html.

Gouveia, Lourdes, and Donald D. Stull. "Latino Immigrants, Meatpacking, and Rural Communities: A Case Study of Lexington, Nebraska." JSRI Research Report. East Lansing: The Julian Samora Research Institute. Michigan State University, 1997.

Greene, Christina. *Our Separate Ways: Women and the Black Freedom Movement in Durham, North Carolina*. Chapel Hill: University of North Carolina Press, 2005.

Greer, Christina M. *Black Ethnics: Race, Immigration and the Pursuit of the American Dream*. New York: Oxford University Press, 2013.

Greeson, Jennifer Rae. "'The Mysteries and Miseries' of North Carolina: New York City, Urban Gothic Fiction, and Incidents in the Life of a Slave Girl." *American Literature* 73, no. 2 (2001): 271–309.

Griffin, Farah Jasmine. "Black Feminists and Du Bois: Respectability, Protection, and Beyond." *The ANNALS of the American Academy of Political and Social Science* 568, no. 1 (2000): 28–40.

Griffin, Larry J., and Robert R. Korstad. "Class as Race and Gender|Making and Breaking a Labor Union in the Jim Crow South." *Social Science History* 19, no. 4 (1995): 425–454. https://doi.org/10.1017/S0145553200017454.

Griffin, Larry J., and Ashley B. Thompson. "Enough about the Disappearing South: What about the Disappearing Southerner?" *Southern Cultures* 9, no. 3 (2003): 51–65.

Griffith, David. *Jones's Minimal: Low-Wage Labor in the United States*. Albany: SUNY Press, 1993.

Griffith, David C. "Rural Industry and Mexican Immigration and Settlement in North Carolina." In *New Destinations: Mexican Immigration in the United States*, edited by Victor Zúñiga and Rubén Hernández-León, 50–75. New York, NY: Russell Sage Foundation, 2006.

Gross, Ariela J. "Texas Mexicans and the Politics of Whiteness." *Law and History Review* 21, no. 1 (2003): 195–205. https://doi.org/10.2307/3595072.

Grossman, James R. *Land of Hope: Chicago, Black Southerners, and the Great Migration*. Chicago: University of Chicago Press, 1989. http://hdl.handle.net/2027/heb.01940.

Grow, Matthew. "The Shadow of the Civil War: A Historiography of Civil War Memory." *American Nineteenth Century History* 4, no. 2 (June 1, 2003): 77–103. https://doi.org/10.1080/14664650312331294324.

Guest, Greg, Arwen Bruce, and Laura Johnson. "How Many Interviews Are Enough? An Experiment with Data Saturation and Variability." *Field Methods* 18, no. 1 (2006): 59–82. https://doi.org/10.1177/1525822X05279903.

Guglielmo, Thomas A. *White on Arrival: Italians, Race, Color, and Power in Chicago, 1890–1945*. New York: Oxford University Press, 2003.

Gurin, Patricia., Shirley Hatchett, and James S. Jackson. *Hope and Independence: Blacks' Response to Electoral and Party Politics*. New York: Russell Sage Foundation, 1989.

Gyory, Andrew. *Closing the Gate: Race, Politics, and the Chinese Exclusion Act*. Chapel Hill: The University of North Carolina Press, 1998.

Hacker, Andrew. *Two Nations: Black and White, Separate, Hostile, and Unequal*. Revised ed. New York: Simon & Schuster, 2003.

Hackney, Sheldon. "The Contradictory South." *Southern Cultures* 7, no. 4 (November 1, 2001): 65–80. https://doi.org/10.1353/scu.2001.0050.

Hajnal, Zoltan L., Elisabeth R. Gerber, and Hugh Louch. "Minorities and Direct Legislation: Evidence from California Ballot Proposition Elections." *Journal of Politics* 64, no. 1 (February 1, 2002): 154–177. https://doi.org/10.1111/1468-2508.00122.

Hale, Grace Elizabeth. *Making Whiteness: The Culture of Segregation in the South, 1890-1940*. New York, NY: Pantheon Books, 1998. http://catdir.loc.gov/catdir/bios/random058/97040906.html.

Hall, Stuart. "Cultural Identity and Diaspora." In *Colonial Discourse and Post-Colonial Theory: A Reader*, edited by introduced by Patrick Williams and Laura Chrisman, 392–403. New York: Columbia University Press, 1990.

Hamilton, Darrick, William Darrity, Jr., Anne E. Price, Vishnu Shridharan, and Rebecca Tippett. "Umbrellas Don't Make It Rain: Why Studying and Working Hard Isn't Enough for Black Americans." The New School, The Duke University Center for Social Equity and Insight Center for Community Economic Development, April 2015. http://ww1.insightcced.org/uploads/CRWG/Umbrellas-Dont-Make-It-Rain8.pdf.

Hanagan, Michael. "Irish Transnational Social Movements, Deterritorialized Migrants, and the State System: The Last One Hundred and Forty Years." *Mobilization: An International Quarterly* 3, no. 1 (1998): 107–126.

Hanchard, Michael. "Identity, Meaning and the African-American." *Social Text*, no. 24 (1990): 31–42. https://doi.org/10.2307/827825.

Hancock, Ange-Marie. *The Politics of Disgust: The Public Identity of the Welfare Queen*. New York: New York University Press, 2004.

Haney-López, Ian. *White by Law: The Legal Construction of Race*. Critical America. New York: New York University Press, 1996.

Harper, Phillip Brian. *Are We Not Men?: Masculine Anxiety and the Problem of African-American Identity*. New York: Oxford University Press, 1996.

Harrington, Michael. *The Other America: Poverty in the United States*. New York: Simon & Schuster, 1997.

Harris, Cheryl I. "Whiteness as Property." *Harvard Law Review* 106, no. 8 (1992): 1707–1791.

Harris, Frederick C., Valeria Sinclair-Chapman, and Brian McKenzie. *Countervailing Forces in African-American Civic Activism, 1973–1994*. Cambridge: Cambridge University Press, 2006.

Harris, J. John. "Education, Society, and the Brown Decision: Historical Principles Versus Legal Mandates." *Journal of Black Studies* 13, no. 2 (1982): 141–154.

Harris-Lacewell, Melissa V. "The Heart of the Politics of Race: Centering Black People in the Study of White Racial Attitudes." *Journal of Black Studies* 34, no. 2 (2003): 222–249. https://doi.org/10.1177/0021934703255596.

Harris-Lacewell, Melissa V. *Barbershops, Bibles, and BET: Everyday Talk and Black Political Thought*. New Jersey: Princeton University Press, 2004. http://catdir.loc.gov/catdir/toc/prin051/2003055452.html.

Harris-Perry, Melissa V. *Sister Citizen: Shame, Stereotypes, and Black Women in America*. New Haven: Yale University Press, 2013.

Harrison, Faye V. "The Persistent Power of 'Race' in the Cultural and Political Economy of Racism." *Annual Review of Anthropology* 24 (1995): 47–74.

Harrison, Faye V. "Introduction: Expanding the Discourse on 'Race.'" *American Anthropologist* 100, no. 3 (1998): 609–631.

Hartigan Jr., John. "Establishing the Fact of Whiteness." *American Anthropologist* 99, no. 3 (1997): 495–505. https://doi.org/10.1525/aa.1997.99.3.495.

Hartz, Louis. *The Liberal Tradition in America: An Interpretation of American Political Thought since the Revolution*. San Diego: Harcourt Brace Jovanovich, 1991.

Harvey, William B., Adia M. Harvey, and Mark King. "The Impact *of Brown v. Board of Education* Decision on Postsecondary Participation of African Americans." *Journal of Negro Education* 73, no. 3 (2004): 328–340. https://doi.org/10.2307/4129615.

Harwood, Edwin. "American Public Opinion and U. S. Immigration Policy." *The Annals of the American Academy of Political and Social Science* 487 (1986): 201–212.

Heckman, James, and Brook Payner. "Determining the Impact of Federal Antidiscrimination Policy on the Economic Status of Blacks: A Study of South Carolina." *American Economic Review* 79, no. 1 (1989): 138–177.

Hellwig, David. "The Afro-American and the Immigrant, 1880–1930: A Study of Black Social Thought." PhD Dissertation (History), Syracuse University, 1973. https://surface.syr.edu/hst_etd/49.

Hellwig, David J. "Afro-American Reactions to the Japanese and the Anti-Japanese Movement, 1906–1924." *Phylon* 38, no. 1 (1977): 93–104. https://doi.org/10.2307/274447.

Hellwig, David J. "Black Meets Black: Afro American Reactions to West-Indian Immigrants in the 1920s." *South Atlantic Quarterly* 77, no. 2 (1978): 206–224.

Hellwig, David J. "Black Attitudes Toward Immigrant Labor in the South, 1865–1910." *The Filson Club History Quarterly* 54, no. 2 (1980): 151–168.

Hellwig, David J. "Black Leaders and United States Immigration Policy, 1917-1929." *The Journal of Negro History* 66, no. 2 (1981): 110–127. https://doi.org/10.2307/2717281.

Hellwig, David J. "Strangers in Their Own Land: Patterns of Black Nativism, 1830–1930." *American Studies* 23, no. 1 (1982): 85–98.

Hellwig, David J. "The Afro-American Press and Woodrow Wilson's Mexican Policy, 1913-1917." *Phylon* 48, no. 4 (1987): 261–270. https://doi.org/10.2307/274483.

Henderson, Carol E. "Guest Editor's Introduction: The Bodies of Black Folks: The Flesh Manifested in Words, Pictures, and Sound." *Melus* 35, no. 4 (Winter 2010): 5–13.

Henry, Charles, and Jr. Munoz Carlos. "Ideological and Interest Linkages in California Rainbow Politics." In *Racial and Ethnic Politics in California*, edited by Byran O. Jackson and Michael B. Preston, 2:323–328. Berkeley, CA: IGS Press, 1991.

Hergenhahn, B. R., Ken Cramer, and Matthew H. Olson. *An Introduction to Theories of Personality*. Toronto: Pearson Education Canada, 2002.

Hernández-León, Rubén, and Víctor Zúñiga. "'Making Carpet by the Mile': The Emergence of a Mexican Immigrant Community in an Industrial Region of the U.S. Historic South." *Social Science Quarterly* 81, no. 1 (2000): 49–66.

Hero, Rodney E., and Caroline J. Tolbert. "A Racial/Ethnic Diversity Interpretation of Politics and Policy in the States of the U.S." *American Journal of Political Science* 40, no. 3 (1996): 851–871. https://doi.org/10.2307/2111798.

Herriott, James. "Race Splits Durham School Board." *Duke Chronicle*. May 23, 2001.

Hershberg, Theodore. "Free Blacks in Antebellum Philadelphia: A Study of Ex-Slaves, Freeborn, and Socioeconomic Decline." *Journal of Social History* 5, no. 2 (1971): 183–209.

Hershberg, Theodore, Alan N. Burstein, Eugene P. Ericksen, Stephanie Greenberg, and William L. Yancey. "A Tale of Three Cities: Blacks and Immigrants in Philadelphia: 1850–1880, 1930 and 1970." *The Annals of the American Academy of Political and Social Science* 441 (1979): 55–81.

Higginbotham, Jr., A. Leon, and Anne F. Jacobs. "Law Only as an Enemy: The Legitimization of Racial Powerlessness through the Colonial and Antebellum Criminal Laws of Virginia." *The North Carolina Law Review* 70, no. 4 (April 1992): 969–1070. https://heinonline.org/HOL/P?h=hein.journals/nclr70&i=997.

Higgins, George E., and Shaun L. Gabbidon. "Perceptions of Consumer Racial Profiling and Negative Emotions: An Exploratory Study." *Criminal Justice and Behavior* 36, no. 1 (2009): 77–88. https://doi.org/10.1177/0093854808325686.

Higham, John. *Strangers in the Land: Patterns of American Nativism, 1860–1925.* New York: Atheneum, 1970.

Higham, John. *Send These to Me: Jews and Other Immigrants in Urban America.* New York: Atheneum, 1975.

Hine, Darlene Clark. "Rape and the Inner Lives of Black Women in the Middle West." *Signs* 14, no. 4 (1989): 912–920.

Hochschild, Jennifer L. *Facing up to the American Dream : Race, Class, and the Soul of the Nation.* Princeton Studies in American Politics. Princeton: Princeton University Press, 1996.

Hochschild, Jennifer L. "Ambivalence about Equality in the United States or, Did Tocqueville Get It Wrong and Why Does That Matter?" *Social Justice Research* 19, no. 1 (2006): 43–62.

Hochschild, Jennifer L. *Facing up to the American Dream: Race, Class, and the Soul of the Nation.* Princeton Studies in American Politics. Princeton, NJ: Princeton University Press, 1995.

Hodes, Martha. "The Sexualization of Reconstruction Politics: White Women and Black Men in the South after the Civil War." *Journal of the History of Sexuality* 3, no. 3 (1993): 402–417.

Hodes, Martha. *White Women, Black Men: Illicit Sex in the 19th-Century South.* Yale University Press, 1997.

Hodes, Martha Elizabeth. *Sex, Love, Race: Crossing Boundaries in North American History.* New York: New York University Press, 1999.

Hoelscher, Steven. "Making Place, Making Race: Performances of Whiteness in the Jim Crow South." *Annals of the Association of American Geographers* 93, no. 3 (September 1, 2003): 657–686. https://doi.org/10.1111/1467-8306.9303008.

Holland, Sharon Patricia. *The Erotic Life of Racism.* Durham: Duke University Press, 2012.

Hollinger, David A. "Amalgamation and Hypodescent: The Question of Ethnoracial Mixture in the History of the United States." *The American Historical Review* 108, no. 5 (December 1, 2003): 1363–1390. https://doi.org/10.1086/ahr/108.5.1363.

Holloway, Karla F. C. *Passed on: African American Mourning Stories: A Memorial.* Durham: Duke University Press, 2002.

Honig, Bonnie. *Democracy and the Foreigner.* Princeton: Princeton University Press, 2001.

Hood, M. V., and Irwin L. Morris. "¿Amigo o Enemigo?: Context, Attitudes, and Anglo Public Opinion toward Immigration." *Social Science Quarterly* 78, no. 2 (1997): 309–323.

Horne, Gerald. *The Fire This Time: The Watts Uprising and the 1960s.* Charlottesville: University of Virginia Press, 1997.

Horton, James Oliver. "Freedom's Yoke: Gender Conventions among Antebellum Free Blacks." *Feminist Studies* 12, no. 1 (1986): 51–76. https://doi.org/10.2307/3177983.

HoSang, Daniel Martinez. *Racial Propositions: Ballot Initiatives and the Making of Postwar California.* Berkeley: University of California Press, 2010.

Huddy, Leonie, and Nadia Khatib. "American Patriotism, National Identity, and Political Involvement." *American Journal of Political Science* 51, no. 1 (2007): 63–77.

Hugenberg, Kurt, and Galen V. Bodenhausen. "Facing Prejudice: Implicit Prejudice and the Perception of Facial Threat." *Psychological Science* 14, no. 6 (2003): 640–643.

Hull, Akasha (Gloria T.), Patricia Bell-Scott, and Barbara Smith. *All the Women Are White, All the Blacks Are Men, but Some of Us Are Brave: Black Women's Studies.* Old Westbury, NY: Feminist Press, 1982.

Hunter, Andrea G., and Sherrill Sellers. "Feminist Attitudes Among African American Women and Men." *Gender & Society* 12, no. 1 (February 1, 1998): 81–99. https://doi.org/10.1177/089124398012001005.

Hunter, Tera W. *To 'joy My Freedom: Southern Black Women's Lives and Labors after the Civil War.* Cambridge: Harvard University Press, 1997.

Huntington, Samuel P. *Who Are We?: The Challenges to America's National Identity.* New York: Simon & Schuster, 2004.

Hurwitz, Jon, and Mark Peffley. "International Attitudes." In *Measures of Political Attitudes,* edited by John P. Robinson, Phillip R. Shaver, and Lawrence S. Wrightsman, 533–590. San Diego: Academic Press, 1999.

Hutchings, Vincent L., and Nicholas A. Valentino. "The Centrality of Race in American Politics." *Annual Review of Political Science* 7, no. 1 (2004): 383–408. https://doi.org/10.1146/annurev.polisci.7.012003.104859.

Ignatiev, Noel. *How the Irish Became White.* New York: Routledge, 1996.

Iijima, Chris K. "The Era of We-Construction: Reclaiming the Politics of Asian Pacific American Identity and Reflections on the Critique of the Black/White Paradigm." *Columbia Human Rights Law Review* 29, no. 1 (Fall 1997): 47–90.

Ikemoto, Lisa C. "Traces of the Master Narrative in the Story of African American/Korean Conflict: How We Constructed Los Angeles." *Southern California Law Review* 66, no. 4 (1993): 1581–1598.

Jackson, Byran O., Elisabeth R. Gerber, and Bruce E. Cain. "Coalitional Prospects in a Multi-Racial Society: African-American Attitudes Toward Other Minority Groups." *Political Research Quarterly* 47, no. 2 (June 1, 1994): 277–294. https://doi.org/10.1177/106591299404700202.

Jacobs, Ronald N. *Race, Media, and the Crisis of Civil Society: From Watts to Rodney King.* Cambridge Cultural Social Studies. Cambridge: Cambridge University Press, 2000.

Jacobson, Matthew Frye. *Whiteness of a Different Color European Immigrants and the Alchemy of Race.* Cambridge: Harvard University Press, 2001.

Jahoda, Gustav. *Images of Savages: Ancients [Sic] Roots of Modern Prejudice in Western Culture*. London: Routledge, 1999.

Jaynes, Gerald David. *Immigration and Race: New Challenges for American Democracy*. 1 online resource (vii, 327 pages): illustrations vols. New Haven: Yale University Press, 2000. http://site.ebrary.com/id/10579359.

Jenkins, Lee. "'The Black O'Connell': Frederick Douglass and Ireland." *Nineteenth Century Studies* 13 (1999): 22–46.

Jennings, James. *Blacks, Latinos, and Asians in Urban America: Status and Prospects for Politics and Activism*. Westport, Conn.: Praeger, 1994.

Johnson, Guion Griffis. *Ante-Bellum North Carolina; a Social History*. Chapel Hill: University of North Carolina Press, 1937.

Johnson, James H., Walter C. Farrell, and Chandra Guinn. "Immigration Reform and the Browning of America: Tensions, Conflicts and Community Instability in Metropolitan Los Angeles." *The International Migration Review* 31, no. 4 (1997): 1055–1095. https://doi.org/10.2307/2547424.

Johnson, James, Karen Johnson-Webb, and Walter C. Farrell. "A Profile of Hispanic Newcomers to North Carolina." *Popular Government* 65, no. 1 (1999): 2–12.

Johnson, Kevin R. "Law and Politics in Post-Modern California: Coalition or Conflict between African Americans, Asian Americans, and Latina/Os?" *Ethnicities* 4, no. 3 (September 1, 2004): 381–401. https://doi.org/10.1177/1468796804045240.

Johnson–Webb, Karen D. "Employer Recruitment and Hispanic Labor Migration: North Carolina Urban Areas at the End of the Millennium." *The Professional Geographer* 54, no. 3 (August 1, 2002): 406–421. https://doi.org/10.1111/0033-0124.00339.

Jones, Beverly W. "Race, Sex, and Class: Black Female Tobacco Workers in Durham, North Carolina, 1920-1940, and the Development of Female Consciousness." *Feminist Studies* 10, no. 3 (1984): 441–451. https://doi.org/10.2307/3178034.

Jones, Jacqueline. *Labor of Love, Labor of Sorrow: Black Women, Work, and the Family from Slavery to the Present*. 2nd ed. New York: Basic Books, 2009.

Jones, Jeffrey M. "Americans Less Satisfied with Treatment of Minority Groups." Washington, DC: Gallup, February 20, 2019. https://news.gallup.com/poll/246866/americans-less-satisfied-treatment-minority-groups.aspx.

Jordan-Zachery, Julia S. *Black Women, Cultural Images, and Social Policy*. New York and London: Routledge, 2009.

Joyce, Patrick D. *No Fire next Time: Black-Korean Conflicts and the Future of America's Cities*. Ithaca: Cornell University Press, 2003.

Junn, Jane. "Mobilizing Group Consciousness: When Does Ethnicity Have Political Consequences." In *Transforming Politics, Transforming America: The Political and Civic Incorporation of Immigrants in the United States*, edited by Taeku Lee, S. Karthick Ramakrishnan, and Ricardo Ramirez, 32–48. Charlottesville: University of Virginia Press, 2006.

Kachun, Mitch. "From Forgotten Founder to Indispensable Icon: Crispus Attucks, Black Citizenship, and Collective Memory, 1770–1865." *Journal of the Early Republic* 29, no. 2 (2009): 249–286. https://doi.org/10.1353/jer.0.0072.

Kadlec, David. "Marianne Moore, Immigration, and Eugenics." *Modernism/Modernity* 1, no. 2 (April 1, 1994): 21–49. https://doi.org/10.1353/mod.1994.0031.

Kadushin, Charles, Matthew Lindholm, Dan Ryan, Archie Brodsky, and Leonard Saxe. "Why It Is so Difficult to Form Effective Community Coalitions." *City and Community* 4, no. 3 (2005): 255–275.

Kanazawa, Mark. "Immigration, Exclusion, and Taxation: Anti-Chinese Legislation in Gold Rush California." *The Journal of Economic History* 65, no. 3 (2005): 779–805.

Kandel, William, and Emilio A. Parrado. "Hispanics in the American South and the Transformation of the Poultry Industry." In *Hispanic Spaces, Latino Places: Community and Cultural Diversity in Contemporary America*, edited by Daniel D. Arreola, 1st ed., 255–276. Austin: University of Texas Press, 2004. http://public.eblib.com/choice/publicfullrecord.aspx?p=3442984.

Kantrowitz, Nathan. "Racial and Ethnic Residential Segregation in Boston 1830-1970." *The ANNALS of the American Academy of Political and Social Science* 441, no. 1 (January 1, 1979): 41–54. https://doi.org/10.1177/000271627944100105.

Kasinitz, Philip. *Caribbean New York: Black Immigrants and the Politics of Race*. 1 edition. Ithaca: Cornell University Press, 1992.

Kates, Don B. "Handgun Prohibition and the Original Meaning of the Second Amendment." *Michigan Law Review* 82, no. 2 (April 15, 1983): 204–273.

Katznelson, Ira. *When Affirmative Action Was White: An Untold Story of Racial Inequality in Twentieth-Century America*. New York: W.W. Norton & Company, 2006.

Kaufmann, Karen M. "Cracks in the Rainbow: Group Commonality as a Basis for Latino and African-American Political Coalitions." *Political Research Quarterly* 56, no. 2 (2003): 199–210. https://doi.org/10.2307/3219898.

Keech, William R. *The Impact of Negro Voting; the Role of the Vote in the Quest for Equality*. American Politics Research Series. Chicago: Rand McNally, 1968.

Kelley, Robin D. G. *Hammer and Hoe: Alabama Communists during the Great Depression*. Chapel Hill: University of North Carolina Press, 1990.

Kelley, Robin D. G. "'We Are Not What We Seem': Rethinking Black Working-Class Opposition in the Jim Crow South." *Journal of American History* 80, no. 1 (1993): 75–112. https://doi.org/10.2307/2079698.

Kelley, Robin D. G. *Race Rebels: Culture, Politics, and the Black Working Class*. New York: Free Press, 1996.

Kelley, Robin D. G. "'But a Local Phase of a World Problem': Black History's Global Vision, 1883-1950." *The Journal of American History* 86, no. 3 (1999): 1045–1077. https://doi.org/10.2307/2568605.

Kelley, Robin D. G. *Freedom Dreams: The Black Radical Imagination*. Boston, Mass.: Beacon, 2003.

Kellstedt, Paul M. "Media Framing and the Dynamics of Racial Policy Preferences." *American Journal of Political Science* 44, no. 2 (2000): 245–260. https://doi.org/10.2307/2669308.

Kelly, Hilton. *Race, Remembering, and Jim Crow's Teachers.* New York: Routledge, 2010.

Kelsey, Carl. "Immigration and Crime." *The Annals of the American Academy of Political and Social Science* 125, no. 1 (May 1, 1926): 165–174. https://doi.org/10.1177/000271622612500132.

Kendi, Ibram X. *Stamped from the Beginning: A History of Racist Ideas in America.* New York: Nation Books, 2016.

Kennelly, Ivy. "That Single-Mother Element: How White Employers Typify Black Women." *Gender & Society* 13, no. 2 (1999): 168–192. https://doi.org/10.1177/089124399013002002.

Kessler-Harris, Alice. *Out to Work: A History of Wage-Earning Women in the United States.* Oxford, UK; New York: Oxford University Press, 2003.

Key, V. O. *Southern Politics in State and Nation.* Knoxville: University of Tennessee Press, 1996.

Kim, Claire Jean. "The Racial Triangulation of Asian Americans." *Politics and Society* 27, no. 1 (1999): 105–138.

Kim, Claire Jean. *Bitter Fruit: The Politics of Black-Korean Conflict in New York City.* New Haven: Yale University Press, 2000.

Kim, Claire Jean. "Imagining Race and Nation in Multiculturalist America." *Ethnic and Racial Studies* 27, no. 6 (November 1, 2004): 987–1005. https://doi.org/10.1080/0141987042000268567.

Kim, Elaine H. "'At Least You're Not Black': Asian Americans in U.S. Race Relations." *Social Justice* 25, no. 3 (73) (1998): 3–12.

Kim, Janine Young. "Are Asians Black?: The Asian-American Civil Rights Agenda and the Contemporary Significance of the Black/White Paradigm." *Yale Law Journal* 108, no. 8 (1999): 2385–2412.

Kinder, Donald R., and Cindy D. Kam. *Us against Them: Ethnocentric Foundations of American Opinion.* Chicago: University of Chicago Press, 2010.

Kinder, Donald R., and Lynn M. Sanders. *Divided by Color: Racial Politics and Democratic Ideals.* Chicago: The University of Chicago Press, 1996.

King, Deborah K. "Multiple Jeopardy, Multiple Consciousness: The Context of a Black Feminist Ideology." *Signs* 14, no. 1 (1988): 42–72.

King, Desmond. *Making Americans: Immigration, Race, and the Origins of the Diverse Democracy.* Cambridge, MA: Harvard University Press, 2002.

King, Desmond S., and Rogers M. Smith. "Racial Orders in American Political Development." *American Political Science Review* 99, no. 1 (2005): 75–92. https://doi.org/10.1017/S0003055405051506.

Kirby, John B. "Ralph J. Bunche and Black Radical Thought in the 1930s." *Phylon* 35, no. 2 (1974): 129–141. https://doi.org/10.2307/274702.

Kirschenman, Joleen, and Kathryn M. Neckerman. "We'd Love to Hire Them, but...: The Meaning of Race for Employers." In *The Urban Underclass*, edited by Christopher Jencks and Paul E. Peterson, 203–232. Washington, DC: The Brookings Institution, 1991.

Klarman, Michael J. "The Racial Origins of Modern Criminal Procedure." *Michigan Law Review* 99, no. 1 (2000): 48–97. https://doi.org/10.2307/1290325.

Klinkner, Philip. "The Easiest Way to Guess If Someone Supports Trump? Ask If Obama Is a Muslim." *Vox*, June 2, 2016. https://www.vox.com/2016/6/2/11833548/donald-trump-support-race-religion-economy.

Klinkner, Philip A., and Rogers M. Smith. *The Unsteady March: The Rise and Decline of Racial Equality in America*. Chicago: University of Chicago Press, 1999. http://catdir.loc.gov/catdir/toc/uchi052/99023195.html.

Knobel, Dale T. *America for the Americans: The Nativist Movement in the United States*. New York: Twayne Pub, 1996.

Kochhar, Rakesh., Roberto Suro, Sonya M. Tafoya, and Pew Hispanic Center. *The New Latino South: The Context and Consequences of Rapid Population Growth*. Washington, DC: Pew Hispanic Center, 2005. http://pewhispanic.org/reports/report.php?ReportID=50.

Kousser, J. Morgan. *Colorblind Injustice: Minority Voting Rights and the Undoing of the Second Reconstruction*. Chapel Hill: University of North Carolina Press, 1999.

Krogstad, Jens Mauel. "U.S. Hispanic Population Growth Has Leveled Off." Washington, DC: Pew Charitable Trusts, August 3, 2017. https://www.pewresearch.org/fact-tank/2017/08/03/u-s-hispanic-population-growth-has-leveled-off/.

Krysan, Maria. "Prejudice, Politics, and Public Opinion: Understanding the Sources of Racial Policy Attitudes." *Annual Review of Sociology* 26, no. 1 (2000): 135–168. https://doi.org/ttps://doi.org/10.1146/annurev.soc.26.1.135.

Kuklinski, James H., Michael D. Cobb, and Martin Gilens. "Racial Attitudes and the 'New South.'" *The Journal of Politics* 59, no. 2 (1997): 323–349. https://doi.org/10.1017/S0022381600053470.

Kusmer, Kenneth L. *A Ghetto Takes Shape: Black Cleveland, 1870–1930*. Champaign: University of Illinois Press, 1978.

Lacy, Karyn R. *Blue-Chip Black: Race, Class, and Status in the New Black Middle Class*. Berkeley: University of California Press, 2007.

Ladd, Everett Carll. *Negro Political Leadership in the South*. Ithaca: Cornell University Press, 1966.

LeDuff, Charlie. "At a Slaughterhouse, Some Things Never Die." In *How Race Is Lived in America: Pulling Together, Pulling Apart*, edited by correspondents of *The New York Times*, 79–96. London: Macmillan, 2002.

Lee, Erika. "Enforcing the Borders: Chinese Exclusion along the U.S. Borders with Canada and Mexico, 1882–1924." *The Journal of American History* 89, no. 1 (2002a): 54–86. https://doi.org/10.2307/2700784.

Lee, Erika. "The Chinese Exclusion Example: Race, Immigration, and American Gatekeeping, 1882-1924." *Journal of American Ethnic History* 21, no. 3 (2002b): 36–62.

Lee, Jennifer, and Frank D. Bean. "Reinventing the Color Line: Immigration and America's New Racial/Ethnic Divide." *Social Forces* 86, no. 2 (December 1, 2007): 561–586. https://doi.org/10.1093/sf/86.2.561.

Lee, Karen. "Asian and African American Co-Operation and Competition in Nineteenth Century USA." *Graduate Journal of Asia-Pacific Studies* 4, no. 1 (2006): 82–91.

Leiter, Jeffrey, Leslie Hossfeld, and Donald Tomaskovic-Devey. "North Carolina Employers Look at Latino Workers." Atlanta, GA: Annual Conference of the Southern Sociological Society, 2001.

Leitner, Helga. "Spaces of Encounters: Immigration, Race, Class, and the Politics of Belonging in Small-Town America." *Annals of the Association of American Geographers* 102, no. 4 (2012): 828–846. https://doi.org/10.1080/00045608.2011.601204.

Leonard, Thomas. "Mistaking Eugenics for Social Darwinism: Why Eugenics Is Missing from the History of American Economics." *History of Political Economy* 37, no. 5 (2005): 200–233.

Lesniewski, Niels. "Lindsey Graham Seconds Trump Proposal to End Birthright Citizenship." *Roll Call*, October 30, 2018, sec. Politics. https://www.rollcall.com/news/politics/lindsey-graham-trump-birthright-citizenship.

Lewis, David Levering, ed. *W.E.B. Du Bois: A Reader*. New York: Holt Paperbacks, 1995.

Lichtenstein, Alex. "Ned Cobb's Children: A New Look at White Supremacy in the Rural Southern US." *The Journal of Peasant Studies* 33, no. 1 (January 1, 2006): 124–139. https://doi.org/10.1080/03066150600624579.

Lieberman, Robert C. "Private Power and the American Bureaucracy: The EEOC and Civil Rights Enforcement." American Political Development Colloquium. Charlottesville: Miller Center of Public Affairs, University of Virginia, March 18, 2005.

Lieberson, Stanley. *A Piece of the Pie: Blacks and White Immigrants Since 1880*. Berkeley: University of California Press, 1980.

Light, Ivan. "Immigrant Place Entrepreneurs in Los Angeles, 1970–99." *International Journal of Urban and Regional Research* 26, no. 2 (June 1, 2002): 215–228. https://doi.org/10.1111/1468-2427.00376.

Lincoln, C. Eric, and Lawrence H. Mamiya. *The Black Church in the African American Experience*. Durham, NC: Duke University Press, 1990.

Lindsay, Matthew J. "Reproducing a Fit Citizenry: Dependency, Eugenics, and the Law of Marriage in the United States, 1860–1920." *Law & Social Inquiry* 23, no. 3 (1998): 541–585. https://doi.org/10.1111/j.1747-4469.1998.tb00121.x.

Lipka, Michael. "Muslims and Islam: Key Findings in the U.S. and Around the World." Washington, DC: Pew Research Center, August 9, 2017. https://

www.pewresearch.org/fact-tank/2017/08/09/muslims-and-islam-key-findings-in-the-u-s-and-around-the-world/.

Lipman, Francine. "The Taxation of Undocumented Immigrants: Separate, Unequal, and Without Representation." *Harvard Latino Law Review* 9 (February 15, 2006): 59–90.

Lipsitz, George. "The Possessive Investment in Whiteness: Racialized Social Democracy and the 'White' Problem in American Studies." *American Quarterly* 47, no. 3 (1995): 369–387. https://doi.org/10.2307/2713291.

Litwack, Leon F. "Jim Crow Blues." *OAH Magazine of History* 18, no. 2 (January 1, 2004): 7–58. https://doi.org/10.1093/maghis/18.2.7.

Loewen, James W. *The Mississippi Chinese: Between Black and White*. First. Prospect Heights, IL: Waveland Press, Inc., 1988.

Loewenberg, Bert James. "Efforts of the South to Encourage Immigration, 1865–1900." *South Atlantic Quarterly* 33 (1934): 363–385.

Logan, Rayford W. *The Negro in American Life and Thought; The Nadir, 1877–1901*. New York: Dial Press, 1954.

Logan, Rayford W. *The Betrayal of the Negro: From Rutherford B. Hayes to Woodrow Wilson*. New York: Da Capo Press, 1997.

Lopez, Linda, and Adrian D. Pantoja. "Beyond Black and White: General Support for Race-Conscious Policies Among African Americans, Latinos, Asian Americans and Whites." *Political Research Quarterly* 57, no. 4 (December 1, 2004): 633–642. https://doi.org/10.1177/106591290405700411.

Lott, Eric. "Love and Theft: The Racial Unconscious of Blackface Minstrelsy." *Representations* 39 (1992): 23–50.

Loury, Glenn C. "Discrimination in the Post-Civil Rights Era: Beyond Market Interactions." *The Journal of Economic Perspectives* 12, no. 2 (1998): 117–126.

Lui, Mary. "Saving Young Girls from Chinatown: White Slavery and Woman Suffrage, 1910–1920." *Journal of the History of Sexuality* 18, no. 3 (2009): 393–417. https://doi.org/10.5555/jhs.2009.18.3.393.

Lui, Meizhu, Barbara Robles, Betsy Leondar-Wright, Rose Brewer, and Rebecca Adamson. *The Color of Wealth: The Story Behind the U.S. Racial Wealth Divide*. New York: The New Press, 2006.

Lyman, Stanford M. "The 'Yellow Peril' Mystique: Origins and Vicissitudes of a Racist Discourse." *International Journal of Politics, Culture, and Society* 13, no. 4 (2000): 683–747.

Mabry, William Alexander. "Disfranchisement of the Negro in Mississippi." *The Journal of Southern History* 4, no. 3 (1938): 318–333. https://doi.org/10.2307/2191292.

MacDorman, Marian F., and T. J. Matthews. "Understanding Racial and Ethnic Disparities in U.S. Infant Mortality Rates." *NCHS Data Brief* 74 (2011): 1–8.

MacGill, C. E. "Immigration to the Southern States." In *The South in the Building of the Nation*, edited by Walter L Fleming, 584–594. Richmond: Southern Historical Publication Society, 1905. http://archive.org/details/jstor-2140401.

Maeda, Daryl J. "Black Panthers, Red Guards, and Chinamen: Constructing Asian American Identity through Performing Blackness, 1969–1972." *American Quarterly* 57, no. 4 (2005): 1079–1103.

Maldonado, Marta Maria. "Racial Triangulation of Latino/a Workers by Agricultural Employers." *Human Organization* 65, no. 4 (Winter 2006): 353–361. https://doi.org/10.17730/humo.65.4.a84b5xykrodvp91l.

Malloy, Robert. "Cast Down Your Buckets Where You Are: Black Americans on Immigration." CIS Paper. Washington, DC: Center for Immigration Studies, 1996.

Malone, Tara L. "Family Joins U-46 Lawsuit; District's Problems Affect All Minorities, Lawyer Says." *Chicago Daily Herald*, May 27, 2005. https://newspaperarchive.com/daily-herald-suburban-chicago-aug-28-2003-p-189/.

Maloney, Thomas N. "Degrees of Inequality: The Advance of Black Male Workers in the Northern Meat Packing and Steel Industries before World War II." *Social Science History* 19, no. 1 (1995): 31–62. https://doi.org/10.1017/S0145553200017211.

Maloney, Thomas N., and Warren C. Whatley. "Making the Effort: The Contours of Racial Discrimination in Detroit's Labor Markets, 1920-1940." *The Journal of Economic History* 55, no. 3 (1995): 465–493.

Malzberg, Benjamin. "Mental Disease Among Foreign-Born Whites, with Special Reference to Natives of Russia and Poland." *American Journal of Psychiatry* 92, no. 3 (November 1, 1935): 627–640. https://doi.org/10.1176/ajp.92.3.627.

Manza, Jeff, and Christopher Uggen. *Locked Out: Felon Disenfranchisement and American Democracy*. New York: Oxford University Press, 2006.

Marable, Manning. *Black Leadership*. New York: Columbia University Press, 1998.

Marable, Manning, and Leith Mullings, eds. *Let Nobody Turn Us Around: An African American Anthology*. Lanham: Rowman & Littlefield Publishers, 2000.

Maris-Wolf, Ted. *Family Bonds: Free Blacks and Re-Enslavement Law in Antebellum Virginia*. Chapel Hill: University of North Carolina Press, 2015.

Marrow, Helen B. "What's New? Immigration and Local Receiving Context in the Rural and Small-Town U.S. South." Irvine, CA: Paper presented at the Summer Institute on International Migration, 2005a.

Marrow, Helen B. "New Destinations and Immigrant Incorporation." *Perspectives on Politics* 3, no. 4 (2005b): 781–799.

Martínez, George A. "Immigration and the Meaning of United States Citizenship: Whiteness and Assimilation." *Washburn Law Journal* 46, no. 2 (2007): 335–344.

Marx, Anthony W. *Making Race and Nation: A Comparison of South Africa, the United States, and Brazil*. Cambridge, UK; New York: Cambridge University Press, 1998.

Massey, Douglas. *Political Process and the Development of Black Insurgency, 1930–1970.* Chicago: University of Chicago Press, 1982. https://www.press.uchicago.edu/ucp/books/book/chicago/P/bo5939918.html.

Massey, Douglas S. "American Apartheid: Segregation and the Making of the Underclass." *American Journal of Sociology* 96, no. 2 (1990): 329–357.

Massey, Douglas S. "America's Never-Ending Debate: A Review Essay." Edited by Aristide R. Zolberg. *Population and Development Review* 32, no. 3 (2006): 573–584.

Massey, Douglas, and Nancy Denton. *American Apartheid: Segregation and the Making of the Underclass.* Cambridge: Harvard University Press, 1993.

Massey, Douglas S, Margarita Mooney, Kimberly C. Torres, and Camille Z. Charles. "Black Immigrants and Black Natives Attending Selective Colleges and Universities in the United States." *American Journal of Education* 113, no. 2 (February 2007): 243–271. https://doi.org/10.1086/510167.

Masuoka, Natalie. "Together They Become One: Examining the Predictors of Panethnic Group Consciousness among Asian Americans and Latinos." *Social Science Quarterly* 87, no. 5 (November 16, 2006): 993–1011. https://doi.org/10.1111/j.1540-6237.2006.00412.x.

Masuoka, Natalie, and Jane Junn. *The Politics of Belonging: Race, Public Opinion, and Immigration.* Chicago and London: University of Chicago Press, 2013.

Matthews, Donald R. *Negroes and the New Southern Politics.* San Diego: Harcourt, 1966.

May, Reuben A. Buford. "Race Talk and Local Collective Memory among African American Men in a Neighborhood Tavern." *Qualitative Sociology* 23, no. 2 (June 1, 2000): 201–214. https://doi.org/10.1023/A:1005482816598.

May, Robert E. "Cashing in on Dixie?" *Reviews in American History* 34, no. 3 (2006): 342–349. https://doi.org/10.1353/rah.2006.0043.

Mayfield, Loomis. "Voting Fraud in Early Twentieth-Century Pittsburgh." *The Journal of Interdisciplinary History* 24, no. 1 (1993): 59–84. https://doi.org/10.2307/205101.

McAdam, Doug. *Political Process and the Development of Black Insurgency, 1930–970.* 2nd ed. Chicago: University of Chicago Press, 1999.

McBride, Dwight A. "Can the Queen Speak? Racial Essentialism, Sexuality and the Problem of Authority." *Callaloo* 21, no. 2 (May 1, 1998): 363–379. https://doi.org/10.1353/cal.1998.0112.

McClain, Paula D. "The Changing Dynamics of Urban Politics: Black and Hispanic Municipal Employment—Is There Competition?" *The Journal of Politics* 55, no. 2 (1993): 399–414. https://doi.org/10.2307/2132272.

McClain, Paula D. "Presidential Address. 'Racial Intergroup Relations in a Set of Cities: A Twenty-Year Perspective.'" *The Journal of Politics* 68, no. 4 (2006): 757–770. https://doi.org/10.1111/j.1468-2508.2006.00468.x.

McClain, Paula D., and Albert K. Karnig. "Black and Hispanic Socioeconomic and Political Competition." *American Political Science Review* 84, no. 2 (June 1990): 535–545. https://doi.org/10.2307/1963534.

McClain, Paula D., Niambi M. Carter, and Michael C. Brady. "Gender and Black Presidential Politics: From Chisholm to Moseley Braun." *Journal of Women, Politics & Policy* 27, no. 1–2 (October 13, 2005): 51–68. https://doi.org/10.1300/J501v27n01_04.

McClain, Paula D., Michael C. Brady, Niambi M. Carter, Efrén O. Pérez, and Victoria DeFrancesco Soto. "Rebuilding Black Voting Rights before the Voting Rights Act." In *The Voting Rights Act: Securing the Ballot*, edited by Richard Vallelly, 57–76. Washington, DC: CQ press, 2006a.

McClain, Paula D., Niambi M. Carter, Victoria M. DeFrancesco Soto, Monique L. Lyle, Jeffrey D. Grynaviski, Shayla C. Nunnally, et al. "Racial Distancing in a Southern City: Latino Immigrants' Views of Black Americans." *The Journal of Politics* 68, no. 3 (August 1, 2006b): 571–584. https://doi.org/10.1111/j.1468-2508.2006.00446.x.

McClain, Paula D., Monique L. Lyle, Niambi M. Carter, Victoria M. DeFrancesco Soto, Gerald F. Lackey, Kendra Davenport Cotton, Shayla C. Nunnally, Thomas J. Scotto, Jeffrey D. Grynaviski, and J. Alan Kendrick. "Black Americans and Latino Immigrants in a Southern City: Friendly neighbors or Economic Competitors?." *Du Bois Review: Social Science Research on Race* 4, no. 1 (2007): 97–117. https://doi.org/10.1017/S1742058X07070063.

McClain, Paula Denice, and Joseph Stewart. *"Can We All Get Along?": Racial and Ethnic Minorities in American Politics*. Dilemmas in American Politics. Boulder: Westview Press, 2006. http://catdir.loc.gov/catdir/toc/ecip0511/2005009838.html.

McClain, Paula D., and Steven C. Tauber. "Black and Latino Socioeconomic and Political Competition: Has a Decade Made a Difference." *American Politics Quarterly* 26, no. 2 (1998): 237–252. https://doi.org/10.1177/1532673X9802600206.

McDaniel, Eric Leon, Irfan Nooruddin, and Allyson Faith Shortle. "Divine Boundaries: How Religion Shapes Citizens' Attitudes Toward Immigrants." *American Politics Research* 39, no. 1 (2011): 205–233. https://doi.org/10.1177/1532673X10371300.

McGuire, Danielle L. *At the Dark End of the Street: Black Women, Rape, and Resistance—a New History of the Civil Rights Movement from Rosa Parks to the Rise of Black Power*. Reprint. New York: Vintage Books, 2010.

McGuire, Gail M. "Gender, Race, Ethnicity, and Networks: The Factors Affecting the Status of Employees' Network Members." *Work and Occupations* 27, no. 4 (November 1, 2000): 501–524. https://doi.org/10.1177/0730888400027004004.

McKanders, Karla Mari. "Sustaining Tiered Personhood: Jim Crow and Anti-Immigrant Laws." *Harvard Journal of Racial and Ethnic Justice* 26, no. 1 (Spring 2010): 163–210. https://heinonline.org/HOL/P?h=hein.journals/hblj26&i=165.

McKinnon, Jesse. "The Black Population in the United States: 2002." U.S. Census Bureau, Current Population Reports, April 2003.

McMillen, Neil R. "'Reconstruction and Its Aftermath: Mississippi History, 1865–1890.' Mississippi State Historical Museum, 100 South State St., Jackson, MS

39209." *Journal of American History* 77, no. 1 (June 1, 1990): 239–246. https://doi.org/10.2307/2078658.

McMillen, Neil R. *The Citizens' Council: Organized Resistance to the Second Reconstruction, 1954-64.* Urbana: University of Illinois Press, 1994.

Mehlinger, Louis R. "The Attitude of the Free Negro Toward African Colonization." *The Journal of Negro History* 1, no. 3 (1916): 276–301.

Meier, Kenneth J., Paula D. McClain, J. L. Polinard, and Robert D. Wrinkle. "Divided or Together? Conflict and Cooperation between African Americans and Latinos." *Political Research Quarterly* 57, no. 3 (September 1, 2004): 399–409. https://doi.org/10.1177/106591290405700305.

Meier, Kenneth J., and Joseph Stewart. "Cooperation and Conflict in Multiracial School Districts." *The Journal of Politics* 53, no. 4 (November 1991): 1123–1133. https://doi.org/10.2307/2131870

Melish, Joanne Pope. "The 'Condition' Debate and Racial Discourse in the Antebellum North." *Journal of the Early Republic* 19, no. 4 (1999): 651–672.

Mettler, Suzanne. *Soldiers to Citizens: The G.I. Bill and the Making of the Greatest Generation.* New York: Oxford University Press, 2005.

Mills, Charles W. *The Racial Contract.* Ithaca: Cornell University Press, 1997.

Min, Pyong-Gap, and Andrew Kolodny. "The Middleman Minority Characteristics of Korean Immigrants in the United States." *Korea Journal of Population and Development* 23, no. 2 (1994): 179–202.

Mindiola, Tatcho Jr., Yolanda Flores Niemann, and Nestor Rodriguez. *Black-Brown Relations and Stereotypes.* 1 edition. Austin: University of Texas Press, 2003.

Mitchell, Michele. "Silences Broken, Silences Kept: Gender and Sexuality in African-American History." *Gender History* 11, no. 3 (November 1999): 433–444. https://doi.org/10.1111/1468-0424.00154.

Miyashita, Alex Mineses. "Black, Hispanic Activists Come Together in Wake of Fox's Comments." *Scripps Howard News Service*, May 25, 2005.

Montgomery, David. "Presidential Address: Racism, Immigrants, and Political Reform." *The Journal of American History* 87, no. 4 (2001): 1253–1274. https://doi.org/10.2307/2674728.

Morris, Aldon D. *The Origins of the Civil Rights Movement: Black Communities Organizing for Change.* New York: Free Press, 1986.

Morris, Aldon D. "A Retrospective on the Civil Rights Movement: Political and Intellectual Landmarks." *Annual Review of Sociology* 25, no. 1 (1999): 517–539.

Morris, Irwin L. "African American Voting on Proposition 187: Rethinking the Prevalence of Interminority Conflict." *Political Research Quarterly* 53, no. 1 (March 1, 2000): 77–98. https://doi.org/10.1177/106591290005300104.

Moskos, Charles C. "Success Story: Blacks in the Military." *The Atlantic*, May 1, 1986.

Moye, J. Todd. *Let the People Decide: Black Freedom and White Resistance Movements in Sunflower County, Mississippi, 1945-1986.* Chapel Hill: University of North Carolina Press, 2004.

Muhammad, Khalil Gibran. *The Condemnation of Blackness: Race, Crime, and the Making of Modern Urban America*. Cambridge: Harvard University Press, 2010.

Mukherjee, Roopali. "Antiracism Limited: A Pre-History of Post-Race." *Cultural Studies* 30, no. 1 (2016): 47–77. https://doi.org/10.1080/09502386.2014.935455

Mullen, Robert W. *Blacks in America's Wars; the Shift in Attitudes From the Revolutionary War to Vietnam*. New York: Monad Press, 1973.

Mumford, Kevin. *Interzones: Black/White Sex Districts in Chicago and New York in the Early Twentieth Century*. New York: Columbia University Press, 1997.

Muñoz, Carlos, and Charles Henry. "Rainbow Coalitions in Four Big Cities: San Antonio, Denver, Chicago and Philadelphia." *PS: Political Science & Politics* 19, no. 3 (1986): 598–609. https://doi.org/10.1017/S1049096500018163.

Murray, Pauli. *Proud Shoes: The Story of an American Family*. Boston: Beacon Press, 1999.

Mutua, Athena D. "Shifting Bottoms and Rotating Centers: Reflections on LatCrit III and the Black/White Paradigm." *University of Miami Law Review* 53, no. 4 (1999): 1177–1218.

Myers, Ella. "Beyond the Psychological Wage: Du Bois on White Dominion." *Political Theory* 47, no. 1 (2018): 6–31. https://doi.org/10.1177/0090591718791744.

Myrdal, Gunnar. *An American Dilemma: The Negro Problem and Modern Democracy*. New York: McGraw-Hill, 1962.

Nagel, Joane. *American Indian Ethnic Renewal: Red Power and the Resurgence of Identity and Culture*. New York: Oxford University Press, 1997.

Nagel, Joane. "American Indian Ethnic Renewal: Politics and the Resurgence of Identity." *American Sociological Review* 60, no. 6 (1995): 947–965. https://doi.org/10.2307/2096434.

National Hispanic Media Coalition. "The Impact of Media Stereotypes on Opinions and Attitudes Toward Latinos." September 2012. http://www.nhmc.org/sites/default/files/LD%20NHMC%20Poll%20Results%20Sept.2012.pdf

Neckerman, Kathryn M., and Joleen Kirschenman. "Hiring Strategies, Racial Bias, and Inner-City Workers." *Social Problems* 38, no. 4 (1991): 433–447. https://doi.org/10.2307/800563.

Nelson, Bruce. *Divided We Stand*. Princeton: Princeton University Press, 2001. https://press.princeton.edu/titles/6947.html.

Newton, I. G. "Expansion of Negro Suffrage in North Carolina." *The Journal of Negro Education* 26, no. 3 (1957): 351–358. https://doi.org/10.2307/2293417.

Ngai, Mae M. *Impossible Subjects: Illegal Aliens and the Making of Modern America*. Princeton: Princeton University Press, 2004.

Nobles, Melissa. *Shades of Citizenship: Race and the Census in Modern Politics*. 1 edition. Stanford, Calif: Stanford University Press, 2000.

Nteta, Tatishe. "United We Stand? African Americans, Self-Interest, and Immigration Reform." *American Politics Research* 41, no. 1 (2013): 147–172. https://doi.org/10.1177/1532673X12452909.

Nteta, Tatishe. "The Past Is Prologue: African American Opinion toward Undocumented Immigration." *Social Science History* 38, no. 3–4 (2014): 389–410. https://doi.org/10.1017/ssh.2015.30.

Nunnally, Shayla C. "Learning Race, Socializing Blackness: A Cross-Generational Analysis of Black Americans' Racial Socialization Experiences." *Du Bois Review: Social Science Research on Race* 7, no. 1 (2010): 185–217.

Nunnally, Shayla C. *Trust in Black America: Race, Discrimination, and Politics.* New York: NYU Press, 2012.

Nunnally, Shayla C., and Niambi M. Carter. "Moving from Victims to Victors: African American Attitudes on the 'Culture of Poverty.'" *Journal of African American Studies* 16, no. 3 (2012): 423–455.

O'Brien, Eileen. *The Racial Middle: Latinos and Asian Americans Living Beyond the Racial Divide.* New York: NYU Press, 2008.

Ohl, Jessy J., and Jennifer E. Potter. "United We Lynch: Post-Racism and the (Re) Remembering of Racial Violence in Without Sanctuary: Lynching Photography in America." *Southern Communication Journal* 78, no. 3 (2013): 185–201. https://doi.org/10.1080/1041794X.2012.749297.

Okazawa-Rey, Margo, and Marshall Wong. "Organizing in Communities of Color: Addressing Interethnic Conflicts." *Social Justice* 24, no. 1 (67) (1997): 24–39.

Oliver, J. Eric, and Janelle Wong. "Intergroup Prejudice in Multiethnic Settings." *American Journal of Political Science* 47, no. 4 (October 1, 2003): 567–582. https://doi.org/10.1111/1540-5907.00040.

Oliver, Melvin, and Thomas M. Shapiro, eds. *Black Wealth/White Wealth: A New Perspective on Racial Inequality.* New York, NY: Routledge, 2001.

Olzak, Susan. "Labor Unrest, Immigration, and Ethnic Conflict in Urban America, 1880–1914." *American Journal of Sociology* 94, no. 6 (1989): 1303–1333.

Omi, Michael, and Howard Winant. *Racial Formation in the United States: From the 1960s to the 1990s.* New York: Routledge, 1994.

Ordover, Nancy. *American Eugenics: Race, Queer Anatomy, and the Science of Nationalism.* Minneapolis: University of Minnesota Press, 2003.

Orr, Marion. *Black Social Capital: The Politics of School Reform in Baltimore, 1986-1999.* Lawrence: University Press of Kansas, 1999.

Orsi, Robert. "The Religious Boundaries of an Inbetween People: Street Feste and the Problem of the Dark-Skinned Other in Italian Harlem, 1920–1990." *American Quarterly* 44, no. 3 (1992): 313–347. https://doi.org/10.2307/2712980.

Osajima, Keith. "Asian Americans as the Model Minority: An Analysis of the Popular Press Image in the 1960s and 1980s." In *Reflections on Shattered Windows: Promises and Prospects for Asian American Studies*, edited by Gary Okihiro, Shirley Hune, John Hansen, and John Liu, 165–175. Pullman: Washington State University Press, 1987. https://search.library.wisc.edu/catalog/9995880766021121.

Pager, Devah, Bart Bonikowski, and Bruce Western. "Discrimination in a Low-Wage Labor Market: A Field Experiment." *American Sociological Review* 74, no. 5 (2009): 777–799. https://doi.org/10.1177/000312240907400505.

Painter, Nell Irvin. "'One Drop of Blood: The American Misadventure of Race' (Review)." *The Journal of Southern History* 68, no. 3 (2002): 669–671. https://doi.org/10.2307/3070163.

Palmer, Breanne J. "The Crossroads: Being Black, Immigration, and Undocumented in the Era of #BlackLivesMatter." *Georgetown Journal of Law & Modern Critical Race Perspectives* 9, no. 1 (2017): 99–121.

Pantoja, Adrian D. "Latino Politics in the Era of Bad Feelings." Presented at the Global Awareness Lectures, College of St. Benedict and St. John's University Digital Commons, October 11, 2016. https://digitalcommons.csbsju.edu/polsci_global_awareness/18

Pantoja, Adrian. "Against The Tide? Core American Values and Attitudes Toward US Immigration Policy in the Mid-1990s." *Journal of Ethnic and Migration Studies* 32, no. 3 (April 1, 2006): 515–531. https://doi.org/10.1080/13691830600555111.

Park, Julie. "Poverty Trends for Southeast Asians in the United States, 1990-2000." Philadelphia, PA: Annual Meetings of the Population Association of America, 2005.

Parker, Christopher S. "When Politics Becomes Protest: Black Veterans and Political Activism in the Postwar South." *The Journal of Politics* 71, no. 1 (January 2009): 113–131. https://doi.org/doi:10.1017/S0022381608090087.

Parker, Christopher S. "Symbolic versus Blind Patriotism: Distinction without a Difference?" *Political Research Quarterly* 63, no. 1 (2010): 97–114.

Parker, Frederick B. "The Status of the Foreign Stock in the Southeast: A Region-Nation Comparison." *Social Forces* 27, no. 2 (1948): 136–143.

Parrish, Thomas B., Amy Merickel, Maria Perez, Robert Linquanti, Miguel Socias, Angeline Spain, Cecilia Speroni, Phil Esra, Leslie Brock, and Danielle Delancey. "Effects of the Implementation of Proposition 227 on the Education of English Learners, K-12: Findings from a Five-Year Evaluation. Final Report for AB 56 and AB 1116." Washington, DC: American Institutes for Research, 2006.

Pascoe, Peggy. "Miscegenation Law, Court Cases, and Ideologies of 'Race' in Twentieth-Century America." *Journal of American History* 83, no. 1 (June 1, 1996): 44–69. https://doi.org/10.2307/2945474.

Passel, Jeffrey S. "Illegal Immigration: How Big a Problem?" Washington, DC: Urban Institute, 1995.

Passel, Jeffrey S. "The Size and Characteristics of the Unauthorized Hispanic Population." Washington, DC: Pew Hispanic Center, 2006.

Passel, Jeffrey S., Randolph Capps, and Michael E. Fix. "Undocumented Immigrants: Facts and Figures." Washington, DC: Urban Institute, 2004. https://www.urban.org/research/publication/undocumented-immigrants-facts-and-figures.

Passel, Jeffrey S., and Wendy Zimmermann. "Are Immigrants Leaving California? Settlement Patterns of Immigrants in the Late 1990s." Washington, DC: Urban Institute, 2001. https://eric.ed.gov/?id=ED452333.

Pastor, Manuel, and Enrico Marcelli. "Somewhere over the Rainbow?: African Americans, Unauthorized Mexican Immigration, and Coalition Building." *The Review of Black Political Economy* 31, no. 1–2 (2003): 125–155.

Patram, Sahadeo, Travis Patton, and Obie Clayton. "Immigrants, Economic Opportunity, and Political Influence: Perceptions of Native Born Americans." *Challenge: A Journal of Research on African American Men* 7 (1996): 29–56.

Pattillo, Mary. *Black Picket Fences: Privilege and Peril among the Black Middle Class.* Chicago; London: University of Chicago Press, 2000.

Payne, Charles. "Ella Baker and Models of Social Change." *Signs: Journal of Women in Culture and Society* 14, no. 4 (1989): 885–899.

Payne, Charles M. *I've Got the Light of Freedom: The Organizing Tradition and the Mississippi Freedom Struggle.* Berkeley: University of California Press, 1997.

Payne, Charles M. "'The Whole United States Is Southern!': Brown v. Board and the Mystification of Race." *The Journal of American History* 91, no. 1 (2004): 83–91. https://doi.org/10.2307/3659615.

Peach, Ceri. "Good Segregation, Bad Segregation." *Planning Perspectives* 11, no. 4 (December 1, 1996): 379–398. https://doi.org/10.1080/026654396364817.

Pedriana, Nicholas, and Robin Stryker. "The Strength of a Weak Agency: Enforcement of Title VII of the 1964 Civil Rights Act and the Expansion of State Capacity, 1965-1971." *American Journal of Sociology* 110, no. 3 (November 1, 2004): 709–760. https://doi.org/10.1086/422588.

Peffley, Mark, Jon Hurwitz, and Paul M. Sniderman. "Racial Stereotypes and Whites' Political Views of Blacks in the Context of Welfare and Crime." *American Journal of Political Science* 41, no. 1 (1997): 30–60. https://doi.org/10.2307/2111708.

Pennebaker, James W., Bernard Rim, and Dario Paez, eds. *Collective Memory of Political Events: Social Psychological Perspectives.* Mahwah, NJ: Psychology Press, 2013.

Perea, Juan F. "The Black/White Binary Paradigm of Race: The 'Normal Science' of American Racial Thought." *California Law Review* 85, no. 5 (1997): 1213–1258. https://doi.org/10.2307/3481059.

Pérez, Efrén O. *Unspoken Politics: Implicit Attitudes and Political Thinking.* Cambridge: Cambridge University Press, 2016.

Perlmann, Joel. *Ethnic Differences: Schooling and Social Structure among the Irish, Italians, Jews, and Blacks in an American City, 1880–1935.* Cambridge: Cambridge University Press, 1989.

Perman, Michael. *Struggle for Mastery: Disfranchisement in the South, 1888–1908.* Chapel Hill: University of North Carolina Press, 2001.

Perry, Andre, Jonathan Rothwell, and David Harshbarger. "The Devaluation of Assets in Black Neighborhoods: The Case of Residential Property." Washington,

DC: Metropolitan Policy Program at The Brookings Institution, November 2018. https://www.brookings.edu/wp-content/uploads/2018/11/2018.11_Brookings-Metro_Devaluation-Assets-Black-Neighborhoods_final.pdf.

Perry, Huey. "The Evolution and Impact of Biracial Coalitions and Black Mayors in Birmingham and New Orleans." In *Racial Politics in American Cities*, edited by Rufus P Browning, Dale Rogers Marshall, and David H Tabb, 179–200. New York: Longman, 2003.

Pettit, Becky, and Bruce Western. "Mass Imprisonment and the Life Course: Race and Class Inequality in US Incarceration." *American Sociological Review* 69, no. 2 (2004): 151–169. https://doi.org/10.1177/000312240406900201.

Pew Research Center. "Blacks Upbeat about Black Progress, Prospects." Washington, DC. January 2, 2010. https://www.pewresearch.org/wp-content/uploads/sites/3/2010/10/blacks-upbeat-about-black-progress-prospects.pdf.

Pew Research Center. "On Views of Race and Inequality, Blacks and Whites are Worlds Apart." Washington, DC. June 27, 2016. https://www.pewsocialtrends.org/2016/06/27/on-views-of-race-and-inequality-blacks-and-whites-are-worlds-apart/.

Pinderhughes, Dianne M. *Race and Ethnicity in Chicago Politics: A Reexamination of Pluralist Theory*. Urbana: University of Illinois Press, 1987.

Plummer, Brenda Gayle. *Rising Wind: Black Americans and US Foreign Affairs, 1935–1960*. Chapel Hill: The University of North Carolina Press, 1996.

Polinard, Jerry L., Robert D. Wrinkle, and Rodolfo de la Garza. "Attitudes of Mexican Americans toward Irregular Mexican Immigration." *The International Migration Review* 18, no. 3 (1984): 782–799. https://doi.org/10.2307/2545898.

Portes, Alejandro. *City on the Edge*. Berkeley: University of California Press, 1993.

Posadas, Barbara M. "The Hierarchy of Color and Psychological Adjustment in an Industrial Environment: Filipinos, the Pullman Company and the Brotherhood of Sleeping Car Porters." *Labor History* 23, no. 3 (1982): 349–373.

Powers, Daniel A., and Christopher G. Ellison. "Interracial Contact and Black Racial Attitudes: The Contact Hypothesis and Selectivity Bias." *Social Forces* 74, no. 1 (1995): 205–226. https://doi.org/10.2307/2580629.

Powers, Rebecca S. "Working It out in North Carolina: Employers and Hispanic/Latino Immigrants." *Sociation Today* 3, no. 2 (2005): 1–23.

Preston, William. *Aliens and Dissenters: Federal Suppression of Radicals, 1903-1933*. Urbana: University of Illinois Press, 1994.

Price, Melanye T. *Dreaming Blackness: Black Nationalism and African American Public Opinion*. New York: New York University Press, 2009.

Pritchard, Justin. "Mexican-Worker Deaths Are Rising Sharply in U.S." *Associated Press*, March 19, 2004. https://www.deseretnews.com/article/595048917/Mexican-worker-deaths-are-rising-sharply-in-US.html.

Pugliese, Joseph. "Race as Category Crisis: Whiteness and the Topical Assignation of Race." *Social Semiotics* 12, no. 2 (August 1, 2002): 149–168. https://doi.org/10.1080/1035033027602120.78.

Qian, Z. "Breaking the Racial Barriers: Variations in Interracial Marriage between 1980 and 1990." *Demography* 34, no. 2 (May 1997): 263–276.

Quan, Robert Seto. *Lotus among the Magnolias: The Mississippi Chinese.* Jackson: University Press of Mississippi, 2007.

Quarles, Benjamin. *The Negro in the American Revolution.* Chapel Hill: Omohundro Institute and University of North Carolina Press, 1961.

Quarles, Benjamin. *Black Mosaic: Essays in Afro-American History and Historiography.* Amherst: University of Massachusetts Press, 1988.

Quillian, Lincoln. "Group Threat and Regional Change in Attitudes Toward African-Americans." *American Journal of Sociology* 102, no. 3 (1996): 816–860.

Quillian, Lincoln, and Devah Pager. "Black Neighbors, Higher Crime? The Role of Racial Stereotypes in Evaluations of Neighborhood Crime." *American Journal of Sociology* 107, no. 3 (November 2001): 717–767. https://doi.org/10.1086/338938.

Rabinowitz, Howard N. "From Exclusion to Segregation: Health and Welfare Services for Southern Blacks, 1865–1890." *Social Science Review* 48, no. 3 (1974): 327–354. https://doi.org/10.1086/643148.

Rabinowitz, Howard N. "From Exclusion to Segregation: Southern Race Relations, 1865–1890." *The Journal of American History* 63, no. 2 (1976): 325–350. https://doi.org/10.2307/1899640.

Ransby, Barbara. *Ella Baker and the Black Freedom Movement: A Radical Democratic Vision.* Chapel Hill: University of North Carolina Press, 2003.

Reed, John Shelton. "'The Cardinal Test of a Southerner:' Not Race But Geography." *The Public Opinion Quarterly* 37, no. 2 (1973): 232–240.

Reich, Steven A. "Soldiers of Democracy: Black Texans and the Fight for Citizenship, 1917–1921." *Journal of American History* 82, no. 4 (March 1, 1996): 1478–1504. https://doi.org/10.2307/2945308.

Reimers, David. *Unwelcome Strangers: American Identity and the Turn Against Immigration.* New York: Columbia University Press, 1998.

Rhee, Jeannie. "In Black and White: Chinese in the Mississippi Delta." *Journal of Supreme Court History* 19, no. 1 (1994): 117–132.

Rimer, Sara, and Karen W. Arenson. "Top Colleges Take More Blacks, but Which Ones?" *New York Times*, June 24, 2004, sec. Education.

Rives, Karin. "Jobs Lure Illegal Immigrants to the State." *The News and Observer.* February 26, 2006.

Roberts, Dorothy. *Killing the Black Body: Race, Reproduction, and the Meaning of Liberty.* 1 edition. New York: Pantheon, 1997.

Rocco, Raymond. "Transforming Citizenship: Membership, Strategies of Containment, and the Public Sphere in Latino Communities." *Latino Studies* 2, no. 1 (April 1, 2004): 4–25. https://doi.org/10.1057/palgrave.lst.8600058.

Rochin, Refugio I. "Rural Latinos: Evolving Conditions and Issues." In *The Changing American Countryside: Rural People and Places,* edited by E. N. Castle, 286–302. Lawrence: University Press of Kansas, 1995.

Rodrigues, Helen A., and Gary Segura. "A Place at the Lunch Counter: Latinos, African Americans, and the Dynamics of American Race Politics." In *Latino Politics: Identity, Mobilization, and Representation*, edited by Rodolfo Espino, David Leal, and Kenneth Meier, 27–43. Charlottesville: University of Virginia, 2007.

Rodríguez, Clara E. *Changing Race: Latinos, the Census and the History of Ethnicity*. New York: NYU Press, 2000.

Rodriguez, Richard. *Brown: The Last Discovery of America*. New York: Viking Adult, 2002.

Roediger, David R. *The Wages of Whiteness: Race and the Making of the American Working Class*. London; New York: Verso, 1999.

Rogers, Reuel R. *Afro-Caribbean Immigrants and the Politics of Incorporation: Ethnicity, Exception, or Exit*. Cambridge: Cambridge University Press, 2006.

Rogers, Reuel R. "Afro-Caribbean Immigrants, African Americans, and the Politics of Group Identity." In *Black and Multiracial Politics in America*, edited by Yvette Marie Alex-Assensoh and Lawrence J. Hanks, 15–59. New York: NYU Press, 2000.

Rogers, Reuel R. "Race-Based Coalitions Among Minority Groups: Afro-Caribbean Immigrants and African-Americans in New York City." *Urban Affairs Review* 39, no. 3 (January 1, 2004): 283–317. https://doi.org/10.1177/1078087403258960.

Rogin, Michael Paul. *Fathers and Children: Andrew Jackson and the Subjugation of the American Indian*. New Brunswick, U.S.A: Transaction Publishers, 1975.

Rogoff, Leonard. "Is the Jew White?: The Racial Place of the Southern Jew." *American Jewish History* 85, no. 3 (September 1, 1997): 195–230. https://doi.org/10.1353/ajh.1997.0025.

Rosenbaum, Rene Perez. "Migration and Integration of Latinos into Rural Midwestern Communities: The Case of Mexicans in Adrian, Michigan" JSRI Research Report No. 19. East Lansing: Julian Samora Research Institute, Michigan State University, 1997. https://migration.ucdavis.edu/cf/more.php?id=156.

Rosenfeld, Michael J., and Marta Tienda. "Mexican Immigration, Occupational Niches, and Labor-Market Competition: Evidence from Los Angeles, Chicago, and Atlanta, 1970 to 1990." In *Immigration and Opportunity: Race, Ethnicity, and Employment in the United States*, edited by Frank D. Bean and Stephanie Bell-Rose, 64–105. New York, NY: Russell Sage Foundation, 1999.

Rothstein, Richard. *The Color of Law: A Forgotten History of How Our Government Segregated America*. New York: Liveright Publishing Corporation, 2017.

Roucek, Joseph S. "The Image of the Slav in U.S. History and in Immigration Policy." *American Journal of Economics and Sociology* 28, no. 1 (January 1, 1969): 29–48. https://doi.org/10.1111/j.1536-7150.1969.tb03093.x.

Rubin, Jay. "Black Nativism: The European Immigrant in Negro Thought, 1830-1860." *Phylon* 39, no. 3 (1978): 193–202. https://doi.org/10.2307/274515.

Rusk, David. "The 'Segregation Tax': The Cost of Racial Segregation to Black Homeowners." Washington, DC: The Brookings Institution, 2001. https://www.brookings.edu/wp-content/uploads/2016/06/rusk.pdf.

Russell-Brown, Katheryn. *The Color of Crime.* 2nd ed. New York: NYU Press, 2009.

Rustin, Bayard. *Down the Line.* Chicago: Quadrangle Books, 1971.

Ryan, James E. "'Brown,' School Choice, and the Suburban Veto." *Virginia Law Review* 90, no. 6 (2004): 1635–1647. https://doi.org/10.2307/3202408.

Sahgal, Neha, and Greg Smith. "A Religious Portrait of African Americans." Washington, DC: Pew Research Center, January 30, 2009. https://www.pewforum.org/2009/01/30/a-religious-portrait-of-african-americans/

Said, Edward W. *Orientalism.* New York: Vintage, 1978.

Saito, Leland T. *Race and Politics: Asian Americans, Latinos, and Whites in a Los Angeles Suburb.* The Asian American Experience. Urbana: University of Illinois Press, 1998. http://catdir.loc.gov/catdir/toc/fy0603/97045435.html.

Sanchez, Gabriel R., and Natalie Masuoka. "Brown Utility Heuristic? The Presence and Contribution Factors of Latino Linked Fate." *Hispanic Journal of Behavioral Sciences* 32, no. 4 (2010): 519–531. https://doi.org/10.1177/0739986310383129.

Sanchez, George J. "Face the Nation: Race, Immigration, and the Rise of Nativism in Late Twentieth Century America." *The International Migration Review* 31, no. 4 (1997): 1009–1030. https://doi.org/10.2307/2547422.

Sanchez, George J. "Race and Immigration in Changing Communities of the United States." *Japanese Journal of American Studies* 14 (2003): 7–20.

Sansone, Livio. *Blackness Without Ethnicity: Constructing Race in Brazil.* New York: Palgrave Macmillan, 2003.

Saucedo, Leticia M. "The Employer Preference for the Subservient Worker and the Making of the Brown Collar Workplace." *Ohio State Law Journal* 67, no. 5 (2006): 961–1022.

Sawyer, Mark Q. *Racial Politics in Post-Revolutionary Cuba.* Cambridge, UK; New York: Cambridge University Press, 2005.

Saxton, Alexander. *The Indispensable Enemy: Labor and the Anti-Chinese Movement in California.* Berkeley: University of California Press, 1975.

Schatz, Robert T., Ervin Staub, and Howard Lavine. "On the Varieties of National Attachment: Blind Versus Constructive Patriotism." *Political Psychology* 20, no. 1 (March 1, 1999): 151–174. https://doi.org/10.1111/0162-895X.00140.

Schlesinger, Arthur M. Jr. *The Disuniting of America: Reflections on a Multicultural Society.* New York: W.W. Norton, 1998.

Schmid, Carol. "Immigration and Asian and Hispanic Minorities in the New South: An Exploration of History, Attitudes, and Demographic Trends." *Sociological Spectrum* 23, no. 2 (April 2003): 129–157. https://doi.org/10.1080/02732170309212.

Schmidt, Peter. "2 Suits, Board Rift Strain Durham, N.C., Merger." *Education Week,* September 20, 1995. https://www.edweek.org/ew/articles/1995/09/20/03nc.h15.html.

Schultz, Bud, and Schultz Ruth. *It Did Happen Here.* Berkeley and Los Angeles: University of California Press, 1989.

Schuman, Howard, Charlotte Steeh, Lawrence Bobo, and Maria Krysan. *Racial Attitudes in America: Trends and Interpretations.* Revised edition. Cambridge: Harvard University Press, 1997.

Schwartz, Barry. "Collective Memory and History: How Abraham Lincoln Became a Symbol of Racial Equality." *The Sociological Quarterly* 38, no. 3 (1997): 469–496.

Scott, Daryl Michael. "'Immigrant Indigestion': A. Philip Randolph, Radical and Restrictionist." Backgrounder. Washington, DC: Center for Immigration Studies, 1999.

Sears, David O. "Symbolic Racism." In *Eliminating Racism: Profiles in Controversy (Perspectives in Social Psychology),* edited by Phyllis A. Katz and Dalmas A. Taylor, 53–84. Boston: Springer, 1988.

Sears, David O., and Jack Citrin. *Tax Revolt: Something for Nothing in California.* Cambridge: Harvard University Press, 1982.

Sears, David O., and John B. McConahay. *The Politics of Violence: The New Urban Blacks and the Watts Riot.* Boston: Houghton Mifflin, 1973.

Sekhon, Vijay. "The Civil Rights of Others: Antiterrorism, the Patriot Act, and Arab and South Asian American Rights in Post-9/11 American Society." *Texas Journal on Civil Liberties & Civil Rights* 8, no. 1 (2003): 117–148.

Shackel, Paul A. *Memory in Black and White: Race, Commemoration, and the Post-Bellum Landscape.* 5th ed. Lanham: Altamira Press, 2003.

Shams, Tahseen. "The Declining Significance of Race or the Persistent Racialization of Blacks? A Conceptual, Empirical, and Methodological Review of Today's Race Debate in America." *Journal of Black Studies* 46, no. 3 (2015): 282–296. https://doi.org/10.1177/0021934714568566.

Shankman, Arnold. "Black on Yellow: Afro-Americans View Chinese-Americans, 1850-1935." *Phylon* 39, no. 1 (1978): 1–17. https://doi.org/10.2307/274429.

Shankman, Arnold. "Black on Green: Afro-American Editors on Irish Independence, 1840–1921." *Phylon* 41, no. 3 (1980): 284–299. https://doi.org/10.2307/274792.

Shankman, Arnold M. *Ambivalent Friends: Afro-Americans View the Immigrant.* Westport: Greenwood Press, 1982.

Shapiro, Thomas M. "Race, Homeownership, and Wealth." *Washington University Journal of Law & Policy* 20 (2006): 53–74.

Shapiro, Thomas, Tatjana Meschede, and Sam Osoro. "The Roots of the Widening Racial Wealth Gap: Explaining the Black-White Economic Divide." Waltham, MA: Institute of Assets and Social Policy, Brandeis University, February 2013.

Shaw, Todd C. "'Two Warring Ideals': Double Consciousness, Dialogue, and African American Patriotism Post-9/11." *Journal of African American Studies* 8, nos. 1–2 (2004): 20–37. https://doi.org/10.1007/s12111-004-1002-4.

Shelby County, Alabama v. Eric Holder, Jr. Attorney General, Docket Number 12–96, 570 U.S, (2013).

Shelby, Tommie. *We Who are Dark: The Philosophical Foundations of Black Solidarity.* Cambridge: Harvard University Press, 2005.

Sheridan, Clare. "Contested Citizenship: National Identity and the Mexican Immigration Debates of the 1920s." *Journal of American Ethnic History* 21, no. 3 (2002): 3–35.

Sherwood, Henry Noble. "The Formation of the American Colonization Society." *The Journal of Negro History* 2, no. 3 (July 1917): 209–228.

Shingles, Richard D. "Black Consciousness and Political Participation: The Missing Link." *The American Political Science Review* 75, no. 1 (1981): 76–91. https://doi.org/10.2307/1962160.

Short, Robert, and Lisa Magaña. "Political Rhetoric, Immigration Attitudes, and Contemporary Prejudice: A Mexican American Dilemma." *The Journal of Social Psychology* 142, no. 6 (2002): 701–712. https://doi.org/10.1080/00224540209603930.

Sidanius, Jim, Seymour Feshbach, Shana Levin, and Felicia Pratto. "The Interface Between Ethnic and National Attachment: Ethnic Pluralism or Ethnic Dominance?" *The Public Opinion Quarterly* 61, no. 1 (1997): 102–133.

Sidanius, Jim, and Felicia Pratto. *Social Dominance: An Intergroup Theory of Social Hierarchy and Oppression.* Cambridge: Cambridge University Press, 2001

Sigelman, Lee, Timothy Bledsoe, Susan Welch, and Michael W. Combs. "Making Contact? Black-White Social Interaction in an Urban Setting." *American Journal of Sociology* 101, no. 5 (1996): 1306–1332.

Sigelman, Lee, and Steven A. Tuch. "Metastereotypes: Blacks' Perceptions of Whites' Stereotypes of Blacks." *Public Opinion Quarterly* 61, no. 1 (May 1, 1997): 87–101. https://doi.org/10.1086/297788.

Silverman, Robert Mark. "The Effects of Racism and Racial Discrimination on Minority Business Development: The Case of Black Manufacturers in Chicago's Ethnic Beauty Aids Industry." *Journal of Social History* 31, no. 3 (1998): 571–597.

Singer, Audrey. "Twenty-First Century Gateways." In *Twenty-First Century Gateways: Immigrant Incorporation in Suburban America*, edited by Audrey Singer, Caroline B. Brettell, and Susan W. Hardwick, 3–30. Washington, DC: Brookings Institution Press, 2008.

Singer, Audrey. "The Rise of New Immigrant Gateways." Center on Urban and Metropolitan Policy. Washington, DC: The Brookings Institution, 2004. https://www.brookings.edu/wp-content/uploads/2016/06/20040301_gateways.pdf

Singh, Gopal K., and Stella M. Yu. "Infant Mortality in the United States: Trends, Differentials, and Projections, 1950 through 2010." *American Journal of Public Health* 85, no. 7 (1995): 957–964.

Singh, Nikhil Pal. *Black Is a Country: Race and the Unfinished Struggle for Democracy.* Cambridge: Harvard University Press, 2005.

Skrentny, John D. *The Ironies of Affirmative Action: Politics, Culture, and Justice in America.* 1 edition. Chicago: University of Chicago Press, 1996.

Smith, Jamil. "Stacy Abrams: The Exit Interview." *Rolling Stone*, November 19, 2018. https://www.rollingstone.com/politics/politics-features/stacey-abrams-voter-suppression-758361/.

Smith, Robert C. "Black Power and the Transformation from Protest to Policies." *Political Science Quarterly* 96, no. 3 (1981): 431–443. https://doi.org/10.2307/2150554.

Smith, Rogers M. "The 'American Creed' and American Identity: The Limits of Liberal Citizenship in the United States." *Western Political Quarterly* 41, no. 2 (June 1, 1988): 225–251. https://doi.org/10.1177/106591298804100202.

Smith, Rogers M. "Beyond Tocqueville, Myrdal, and Hartz: The Multiple Traditions in America." *The American Political Science Review* 87, no. 3 (1993): 549–566. https://doi.org/10.2307/2938735.

Smith, Rogers M. *Civic Ideals: Conflicting Visions of Citizenship in U.S. History*. The Yale ISPS Series. New Haven: Yale University Press, 1997.

Smith, Rogers M. "Citizenship and the Politics of People-Building." *Citizenship Studies* 5, no. 1 (2001): 73–96.

Sonenshein, Raphael J. "The Dynamics of Biracial Coalitions: Crossover Politics in Los Angeles." *Western Political Quarterly* 42, no. 2 (1989): 333–353.

Sonenshein, Raphael J. *Politics in Black and White: Race and Power in Los Angeles*. Princeton: Princeton University Press, 1993.

Sonenshein, Raphael J. "The Prospects for Multiracial Politics: Lessons from America's Three Largest Cities." In *Racial Politics in American Cities*, edited by Rufus P Browning, Dale Rogers Marshall, and David H Tabb, 41–65. New York: Longman Publishing Group, 2003.

Sonenshein, Raphael J., and Susan H. Pinkus. "The Dynamics of Latino Political Incorporation: The 2001 Los Angeles Mayoral Election as Seen in Los Angeles Times Exit Polls." *PS: Political Science & Politics* 35, no. 1 (2002): 67–74.

Sonenshein, Raphael J., and Susan H Pinkus. "Latino Incorporation Reaches the Urban Summit: How Antonio Villaraigosa Won the 2005 Los Angeles Mayor's Race." *PS: Political Science & Politics* 38, no. 4 (2005): 713–721.

Song, Miri. "Introduction: Who's at the Bottom? Examining Claims about Racial Hierarchy." *Ethnic and Racial Studies* 27, no. 6 (2004): 859–877.

Squires, Catherine R. "Rethinking the Black Public Sphere: An Alternative Vocabulary for Multiple Public Spheres." *Communication Theory* 12, no. 4 (2002): 446–468. https://doi.org/10.1111/j.1468-2885.2002.tb00278.x

Stallings, D. T. "A Statistical Overview of Latino Achievement in North Carolina." Duke University, Durham, NC: Supporting Latino Achievement Conference, 2003.

Steeh, Charlotte, and Maria Krysan. "Trends: Affirmative Action and the Public, 1970–1995." *The Public Opinion Quarterly* 60, no. 1 (1996): 128–158. https://www.jstor.org/stable/2749501

Steele, Claude M. "A Threat in the Air: How Stereotypes Shape Intellectual Identity and Performance." *American Psychologist* 52, no. 6 (1997): 613–629. http://dx.doi.org/10.1037/0003-066X.52.6.613.

Steffensmeier, Darrell, Jeffrey Ulmer, and John Kramer. "The Interaction of Race, Gender, and Age in Criminal Sentencing: The Punishment Cost of Being Young, Black, and Male." *Criminology* 36, no. 4 (1998): 763–798. https://doi.org/10.1111/j.1745-9125.1998.tb01265.x.

Steinberg, Stephen. "Immigration, African Americans, and Race Discourse." *New Politics* 10, no. 3 (2005): 42–53.

Stevenson, Brenda. *The Contested Murder of Latasha Harlins: Justice, Gender, and the Origins of the LA Riots.* New York: Oxford University Press, 2015.

Stone, Clarence Nathan. *Regime Politics: Governing Atlanta, 1946–1988.* Lawrence: University Press of Kansas, 1989.

Strom, Jennifer. "The Conflicting Agendas of Lavonia Allison." *IndyWeek.* November 21, 2001. https://indyweek.com/news/conflicting-agendas-lavonia-allison/

Suarez-Orozco, Marcelo, and Mariela Páez. *Latinos: Remaking America.* Berkeley and Los Angeles: University of California Press, 2002.

Sugrue, Thomas J. *The Origins of the Urban Crisis: Race and Inequality in Postwar Detroit.* New Jersey: Princeton University Press, 1996.

Sugrue, Thomas J. "Affirmative Action from Below: Civil Rights, the Building Trades, and the Politics of Racial Equality in the Urban North, 1945–1969." *The Journal of American History* 91, no. 1 (2004): 145–173. https://doi.org/10.2307/3659618.

Suro, Roberto, and Audrey Singer. "Latino Growth in Metropolitan America: Changing Patterns, New Locations." Washington, DC: The Brookings Institution, November 30, 2001. https://www.brookings.edu/research/latino-growth-in-metropolitan-america-changing-patterns-new-locations/.

Tabak, Ronald J. "The Continuing Role of Race in Capital Cases, Notwithstanding President Obama's Election." *Northern Kentucky Law Review* 37, no. 2 (2010): 243–272.

Takaki, Ronald. "The Tempest in the Wilderness: The Racialization of Savagery." *The Journal of American History* 79, no. 3 (1992): 892–912. https://doi.org/10.2307/2080792.

Tamayo, William R. "When the Coloreds Are Neither Black nor Citizens: The United States Civil Rights Movement and Global Migration." *Asian Law Journal* 2 (1995): 1–32.

Tate, Gayle T. "Free Black Resistance in the Antebellum Era, 1830-1860." *Journal of Black Studies* 28, no. 6 (1998): 764–782.

Tate, Katherine. *From Protest to Politics: The New Black Voters in American Elections.* Cambridge: Harvard University Press, 1994.

Tate, Katherine. *Black Faces in the Mirror: African Americans and Their Representatives in the U.S. Congress.* New Jersey: Princeton University Press, 2003.

Telles, Edward. "Ethnic Boundaries and Political Mobilization among African Brazilians: Comparisons with the US Case." In *Racial Politics in Contemporary Brazil*, edited by Michael Hanchard, 82–97. Durham: Duke University Press, 1999.

Telles, Edward, Mark Q. Sawyer, and Gaspar Rivera-Salgado, eds. *Just Neighbors? Research on African American and Latino Relations in the United States*. New York: Russell Sage Foundation, 2011.

Thelen, David. "The Nation and Beyond." *Journal of American History* 86, no. 3 (1999): 965–975.

Thornell, John. "Struggle for Identity in the Most Southern Place on Earth: The Chinese in the Mississippi Delta." *Chinese America: History and Perspectives*, 2003, 63–72.

Thornton, Michael C., and Yuko Mizuno. "Economic Well-Being and Black Adult Feelings toward Immigrants and Whites, 1984." *Journal of Black Studies* 30, no. 1 (1999): 15–44.

Thornton, Michael C., Robert Joseph Taylor, and Linda M. Chatters. "African American and Black Caribbean Mutual Feelings of Closeness: Findings from a National Probability Survey." *Journal of Black Studies* 44, no. 8 (2013): 798–828. https://doi.org/10.1177/0021934713516978.

Tichenor, Daniel J. "The Politics of Immigration Reform in the United States, 1981-1990." *Polity* 26, no. 3 (1994): 333–362.

Tichenor, Daniel J. *Dividing Lines: The Politics of Immigration Control in America*. Princeton: Princeton University Press, 2002.

Tienda, Marta, and Haya Stier. "Generating Labor Market Inequality: Employment Opportunities and the Accumulation of Disadvantage." *Social Problems* 43, no. 2 (1996): 147–165.

Tillery, Jr., Alvin B. *Between Homeland and Motherland: Africa, U.S. Foreign Policy, and Black Leadership in America*. Ithaca: Cornell University Press, 2011.

Tillery, Jr., Alvin B., and Michell Chresfield. "Model Blacks or 'Ras the Exhorter': A Qualitative Analysis of Black Newspapers' Coverage of the First Wave of Afro-Caribbean Immigration to the United States." *Journal of Black Studies* 43, no. 5 (2012): 545–570. https://doi.org/10.1177/0021934712439065.

Timpone, Richard J. "Mass Mobilization or Government Intervention? The Growth of Black Registration in the South." *The Journal of Politics* 57, no. 2 (1995): 425–442.

Tolnay, Stewart E. "The Great Migration Gets Underway: A Comparison of Black Southern Migrants and Nonmigrants in the North, 1920." *Social Science Quarterly* 82, no. 2 (2001): 235–252.

Tolnay, Stewart E., Robert M. Adelman, and Kyle D. Crowder. "Race, Regional Origin, and Residence in Northern Cities at the Beginning of the Great Migration." *American Sociological Review* 67, no. 3 (2002): 456–475. https://doi.org/10.2307/3088966.

Tolnay, Stewart E., and Elwood M. Beck. "Racial Violence and Black Migration in the American South." *American Sociological Review* 57, no. 1 (February 1992): 103–116.

Tolnay, Stewart E., and Suzanne C. Eichenlaub. "Inequality in the West: Racial and Ethnic Variation in Occupational Status and Returns to Education." *Social Science History* 31, no. 4 (2007): 471–507. https://doi.org/10.1017/S0145553200013833.

Tomaskovic-Devey, Donald, and Vincent J. Roscigno. "Racial Economic Subordination and White Gain in the U.S. South." *American Sociological Review* 61, no. 4 (1996): 565–589. https://doi.org/10.2307/2096394

Torres, Cruz C. "Emerging Latino Communities: A New Challenge for the Rural South." Rural South: Preparing for the Challenges of the 21st Century. Mississippi: Southern Rural Development Center, Mississippi State, 2000.

Torres, Kimberly C., and Camille Z. Charles. "Metastereotypes and the Black-White Divide: A Qualitative View of Race on an Elite College Campus." *Du Bois Review: Social Science Research on Race* 1, no. 1 (2004): 115–149. https://doi.org/10.1017/S1742058X0404007X.

Trevor, John B. "An Analysis of the American Immigration Act of 1924." *International Conciliation* 10 (1924): 370–443.

Trotti, Michael. "Freedmen and Enslaved Soil: A Case Study of Manumission, Migration, and Land." *The Virginia Magazine of History and Biography* 104, no. 4 (1996): 455–480.

Tsunokai, Glenn T. "Beyond the Lenses of the 'Model' Minority Myth: A Descriptive Portrait of Asian Gang Members." *Journal of Gang Research* 12, no. 4 (2005): 37–58.

Turner, Sarah, and John Bound. "Closing the Gap or Widening the Divide: The Effects of the GI Bill and World War II on the Educational Outcomes of Black Americans." *The Journal of Economic History* 63, no. 1 (2003): 145–177.

Tyner, James A. "The Geopolitics of Eugenics and the Incarceration of Japanese Americans." *Antipode* 30, no. 3 (1998): 251–269.

Tyson, Timothy B. *Radio Free Dixie: Robert f. Williams and the Roots of Black Power.* Chapel Hill: Univ of North Carolina Press, 2000.

Udani, Adriano, and David C. Kimball. "Immigrant Resentment and Voter Fraud Beliefs in the U.S. Electorate." *American Politics Research* 46, no. 3 (2018): 402–433. https://doi.org/10.1177/1532673X17722988.

Unnever, James D., and Francis T. Cullen. "The Racial Divide in Support for the Death Penalty: Does White Racism Matter?" *Social Forces* 85, no. 3 (2007): 1281–1301. https://doi.org/10.1353/sof.2007.0058.

Vaca, Nicolas C. *The Presumed Alliance: The Unspoken Conflict between Latinos and Blacks and What It Means for America.* New York: Harper Collins, 2004.

Valentino, Nicholas A, Vincent L. Hutchings, and Ismail K. White. "Cues That Matter: How Political Ads Prime Racial Attitudes during Campaigns." *American Political Science Review* 96, no. 1 (2002): 75–90.

Valentino, Nicholas A., and David O. Sears. "Old Times There Are Not Forgotten: Race and Partisan Realignment in the Contemporary South." *American Journal of Political Science* 49, no. 3 (2005): 672–688.

Valverde, Rochelle. "Is Illegal Immigration a Problem in Kansas? Despite Small Numbers, Kobach Says Yes." *Lawrence Journal-World*, September 9, 2018, sec. News. http://www2.ljworld.com/news/2018/sep/09/is-illegal-immigration-a-problem-in-kansas-despite-small-numbers-kobach-says-yes/.

Vander Zanden, James W. "The Ideology of White Supremacy." *Journal of the History of Ideas* 20, no. 3 (1959): 385–402. https://doi.org/10.2307/2708116.

Vann, Andre D., and Beverly Washington-Jones. *Durham's Hayti: An American History*. Charleston: Arcadia Publishing, 1998.

Vasilogambros, Matt. "Polling Places in Black Communities Continue to Close Ahead of November Elections." *Governing Magazine*, September 5, 2018. https://www.governing.com/topics/politics/sl-polling-place-close-ahead-of-november-elections-black-voters.html.

Von Eschen, Penny. *Race against Empire: Black Americans and Anticolonialism, 1937–1957*. Ithaca: Cornell University Press, 1997.

Wagner, Bryan. "Charles Chesnutt and the Epistemology of Racial Violence." *American Literature* 73, no. 2 (2001): 311–337.

Walder, John C., and Allen D. Cleveland. "The South's New Segregation Academies." *The Phi Delta Kappan* 53, no. 4 (1971): 234–249.

Waldinger, Roger. "From Ellis Island to LAX: Immigrant Prospects in the American City." *International Migration Review* 30, no. 4 (1996): 1078–1086.

Waldrep, Christopher. *Lynching in America: A History in Documents*. New York: NYU Press, 2006.

Walker, Iain, and Heather J Smith. *Relative Deprivation: Specification, Development, and Integration*. London; New York: Cambridge University Press, 2001.

Walker, Jack. "Negro Voting in Atlanta: 1953–1961." *Phylon* 24, no. 4 (1963): 379–387.

Wallis, Brian. "Black Bodies, White Science: Louis Agassiz's Slave Daguerreotypes." *American Art* 9, no. 2 (1995): 39–61.

Walters, Ronald. "The Realities Underlying a Black Presidential Candidacy." *PS: Political Science & Politics* 16, no. 3 (1983): 492–494.

Walters, Ronald W. "The Black Initiatives in the Middle East." *Journal of Palestine Studies* 10, no. 2 (1981): 3–13.

Walters, Ronald W. *Black Presidential Politics in America: A Strategic Approach*. Albany: SUNY Press, 1988.

Walters, Ronald W. *The Price of Racial Reconciliation*. Ann Arbor: The University of Michigan Press, 2009.

Walters, Ronald W. "The Impact of Slavery on 20th- and 21st-Century Black Progress." *The Journal of African American History* 97, no. 1–2 (2012): 110–130.

Walton, Hanes Jr. *Black Politics; a Theoretical and Structural Analysis*. The Lippincott Series in American Government. Philadelphia: Lippincott, 1972.

Walton, Hanes Jr. *Invisible Politics: Black Political Behavior.* Albany: SUNY Press, 1985.

Walton, Hanes Jr. *Black Politics and Black Political Behavior: A Linkage Analysis.* Westsport: Prager, 1994.

Walton, Hanes, and Robert C. Smith. *American Politics and the African American Quest for Universal Freedom.* New York: Longman, 2000.

Wang, Dongsheng, and Brian H. Kleiner. "Discrimination against Asian Americans." *Equal Opportunities International* 20, no. 5/6/7 (2001): 64–69.

Warren, Jonathan W., and France Winddance Twine. "White Americans, the New Minority?: Non-Blacks and the Ever Expanding Boundaries of Whiteness." *Journal of Black Studies* 28, no. 2 (1997): 200–218. https://doi.org/10.1177/002193479702800204.

Wasem, Ruth Ellen. "Immigration of Agricultural Guest Workers: Policy, Trends, and Legislative Issues." Washington, DC: *Congressional Research Office,* 2001.

Washburn, Patrick Scott. *A Question of Sedition: The Federal Government's Investigation of the Black Press During World War II.* New York: Oxford University Press, 1986.

Washburn, Wilcomb E. "Indian Removal Policy: Administrative, Historical and Moral Criteria for Judging Its Success or Failure." *Ethnohistory,* 1965, 274–278.

Washington, Booker T. "Atlanta Exposition Address." In *Let Nobody Turn Us Around: An African American Anthology,* edited by Manning Marable and Leith Mullings, 181–197. Lanham: Rowman & Littlefield Publishers, 2000.

Waters, Mary C. "Ethnic and Racial Identities of Second-Generation Black Immigrants in New York City." *International Migration Review* 28, no. 4 (1994): 795–820.

Weare, Walter B. *Black Business in the New South: A Social History of the NC Mutual Life Insurance Company.* Champaign: The University of Illinois Press, 1973.

Weber, Christopher R., Howard Lavine, Leonie Huddy, and Christopher M. Federico. "Placing Racial Stereotypes in Context: Social Desirability and the Politics of Racial Hostility." *American Journal of Political Science* 58, no. 1 (2014): 63–78.

Weill, Susan, and Laura Castañeda. "'Emphathetic Rejectionism' and Inter-Ethnic Agenda Setting: Coverage of Latinos by the Black Press in the American South." *Journalism Studies* 5, no. 4 (2004): 537–550.

Welch, Kelly. "Black Criminal Stereotypes and Racial Profiling." *Journal of Contemporary Criminal Justice* 23, no. 3 (2007): 276–288. https://doi.org/10.1177/1043986207306870.

Weldon, S. Laurel. *When Protest Makes Policy: How Social Movements Represent Disadvantaged Groups.* Ann Arbor: The University of Michigan Press, 2011.

Wells, Amy E. "Good Neighbors? Distance, Resistance, and Desegregation in Metropolitan New Orleans." *Urban Education* 39, no.4 (2004): 408–427. https://doi.org/10.1177/0042085904265108

Wells-Barnett, Ida B. *Southern Horrors: Lynch Law in All Its Phases.* New York: New York Age Print, 1892.

West, Traci C. *Wounds of the Spirit: Black Women, Violence, and Resistance Ethics.* New York: NYU Press, 1999.

White, Ismail K. "When Race Matters and When It Doesn't: Racial Group Differences in Response to Racial Cues." *American Political Science Review* 101, no. 2 (2007): 339–354. https://doi.org/10.1017/S0003055407070177.

Wiegman, Robyn. *American Anatomies: Theorizing Race and Gender.* Durham: Duke University Press, 1995.

Wilkerson, Isabel. *The Warmth of Other Suns: The Epic Story of America's Great Migration.* New York: Vintage Books, 2011.

Willhelm, Sindey M., and Staughton Lynd. *Who Needs the Negro?* 1st edition. New York: Anchor Books/Doubleday, 1971.

Williams, David R., and James S. Jackson. "Race/Ethnicity and the 2000 Census: Recommendations for African American and Other Black Populations in the United States." *American Journal of Public Health* 90, no. 11 (November 2000): 1728–1730.

Williams, Frank B. "The Poll Tax as a Suffrage Requirement in the South, 1870–1901." *The Journal of Southern History* 18, no. 4 (1952): 469–496.

Williams, Melissa S. *Voice, Trust, and Memory: Marginalized Groups and the Failings of Liberal Representation.* Princeton: Princeton University Press, 1998.

Willis, Pauline M. "Who Is a Southerner? It's Your Turn to Tell Us." *Southern Cultures* 11, no. 3 (2005): 1–2.

Wilson, George, Ian Sakura-Lemessy, and Jonathan P West. "Reaching the Top: Racial Differences in Mobility Paths to Upper-Tier Occupations." *Work and Occupations* 26, no. 2 (1999): 165–186.

Winsberg, Morton D. "Ethnic Competition for Residential Space in Miami, Florida, 1970–80." *American Journal of Economics and Sociology* 42, no. 3 (1983): 305–314.

Wintz, Cary D. *African American Political Thought, 1890-1930: Washington, Du Bois, Garvey, and Randolph.* Vol. 157. Armonk: M.E. Sharpe, 1996.

Wolcott, Victoria W. "'Bible, Bath, and Broom': Nannie Helen Burroughs's National Training School and African-American Racial Uplift." *Journal of Women's History* 9, no. 1 (1997): 88–110.

Wolcott, Victoria W. *Remaking Respectability: African American Women in Interwar Detroit.* Chapel Hill: University of North Carolina Press, 2001.

Wolgemuth, Kathleen L. "Woodrow Wilson and Federal Segregation." *The Journal of Negro History* 44, no. 2 (1959): 158–173.

Woliver, Laura R., Angela D. Ledford, and Chris J. Dolan. "The South Carolina Confederate Flag: The Politics of Race and Citizenship." *Politics & Policy* 29, no. 4 (2001): 708–730.

Wong, Janelle S. *Immigrants, Evangelicals, and Politics in an Era of Demographic Change.* New York: Russell Sage Foundation, 2018.

Wong, Morrison G. "Post-1965 Asian Immigrants: Where Do They Come from, Where Are They Now, and Where Are They Going?" *The Annals of the American Academy of Political and Social Science* 487, no. 1 (1986): 150–168.

Wood, B. Dan. "Does Politics Make a Difference at the EEOC?" *American Journal of Political Science*, 1990, 503–530.

Woodard, Komozi. *A Nation within a Nation: Amiri Baraka (LeRoi Jones) and Black Power Politics*. Chapel Hill: University of North Carolina Press, 1999.

Woodson, Carter G. "Fifty Years of Negro Citizenship as Qualified by the United States Supreme Court." *The Journal of Negro History* 6, no. 1 (1921): 1–53.

Woodward, C. Vann. *Origins of the New South, 1877–1913*. Vol. 9. Baton Rouge: Louisiana State University Press, 1951.

Woodward, C. Vann. *The Strange Career of Jim Crow*. Oxford; New York: Oxford University Press, 1974.

Woodward, C. Vann. "Look Away, Look Away." *The Journal of Southern History* 59, no. 3 (1993): 487–504.

Wu, Frank H. "The Arrival of Asian Americans: An Agenda for Legal Scholarship." *Asian Law Journal* 10, no. 1 (2003): 1–12.

Yancey, George. *Who Is White? Latinos, Asians, and the New Black/Nonblack Divide*. Boulder: Lynne Rienner Publishers, 2003.

Yinger, John. *Closed Doors, Opportunities Lost: The Continuing Costs of Housing Discrimination*. New York: Russell Sage Foundation, 1995.

Yoon, In-Jin. "The Growth of Korean Immigrant Entrepreneurship in Chicago." *Ethnic and Racial Studies* 18, no. 2 (1995): 315–335.

Yoon, In-Jin. *On My Own: Korean Businesses and Race Relations in America*. Chicago: University of Chicago Press, 1997.

Yu, Henry. "Orientalizing the Pacific Rim: The Production of Exotic Knowledge by American Missionaries and Sociologists in the 1920s." *The Journal of American-East Asian Relations* 5, no. 3/4 (1996): 331–359.

Yu, Henry. "Mixing Bodies and Cultures: The Meaning of America's Fascination With Sex Between 'Orientals' and 'Whites.'" In *Sex, Love, Race: Crossing Boundaries in North American History*, edited by Martha Hodes, 444–463. New York: NYU Press, 1998.

Zack, Naomi. "White Ideas." In *Whiteness: Feminist Philosophical Reflections*, edited by Chris Cuomo and Kim G. Hall, 77–104. Lanham: Rowman & Littlefield Publishers, 1999.

Zhou, Min. "Are Asian Americans Becoming 'White?'" *Contexts* 3, no. 1 (2004): 29–37.

Zong, Jie, Jeanne Batalova, and Jeffrey Hallock. "Frequently Requested Statistics on Immigrants and Immigration in the United States." Washington, DC: Migration Policy Institute, February 8, 2018. https://www.migrationpolicy.org/article/frequently-requested-statistics-immigrants-and-immigration-united-states-7.

Zúñiga, Víctor, and Rubén Hernández-León. *New Destinations: Mexican Immigration in the United States*. New York: Russell Sage Foundation, 2005.

Index

Tables and map are indicated by an italic *t* and m, respectively, following the page number.

For the benefit of digital users, indexed terms that span two pages (e.g., 52–53) may, on occasion, appear on only one of those pages.

CPSIA information can be obtained
at www.ICGtesting.com
Printed in the USA
BVHW071735020720
582413BV00002B/7